HTML PDF
PDF HTML

Internet Publishing with Acrobat®

Internet Publishing with Acrobat®

A comprehensive reference for creating and integrating PDF files with HTML on the Internet or intranets.

by Gordon Kent

Adobe Press
San Jose, California

Published by Adobe Press, Adobe Systems Incorporated

ISBN: 1-56830-300-9

Library of Congress Catalog No.: 96-77066

10 9 8 7 6 5 4 3 2 First Printing: August 1996

Printed in the United States of America by Shepard Poorman Communications Corporation, Indianapolis, IN. Published simultaneously in Canada.

Cover and text design by Graham Metcalfe and Paula Shuhert.

Adobe Press books are published and distributed by Macmillan Computer Publishing USA. For individual, educational, corporate, or retail sales accounts, call 1-800-428-5331, or 317-581-3500. For information address Macmillan Computer Publishing USA, 201 West 103rd Street, Indianapolis, IN 46290. Macmillan's World Wide Web page URL is www.mcp.com.

Dedication

For my grandmother, father, mother, and family.

Contents

Figures & Tables

Figures

Tables

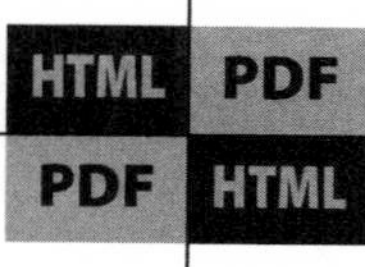

Internet Publishing with Acrobat®

1

Introduction

Adobe Acrobat® software helps you create content for the Internet that is compact, graphically rich, interactive, intuitively navigable, and easy to publish. Portable Document Format (PDF) publishing on the Internet unshackles your creativity from Web-specific publishing applications and allows you to use the almost limitless design capabilities of to-day's powerful print-publishing software. If an application can print, it can be used to create compelling content for the Web.

The World Wide Web introduced most people to Adobe Acrobat and PDF files—and still does. Early in the growth of the Web, Adobe recognized the value of Acrobat and PDF files as a solution for publishing visually complex information on the Internet. PDF files exhibit a number of characteristics that make them well suited for the Internet:

- They are cross-platform binary files, requiring no translation or conversion when moved among popular platforms, such as Windows, Macintosh, UNIX, and other operating systems.

- PDF files are surprisingly compact (in file size) for the amount of visual and contextual content they contain.
- They support text, graphics, and other media formats.
- PDF files are interactive and navigable.

To encourage the use of PDF files on the Internet, Adobe registered the PDF file type as a standard file type (like JPEG graphics and HTML files) for use on the Internet. Adobe published the specification so that others could develop software that utilized the PDF technology. With this evolution of the Acrobat technology, a Web browser could be configured to automatically launch the freely available Acrobat Reader as a helper application and open a PDF file after it was downloaded. Adobe's Weblink plug-in—an add-on module formally introduced with Acrobat 2.1—enabled Reader (and Acrobat Exchange) to communicate with most Web browsers. This communication allowed authors to create links from PDF files to other sites and files on the Web—the same way links are used in HTML documents.

Acrobat 3.0 (originally code-named Acrobat Amber) takes this link in communication among the Web, PDF files, and Acrobat one step further. Acrobat 3.0 integrates the relationship between Web browser and Acrobat Reader by enabling the Web browser to display the PDF file within the Web browser's document window (usually reserved for HTML and image files). Now when viewing a PDF file, the basic Acrobat toolbar appears so the user can navigate and interact with the PDF file as if it were being viewed in Acrobat Reader.

Historically, Web publishers shied away from PDF files, feeling they were simply too large to be useful for publishing on the limited-bandwidth Web. Originally, PDF files were developed for local access networks or large internal networks (intranets), which typically had much greater bandwidth capabilities than the average Internet user. PDF files also can be large because of the types of documents that are published as PDF files. Authors and designers creating PDF files wanted to preserve exactly the electronic magazines, newsletters, technical drawings, and other visually complex documents with their original fonts, extensive use of color, images, graphics, and other design elements. These features included all the attributes that publishers had come to expect from modern page layout, design, and word processing software applications—including large file size. These files had to be completely downloaded before they could be viewed. Ironically, history has shown that PDF files are not significantly larger than HTML files and are sometimes smaller or the same size as most comparable HTML designs.

Adobe Acrobat 3.0 allows the publication of even smaller PDF files than previously thought possible through new compression schemes. Now with Acrobat 3.0, PDF pages render as each page element is downloaded, in much the same manner as HTML files; and, only the pages requested are downloaded—no need to wait until the entire file has downloaded before it can be viewed. This allows PDF pages to be viewed as fast or faster than most image-heavy HTML files.

PDF files are the portable document file format of choice for hundreds of companies that publish documents on the Internet. Other companies also use PDF files as the file format of choice when distributing information via intranets, CD-ROMs, private computer networks, floppy diskettes, and other media formats.

PDF files also are the document format of choice for electronic magazines, technical documentation, books, marketing documents, catalogs, readme files, white papers, and other document types that need to be distributed via various computer platforms, operating systems, media formats, and networks.

From a publisher's perspective, little experience beyond the skills of most print publishers is required for producing PDF files. Every major desktop publishing software package and a number of graphics applications support the PDF file format. Publishing content as PDF files requires no new design training, as HTML did. Many of these software applications have additions, plug-ins, macros, or other utilities that quickly and simply convert document information such as tables of content, cross-references, and notes into intuitively navigable and interactive PDF file objects. Creating PFD files is easy. This book will help you publish PDF files expertly.

1.1 About This Book

Internet Publishing with Acrobat is the essential reference guide for publishers of PDF files on the Internet, or those who want to publish PDF files on the Internet. This book is both a technical reference and a content development guide. It contains the most comprehensive technical information about Acrobat and Internet publishing available to date. Much of this information comes directly from Adobe engineers working on Acrobat, and countless third-party developers, power users, and experts. Unlike the plethora of books on HTML and Web publishing, and the handful of books on Acrobat, this book provides the information necessary to determine how best to serve content: as Portable Document Format (PDF) files, or as Hypertext Markup Language (HTML) files. Many of today's Internet sites created using HTML are ineffective and could benefit dramatically from the addition and integration of PDF files. *Internet Publishing with Acrobat* provides the knowledge a publisher needs to seamlessly integrate PDF and HTML files at both the document and site-wide levels. The efficient exposition of technical information—often compactly in tables or figures—will help the Internet publisher determine the most appropriate Acrobat tool to create compelling PDF files for various document types. The combination of detailed technical information and content development solutions will answer questions, while opening up new content publishing possibilities.

Rather than recycling and repeating the information found in the numerous tutorials, user guides, books, magazine articles, and online discussion groups that focus on using Adobe Acrobat, this book concentrates on what the publisher needs to know to develop content for the Internet. If you are new to Acrobat, you'll find yourself referring back to Adobe's documentation and user guides. If you have limited experience working with HTML files, you may want to take a tutorial in HTML markup before delving into some of the more complex information found in later chapters. This book lists numerous resources for Acrobat-related issues. So if you're not familiar with a topic or concept, you'll know just where to look for more information. *Internet Publishing with Acrobat* has been carefully focused to provide Internet publishers with exactly what they need to expertly publish PDF files on the Internet with Acrobat.

Internet Publishing with Acrobat covers Adobe Acrobat 3.0, a major update of the Adobe Acrobat family of software. Acrobat 3.0 includes a number of new Internet-specific features and enhancements that make publishing with Acrobat more efficient and exciting than ever. However, even users of previous versions of Adobe's Acrobat software (2.1, 2.0, or 1.0) will benefit from the technical information and content development strategies described throughout this book.

Most of Acrobat 3.0's features have been added or enhanced to make publishing and using PDF files on the World Wide Web faster, easier, and more compelling. The Web is by far the most popular service on the Internet. However, rather than limiting the scope of this book to the Web, this book encompasses the whole Internet to include information on sending PDF files as email attachments and serving PDFs on FTP and Gopher sites. There's also technical information and content service strategies and solutions for publishing PDF files on intranets and on-demand print servers that use servers, applications, and applets to generate PDF files dynamically. These non-Web server and distribution strategies offer additional publishing opportunities alone, or in conjunction with Web publishing efforts.

1.2 Using This Book

Put this book near your computer. Undoubtedly, you'll refer to it as you create, design, edit, and prepare to publish PDF files on the Internet. Use this book before you choose a page size, for example; or, refer to it after you've sent your completed document to the printer, and now want to publish it on the Web. You may want to keep this book with your favorite book on HTML, a book on Java, your server's user manual, or some design books—all within easy reach.

The best way to use this book is in conjunction with the Acrobat user guide. The user guide includes much of the how-to information you'll need to perform the actions referred to in this book. In many cases, actual sections of the user guide are replicated so you can quickly find solutions. Also, the user guide has non-Internet publishing-related information, how-tos, and troubleshooting that may prove useful when creating, converting, and publishing PDF files with Acrobat.

The tasks and concepts involved in Internet publishing with Acrobat borrow from a number of disciplines. You should refer to a good book or tutorial on HTML if you haven't published many HTML files. Knowing the basics of HTML will help you better integrate HTML with PDF files. For additional information about related Internet-publishing technologies, see Chapter 10, "Acrobat Resources," for lists of books, publications, recommended Web sites, and discussion groups. The more you experiment with Acrobat and the more you explore the publishing possibilities of Acrobat and PDF files, the more useful you'll find this book.

Internet Publishing with Acrobat is organized sequentially, with each chapter comprising one of the major steps in the Internet publishing process. Chapters and sections are numbered for easy reference. Tables condense highly-technical information into easily digestible chunks, and figures simplify technical concepts. Using the book should be no problem. You may, however, have some questions about how the information is presented in this book and what you will find.

1.2.1 Quick Start Table

If you have a particular task or question in mind, refer to Table 1.2—1 "Quick Start: Common Internet Publishing Tasks and Questions" for a quick way to find the answers within the book.

Note: Throughout this book, references to other sections include the section's number and title heading.

If you want to...	Then...
Learn how to publish existing files on the Web as PDFs...	See Section 3.1, "Content Development Strategies," which describes a number of strategies for converting existing files and paper documents into PDF files for Internet publication.
Learn more about the Internet-specific attributes of Acrobat 3.0 (and earlier versions), and which features are most useful for an Internet publisher...	Read over Section 2.1, "What is Adobe Acrobat?"
Develop a strategy to integrate PDF and HTML files on a Web site...	Start with Section 3.1.4, "Integrating HTML with PDF Files," and then see Section 8.6, "Supporting PDF Files with HTML Markup."
Select the best page size for viewing within a Web browser...	See Section 4.1.1, "Selecting Page Dimensions," which includes specific page sizes for Netscape Navigator and general suggestions for choosing page dimensions.
Use the application in which the file was created to maximize the creator software's feature for saving as a PDF file...	Read both Section 4.2, "Choosing Creator Applications," and Section 4.3, "PDF-Savvy Creator Applications," for help in selecting the best software for creating content to be published on the Internet as PDF files, and how to maximize the use of the creator software to automate the task of adding interactive and navigational objects to PDF files.
Edit or modify PDF files...	See Section 6.2, "Modifying PDF Documents," for strategies on making changes to your PDF files.
Set a link from a PDF file to an HTML file...	Refer to Section 7.1.11, "World Wide Web Link Action."
Have your server process or create form data from a PDF file...	Read Section 8.9, "Processing PDF Forms Data."
Optimize PDF files for progressive rendering...	See Section 7.14, "Optimizing PDF Files for the World Wide Web."

Table 1.2–1 Quick Start: Common Internet Publishing Tasks and Questions

1.2.2 Chapter Summaries

If the specific topic you are interested in doesn't appear in Table 1.2—1, "Quick Start: Common Internet Publishing Tasks and Questions," try checking the table of contents and then referring to the chapter summaries for the most relevant chapter. Each chapter begins with a list that summarizes the most relevant information for Internet publishing in that particular chapter. For a quick reference, the following summaries introduce the concepts and technical information found in the chapters and appendices.

Chapter 2: "Adobe Acrobat and the Portable Document Format." What is Adobe Acrobat 3.0 and the Portable Document Format (PDF), and why are PDF files so well suited for Internet publishing? This chapter discusses the software required to publish electronic documents on the Internet.

Chapter 3: "Selecting Content Strategies, Sources, Formats, and Service." Which publishing strategy and file format (PDF or HTML) best fit the content? What is the source of the content? Given the intended purpose (and use) of the PDF files, what is the best way to serve them to the audience?

Chapter 4: "Designing Content for the Internet." Design content for the screen, as well as for online use within the document window of a Web browser. Capitalize on Acrobat's navigational and interactive features to design the most usable document that can be published on the Internet.

Chapter 5: "Converting PostScript Files to PDF Files." Describes how to convert content to PDF for distribution on the Internet. How to make visually rich, low bandwidth electronic documents also is explained in detail.

Chapter 6: "Fine-Tuning PDF Documents." How to check the PDF file and make changes to whole pages or portions of text. In addition, learn how to examine images, font usage, and other PDF elements with an eye to decreasing bandwidth without sacrificing quality.

Chapter 7: "Adding Interactive and Navigational Objects." Discover the best methods for getting the most out of PDF documents on the Internet by adding interactive and navigational enrichments to PDF documents

Chapter 8: "Publishing PDF files on the Internet." Configure Internet servers (FTP, Gopher, and HTTP) to properly serve PDF files. Includes a section on how to serve progressively rendered PDF files and how to download page-at-a-time (optimized) PDF files.

Chapter 9: "Troubleshooting." Compiles and summarizes the most common user errors in working with Acrobat and Acrobat-related software.

Chapter 10: "Acrobat Resources." Contains comprehensive lists of products, services, and Acrobat resources in and for almost every medium. It even provides information about how to subscribe to reference materials.

1.2.3 Appendices

The appendices include summaries from relevant Adobe technical notes not included with Adobe's software documentation. These appendices provide information that is of particular relevance to many of the concepts found in this book. The full text of the summarized technical documents can be found on the Adobe Web site at http://www.adobe.com/.

Appendix A: "Web Server Software," lists and annotates a number of Web servers that support the new page-on-demand downloading and progressive rendering of Acrobat 3.0 PDF files.

Appendix B: "Internet Searching and Indexing Software," like Appendix A, lists and annotates server-based indexing and search software that supports the PDF file format.

Appendix C: "The Forms Data Format," describes the data format used by PDF file forms and indicates what Web publishers need to know about generating and processing these files.

Appendix D: "Interapplication Communication and Web Browsers," focuses on the language Web browsers and Acrobat viewers use to speak to each other. Interapplication communication allows the integrated viewing of PDF documents directly within World Wide Web browsers.

Appendix E: "Configuring QuarkXPress to Produce PDF Files," explains Quark-specific configuration issues including custom page width and printer-description setup specifications.

Appendix F: "Font Copyrights," contains information about the rights and limitations of embedding fonts within a PDF file. It also includes lists of font companies and designers who allow fonts to be embedded in PDF files.

Appendix G: "Font Embedding Information," explains where embedded fonts are stored in PDF files. Also included is information on how PDF files are viewed and how printers handle embedded or substituted fonts, by platform and font type.

Appendix H: "Setting Options in Distiller's Startup Directory," presents several basic modifications that can be made to the

Acrobat Distiller startup script. These modifications automate page changes when converting PostScript files to PDF files.

Appendix I: "Acrobat Plug-ins," lists plug-ins that are currently available for use with Acrobat Exchange or Acrobat Reader. Additionally, a summary of each plug-in's usefulness to Internet publishers is included.

Appendix J: "Acrobat-Related Creator Application Plug-ins," lists plug-ins that add Acrobat support to popular creator applications (Adobe PageMaker, QuarkXPress, etc.).

Appendix K: "Converting Other File Types to PDF," lists resources, companies, and software products that provide conversion to PDF files from other file formats, including LaTeX and TIFF.

1.2.4 Tables

This book makes extensive use of tables that can be used for quick reference. Each table presents information simply and compactly. The accompanying text fully explains many of the concepts summarized in the tables. Many of these tables can be used in conjunction with the *Portable Document Format Reference Manual* (see Chapter 10, "Acrobat Resources,"), which provides more general technical information about PDF files.

1.2.5 Cross-References

Cross-references, common in most technical references, point to related topics. Herein, the cross-references may be to another page in the book, a site on the World Wide Web, or Acrobat Online documentation. Each cross-reference includes the section number and heading title. The goal is to provide a compact, focused text that allows asynchronous navigation through the book, with tangents to other easily attainable topics and techniques.

Note: World Wide Web locations frequently change, although the information at these sites is current and valid as of the writing of this reference.

1.2.6 Glossary and Index

Terms that are key to understanding electronic publishing concepts are defined in the glossary. Where applicable, how the term relates specifically to Acrobat or Internet publishing is explained. The index provides additional accessibility for locating specific issues—navigating through the book by term, rather than page number.

1.2.7 Other Resources

While this book aims to answer most questions about Internet publishing with Acrobat, as a publisher's need for customized solutions or curiosity grows, other Acrobat and publishing resources will prove useful in expanding a publisher's knowledge. Included are a number of other books on Acrobat, useful World Wide Web sites, Usenet or email discussion groups specific to PDF, and additional resources for information on Acrobat and related technologies.

2

Adobe Acrobat and the Portable Document Format

This chapter introduces Adobe's Acrobat software, which can be used to view, create, author, and index PDF files. Internet publishers may feel they do not need to concern themselves with all the Acrobat tools; however, a firm knowledge of the capabilities of Acrobat tools (applications, utilities, and plug-ins) will assist them in content development. A publisher well grounded in content development will be more effective in the delivery of that content. This chapter provides a context for the development and delivery of content by presenting the following information about Acrobat and PDF files:

- The Internet-specific capabilities and recommended uses of all the Adobe Acrobat software is outlined. For Internet publishing, some features of Acrobat can be more suitable than others. By defining the categories of Acrobat applications and identifying the differences between members of the same category, Internet publishers are able to choose the correct application for the job.

- An overview of the Portable Document Format, including its history, core technology, and its future is discussed.
- Interactive and navigational objects, found in well-designed and constructed PDF files, are identified and defined. An understanding of these objects is key, especially for publishers new to Acrobat.
- Issues of PDF file compatibility with Web browsers and server software is addressed. Backward compatibility of the file format (and software), and describing what makes the PDF file format an open, extendible publishing standard (and why that's important), also is explained.
- This chapter addresses a number of Internet-born concerns about the PDF file format including viewing PDF files, security options, bandwidth use, and new indexing strategies.

This chapter also provides information on platform, operating system, and language availability for all the Acrobat applications. Detailed information is provided on where publishers can get Adobe software and plug-ins, and third-party software that either extends or mirrors the capabilities of Acrobat software.

2.1 What is Adobe Acrobat?

The Adobe Acrobat family of software is a suite of electronic publishing tools. Used together, Acrobat comprises a complete electronic publishing system that can be used individually, or in any combination to match the diverse needs of electronic publishers.

As shown in Table 2.1—1, Acrobat applications fall into three general classifications based on the tasks each application performs.

Classification	Application Name(s)	Description
Viewers	Acrobat Reader Acrobat Exchange Acrobat Player	Viewers display and allow interaction with PDF documents.[2]
Producers	Exchange with Acrobat Capture and Import Plug-ins PDFWriter Acrobat Distiller (with Distiller Assistant) Acrobat Capture	Applications that convert electronic files, or paper documents to PDF files.
Indexer	Acrobat Catalog[1]	Generates indices used by search engines to conduct inquiries.

Table 2.1—1 Adobe Acrobat Software by Class

[1] Other indexing software can create indices that include PDF files, among other file formats. While these products are not part of Adobe's Acrobat software, they can be classified as indexers.

[2] Zeon Corporation's suite of PDF viewing clones are similar to Reader and Exchange (see Section 10.6.1, "Zeon Corporation's DocuComp PDF Viewers and Producers").

Note: Other applications (Adobe Illustrator 5.5 (Mac), Adobe Illustrator 6.0, Transverter Pro, and GhostView) may be able to open, view, print, or edit PDF files. However, these applications may not allow interaction with the content as a viewer does.

2.1.1 Adobe Acrobat Reader

The freely available Acrobat Reader® opens, views, and prints, copies of PDF files, including those downloaded from the Internet. Use Acrobat Reader to navigate through PDF documents with the Reader's toolbar or via interactive objects added to the document.

Reader and Exchange use Adobe's Multiple Master font technology to maintain all line breaks and formatting in order to match the design of the original font.

Acrobat Reader (3.0 and later) works cooperatively with Acrobat 3.0-compatible Web browsers such as Netscape Navigator (2.x or later), Microsoft Internet Explorer (2.0 or later), or other Acrobat 3.0-savvy Web browsers. Users can view, print, and interact seamlessly with PDF documents in an Acrobat 3.0-savvy Web browser window. Reader's capabilities function normally, with the exception of keyboard shortcuts.

Note: The Reader's menus are not visible or functional when viewing a PDF document within a Web browser. Some functions, however, can be controlled by the Menu Action function.

Acrobat Reader is free, shareable, and available on the Internet through the Adobe Acrobat Web site at http://www.adobe.com/acrobat/. It also is bundled with a variety of applications. Table 2.1—2 lists the Acrobat Reader's availability by platform and operating system. For the most complete list of the Reader's availability, check Adobe's Acrobat Web site.

Readers are available in the following languages: Dutch, English (US), French, German, Italian, Spanish, Swedish, UK English, and Asian languages. (For current Reader language availability see the Acrobat Web site at http://www.adobe.com/acrobat/.)

Acrobat Reader also supports a special class of plug-ins configured specifically for use with the Reader. These plug-ins extend the capabilities of Reader and the PDF files they open. Because Reader is for reading PDF files—not for making changes to PDF

Platform	Operating System
680x0 Macintosh and Power Macintosh	Macintosh OS 7.x
PC	Windows 3.x Windows 95 Windows NT 3.5, 4.x OS/2 DOS (Acrobat 1.0 only)
UNIX	SunOS 4.1.3 Sun Solaris 2.3, 2.4, 2.5 Hewlett-Packard-UX 9.03 SGI IRIX 5.3, 6.2 AIX 4.1

Table 2.1—2 Acrobat Reader Availability by Platform and Operating System

---

Note: Support and availability of new Acrobat Reader versions for older operating systems typically diminishes with the support for and use of those systems.

files, most plug-ins are programmed for Exchange, which is used to make changes to PDF files. One exception is the Forms Plug-in which, when installed, enables the user to interact and add data to form fields, although the changes cannot be saved. More information on Acrobat plug-ins can be found later in this chapter and in Appendix I, "Acrobat Plug-ins." (See Adobe's Acrobat Web site at http://www.adobe.com/acrobat/ for a list of plug-ins that work with the free Acrobat Reader.)

Acrobat Reader, widely distributed through many channels, allows users to view PDF documents without investing in software, or requiring the distribution of a viewer with the PDF files. No royalties are collected by Adobe for individual PDF files, thereby encouraging the unlimited publication of any number of PDF documents.

2.1.2 Adobe Acrobat Exchange

Adobe Acrobat Exchange®—like Acrobat Reader—opens, views, and prints PDF files. Exchange differs from the Reader in that it enables the addition of interactive and navigational objects to PDF files; it also allows changes to be saved. Like other Acrobat viewers, Exchange makes use of Adobe's font matching technology to display documents that match the original document's typographical design.

Exchange is an essential tool for Web publishers and for power Web users. Exchange can make whole-page modifications, as well as add or edit the object and interactive features of PDF files. Acrobat Exchange (3.0 and later), and the Touch Up Plug-in can modify portions of text to correct typographical errors, make adjustments, and add visual cues for hypertext links. Exchange enables PDF files to be password protected to allow or to prevent users from printing, making changes, or adding notes to PDF documents.

Table 2.1—3 lists the availability of Acrobat Exchange by platform and operating system.

Acrobat Exchange is available in the following languages: Dutch, English (US), French, German, Italian, Spanish, Swedish, UK English, and Asian languages. (See the Acrobat Web site at http://www.adobe.com/acrobat/ for current Exchange language availability.) In addition to Reader's functions (also found in Exchange), the following list summarizes the capabilities of Acrobat Exchange:

Platform	Operating System
680x0 Macintosh and Power Macintosh	Macintosh OS 7.x
PC	Windows 3.x Windows 95 Windows NT 3.5, 4.x OS/2 DOS (Acrobat 1.0 only)
UNIX	SunOS 4.1.3 Sun Solaris 2.3, 2.4, 2.5 Hewlett-Packard-UX 9.03 AIX 4.1

Table 2.1—3 Acrobat Exchange Availability by Platform and Operating System

- Make whole-page modifications by copying, deleting, cropping, extracting, rotating, replacing, combining, or inserting pages.
- Add interactive features, which can include hypertext links to other locations within the same PDF document, to URLs, to another PDF file, or to other applications' files; create easy-to-view and navigable threads that follow the flow of a story across columns and pages; add sticky-type notes in any color; create or delete thumbnails (small bitmapped previews of pages) in the document; set, move, and delete bookmarks (which act like a table of contents), collapsible outlines, or lists of key features.
- Create user-fillable forms and buttons with the AcroForm Plug-in included with Acrobat 3.0) that can be processed remotely or printed. While Reader users make changes and

print information in form fields, only Acrobat Exchange can save the changes.

- Optimize PDF files to allow the progressive rendering of PDF pages. (This also partially enables on-demand downloading of specified PDF pages from a PDF file.)
- Import images into PDF documents.
- Limit access through a password to prevent access, or secure the document to prevent a user from printing, changing, copying text or graphics, or adding notes to the document.
- Include information about the document such as the author, title, subject, and keywords.
- Summarize or export notes in a document.
- Copy text or graphics to paste into other applications.
- Save PDF files (either incrementally, or as a full save with the same filename, or as a save with another filename).
- With the use of plug-ins and the extensibility they provide, almost anything is possible.

Plug-ins automate or extend the Portable Document Format. Some plug-ins require that the user install the plug-in on his or her machine before the added features can be utilized. If a plug-in is required, but not installed, the features are either ignored by Exchange (and other Acrobat viewers), or displayed with a dummy placeholder.

Adobe's Web site has the most up-to-date information on the platforms for which Exchange is available. Internet publishers frequently use both Exchange and Acrobat Distiller (which converts files to PDF files).

Note: PDF files created on a Macintosh can be edited on the Windows or UNIX platforms (and vice versa), allowing for cross-platform document creation.

2.1.3 Adobe Acrobat Distiller

Adobe Acrobat Distiller interprets and converts PostScript and Encapsulated PostScript (EPS) files into PDF files. PostScript files can be created by almost any software application that can print.

Distiller's function as a converter of PostScript files is essential for Internet publishers. When converting a PostScript file to a PDF file, Distiller compresses both text and graphics. Distiller downsamples and compresses images to save additional file size, and embeds fonts to preserve the document's typographic fidelity. Compression and downsampling allow PDF files to be substantially smaller than the original file size. Resulting file size depends on the number of images in a file and the compression and resolution selected; however, a PDF file can be 10 to 20 times smaller than the PostScript file. Acrobat Distiller 3.0 adds the capability to convert PostScript files to either Acrobat 2.1- or Acrobat 3.0-compatible files. Acrobat 3.0-compatible files are smaller than Acrobat 2.1-compatible files (how small depends on the type of document). Details about the implications of compression, downsampling, and font embedding is explained in detail in Section 5.2, "Using Acrobat Distiller."

Acrobat Distiller is available for most popular platforms and is bundled with some Adobe software applications such as Adobe PageMaker as "Private Editions" (denoted as Acrobat Distiller PE). Private Edition Distillers cannot be used as stand-alone applications. Attempting to convert PostScript files created in any other application than the application with which Distiller PE was bundled, displays a message indicating that the file was not converted and the full version of Distiller is required.

Note: Adobe bundles Acrobat Distiller PE with PageMaker, Persuasion, WebPresenter, and FrameMaker. For users without the retail version of Adobe Acrobat, Distiller PE allows publishers to convert files created in these applications to PDF files. Publishing these same PDF files on the Internet—which requires optimization, the addition of World Wide Web URLs, and more—is accomplished by using Acrobat Exchange. Exchange can be obtained by purchasing the retail version of Adobe Acrobat.

Acrobat Distiller is available in the following languages: Dutch, English (US), French, German, Italian, Spanish, Swedish, UK English, and Asian languages. (See the Acrobat Web site at http://www.adobe.com/acrobat/ for current Distiller language availability.)

Platform	Operating System
680x0 Macintosh and Power Macintosh	Macintosh OS 7.x
PC	Windows 3.x Windows 95 Windows NT 3.5, 4.x OS/2
UNIX	SunOS 4.1.3, 4.1.4 Sun Solaris 2.3, 2.4, 2.5 Hewlett-Packard-UX 9.03 and later AIX 4.1 and later

Table 2.1—4 Acrobat Distiller Availability by Platform and Operating System

Distiller can be used on a network. It can be configured to check and convert PostScript files dropped into defined folders. Also, Distiller can be controlled either over a network or locally with the interapplication communication (IAC) features present in most operating systems, such as AppleEvents on Macintosh computers, or Windows' messages on computers running Windows.

2.1.4 Adobe Acrobat Distiller Assistant

When running, Distiller Assistant converts files to PDF from the application in which they were created, without the added step of first manually printing or saving the files as a PostScript file. Additionally, Distiller Assistant watches designated folders for new files and then launches Distiller to convert the PostScript files to PDF files. Distiller Assistant also launches Distiller to convert files to PDF files when a PostScript file is dragged and dropped on its icon.

Note: While Acrobat Distiller also supports drag-and-drop procedures, it doesn't offer Assistant's customizable viewing, termination, and saving options described below. Drag-and-drop actions vary by platform and operating system. Check Adobe's documentation for system requirements and drag-and-drop actions specific to Distiller.

Distiller Assistant aids in the conversion of application files to PDF files by performing the following tasks:

- Converts PDF files in one easy step by printing directly to the Acrobat Distiller.
- Monitors Distiller's watched folders and Acrobat Distiller for new PostScript files.
- Launches Distiller when PostScript files are dragged and

dropped on the Distiller Assistant program icon (Windows), which then converts the file to a PDF file.

Platform	Operating System
680x0 Macintosh and Power Macintosh	Macintosh OS 7.x[1]
PC[2]	Windows 3.x Windows 95 Windows NT 3.5, 4.x

Table 2.1—5 Acrobat Distiller Assistant 3.0 Availability by Platform and Operating System

[1] Not compatible with QuickDraw GX.

[2] Distiller Assistant 2.1 is available for Windows 3.1 and Windows 95. Distiller Assistant 2.1 is not available for Macintosh.

2.1.5 Adobe Acrobat PDFWriter

PDFWriter® is a print driver-level converter that converts a creator application's files directly to the PDF file format, without first converting the file to a PostScript file. Rather than sending a document to a printer, it can be sent to Acrobat PDFWriter to create a PDF file.

Note: PDFWriter outputs bitmap previews, not the true EPS file, when used in a file and converted to PDF by PDFWriter. Bitmap previews are substantially lower in quality than the true EPS files. For higher output quality, use Distiller to convert files that include EPS graphics.

Internet publishers should use Distiller rather than PDFWriter when converting files to PDF files to allow the greatest degree of control over the PDF conversion process.

When total control over all PDF conversion features is unimportant, PDFWriter is a useful alternative to Distiller. PDFWriter yields satisfactory results for memos, reports, and other text-based documents. For these documents, PDFWriter is much faster and more convenient to use than Distiller, while still producing high-quality PDF files.

Platform	Operating System
680x0 Macintosh and Power Macintosh	Macintosh OS 7.x
PC	Windows 3.x Windows 95 Windows NT 3.5, 4.x

Table 2.1—6 Acrobat PDFWriter 3.0 Availability by Platform and Operating System

2.1.6 Adobe Acrobat Catalog

Acrobat Catalog® generates indices of PDF documents and saves these indices as index-definition files identified by their ".PDX" filename extension. With the Search Plug-in installed, users can search one or more index-definition files with Reader or Exchange. The Search Plug-in supports common keywords and free text searches, allows multiple-term Boolean queries, and can find phonetic matches, related terms, or items near a term or word.

Catalog is a useful tool for managing a large number of PDF files. Unfortunately, it has limited use on the Internet. Catalog can generate indices of PDF files on an Internet site, but the Search Plug-in cannot access indices over the Internet. Only locally-mounted volumes (hard drives, LANs, WANs, or CD-ROMs) may be searched. Additionally, the free Reader doesn't include the Search Plug-in. It is, however, included with the retail version of Adobe Acrobat. As a result, only Exchange users or Reader users with the Search Plug-in may search a locally-mounted index.

Platform	Operating System
680x0 Macintosh and Power Macintosh	Macintosh OS 7.x
PC	Windows 3.x Windows 95 Windows NT 3.5, 4.x

Table 2.1—7 Acrobat Catalog 3.0 Availability by Platform and Operating System

Searching a collection of PDF files on an Internet server requires server-level indexing software that supports the PDF file type. Verity Inc., whose indexing and searching technology are the basis of the Catalog system, has a Web server-based solution to the PDF indexing dilemma. Appendix B, "Internet Searching and Indexing Software," details Verity's TopicSearch, Fulcrum's SurfBoard, and Cascade's MediaSphere, as well as server-level PDF index and search solutions from other vendors.

Note: Some Internet server indexing software (e.g., Verity) can use Acrobat Catalog-generated indices, rather than generating a separate index. Using the same index allows concurrent publishing on other media with exacting search inquiry results, and the need to generate only an index.

2.1.7 Adobe Acrobat Capture

For publishers who need to move large amounts of paper-based content to electronic documents and the Web, Acrobat Capture is an essential tool. Acrobat Capture works with almost all scanners to digitize and convert paper-based documents to PDF files. Through page recognition technology, Capture maintains the document's layout, text, graphics and images, and matches fonts as closely as possible. Words that Capture cannot recognize are not replaced with errors symbols—like most optical character recognition schemes—but are maintained as bitmap images so the document can be read and printed. Capture then adds its closest approximation of the word and places invisible text behind the bitmap image, so the document can be indexed and searched later (by either Acrobat viewer's find command or a search engine).

The accuracy of text recognition can be adjusted by setting Capture's confidence level, which is the level at which it distinguishes text as text or as a bitmapped image. Errors in the Capture process can be corrected with Capture's Reviewer. Reviewer displays the words Capture missed and edits them. Presently, Capture doesn't support color graphics, so it converts color images into grayscale JPEGs. Capture also outputs the files in other file formats such as Microsoft Word, ASCII, and Rich Text Format (RTF).

Capture is a separate Acrobat component that can be purchased separately. It is not included with the retail version of Adobe Acrobat. For occasional conversion of paper documents to PDF files, the Acrobat Capture Plug-in introduced with Acrobat 3.0, performs the basic task of converting scanned documents to PDF files. See Section 2.1.9, "Adobe Acrobat Plug-ins," for more information about the Capture Plug-in.

Note: For scanning multi-page documents or a large number of documents at one time, consider using a scanner with an automatic document feeder attachment or using a service bureau.

Platform	Operating System
PC	Windows 3.x Windows 95 Windows NT 3.5, 4.x

Table 2.1—8 Acrobat Capture Availability by Platform and Operating System

2.1.8 Adobe Acrobat Player

Acrobat Player represents the logical evolution of PDF viewers to meet changing developments in the computer industry. The device-independent Player enables original equipment manufacturers (OEMs) to integrate PDF in set-top boxes, digital billboards, projectors, and in automobile mapping systems.

Extending the PDF file format beyond the personal computer enhances the attractiveness of this technology to publishers.

Detailed technical information about Acrobat Player can be found at Adobe's Acrobat Web site, http://www.adobe.com/acrobat/), or by contacting Adobe's Developer Association at http://www.adobe.com/supportservice/devrelations/.

2.1.9 Adobe Acrobat Plug-ins

Acrobat plug-ins extend the PDF file format and/or the Acrobat software family. The Portable Document Format is extensible, thereby allowing software developers to write plug-ins that add new features, formats, automation, or integration into the PDF file format. Plug-ins for Exchange can automate tasks such as creating bookmarks, or making global changes to link boundary colors. An Adobe Acrobat Software Development Kit (SDK) is available through the Adobe Developer's Association. Developers can build on the sample plug-in source code and the example plug-ins included with the SDK to create custom publishing solutions facilitated by a custom-designed Acrobat plug-in.

The plug-in system has proved successful for other Adobe products such as Adobe Photoshop®, Adobe Illustrator®, and Adobe PageMaker®. Plug-ins for these programs allow integration with PDF files. Adobe PageMaker includes a plug-in that enables publishers to create a PDF file that includes the interactive features of PDF, without ever touching Exchange.

Other software companies extend an application's features to embrace the interactive and navigational objects of PDF with XTensions (used with QuarkXPress), filters, and macros. (See Appendix J, "Acrobat-Related Creator Application Plug-ins," for a list of these companies and their products.)

2.2 What is the Portable Document Format?

The Portable Document Format (PDF) is the file format used by Adobe Acrobat and PDF-compatible products (see Appendix K, "Converting Other File Types to PDF"). It is an open, cross-platform file format that represents documents independent of the software, hardware, and the operating system used to create the file. PDF preserves the fidelity of electronic documents, enabling information to be distributed in a single format across the Internet and other media. This means that a PDF document created on a Macintosh computer can be viewed by a Windows 95 user after downloading the PDF file from a Web site running UNIX.

The Portable Document Format is extensible and supports incremental updating of files. PDF files can be optimized for distribution on a particular medium such as the Web, a CD-ROM, or a commercial online service. Web PDF files are optimized to progressively render page elements (text, images, fonts, and objects, which include links, bookmarks, and buttons) page by page as the file downloads. Furthermore, plug-ins can expand PDF files or add features to the applications that are used to view and enrich them.

The interactive and navigational objects built into PDF allow users to customize their experience with a publication. These objects include the following:

- Links to other PDF pages, application files, Internet sites, and media files.

- Bookmarks that provide links to hierarchically-structured content within a document, as well as several other actions.
- Thumbnails that display a miniature representation of each page.
- Article threads to allow users to follow the flow of a story, which can span multiple columns and pages.
- Form fields that users can fill in, modify, and print out or submit to a server for processing. Forms also can be populated by importing form data into the PDF file.
- Buttons for navigation (buttons are form-field objects).
- Notes that are similar to the digital sticky notes commonly used to annotate information.
- Views to allow a user to magnify or reduce a page to fit within the user's computer screen. Web publishers can emphasize graphics or text areas using Views.

PDF is based on the PostScript® language imaging model. PDF's color and resolution independence enables crisp, color-precise printing on almost all printers. For the screen, device-independent color enables precise color matching regardless of the monitor used. The resolution independence of PDF also enables magnification up to 800% without text or clarity loss in graphics. However, bitmap images display at their own resolutions. Increasing the magnification of a PDF document that contains a bitmap image will display the image clearly until the on screen resolution (typically 72 to 75 dpi at 100%) is greater than the resolution of the image, resulting in image clarity loss.

2.3 Strengths of PDF as an Internet-Publishable File Format

PDF files are well suited for Internet publishing, as well as publishing in other media. HTML and PDF share many characteristics that make them both highly efficient and usable file formats. These features include cross-platform compatibility, support for interactive forms, incremental updates, hypertext, support for other media, other graphic and image file types, and compact file size, to name a few.

2.3.1 Integrated with Web Browsers

As of this writing, Netscape Communications' Netscape Navigator 2.x and 3.x, and Microsoft's Internet Explorer both support Acrobat Reader 3.0 through the PDFViewer Web browser plug-in and ActiveX interapplication communication, respectively. Other Web browser companies have announced their intent to allow users to view PDF files within their Web browsers as a plug-in.

The Acrobat 3.0 PDFViewer Plug-in for Netscape and Netscape API-compatible Web browsers enables the viewing of PDF files within a Web browser's document window. When displaying an HTML document, the interface and interaction are the same; when a PDF file is opened, the Acrobat 3.0 toolbar loads in the browser's document window (usually just under the Web browser's toolbar), along with the PDF file. Opening a PDF file with a Web browser that does not support Acrobat 3.0 downloads the PDF file from the Web and then launches an installed Acrobat viewer—if the browser has been configured to do so.

Viewing PDF files within an Acrobat 3.0-compatible Web browser also enables the user to interact with the content—that is, all the interactive and navigational features found in PDF files work. Additionally, these PDF files can be printed or downloaded (by saving the source file to a local hard drive for later use.)

Note: To completely download an entire PDF file for use off-line within an Acrobat viewer, or to transfer the copy of the file to other media (CD-ROMs, removable drives, etc.), use the Web browser's method of saving files to a local hard drive. For most Web browsers this is accomplished by the Save Link As option. PDF file pages downloaded on demand are cached and viewable only in the Web browser's document window. These cached pages cannot be opened directly within an Acrobat viewer.

2.3.2 Optimizing PDF for Web Browser Viewing

The cooperation between an Acrobat viewer and a Web browser represents the client side of Acrobat 3.0. Any PDF file on any Internet server can be viewed with an Acrobat-compatible Web browser; however, only "optimized" PDF files served by Web servers that serve byte ranges can progressively render each page as it downloads, page-by-page within an Acrobat 3.0-compatible Web browser. Use Acrobat Exchange to optimize PDF files (see Section 7.14, "Optimizing PDF Files for the World Wide Web").

Optimization orders and identifies all the elements (text, images, interactive features, etc.) within a PDF file. This means that the Web server locates and sends only the requested pages—one page at a time—for the user to view, rather than the whole document. In addition, optimization facilitates progressive rendering of page elements as the page downloads. Progressive rendering first displays text, then graphics, then interactive and navigational objects (which can include links, bookmarks, buttons, notes, and more), then images, and finally the true fonts and thumbnails as needed.

Optimization also reduces the size of the PDF file by removing redundant graphics and images. When the image or graphic is displayed again (in another page or by returning to the page originally viewed), both rendering and downloading speeds are increased because the image or graphic already has been read and stored for quick access.

Use HTML for navigation and for short excerpts of information. Use PDF for graphically rich content and for longer pieces or publications that are intended to be downloaded and saved, or printed. The combination of PDF and HTML enables Internet publishers to serve content in its most usable file format, according to the demands of the content—not the technology. With HTML, PDF, and other file formats integrated within a user's browser, publishers are free to use file formats other than HTML for publishing projects.

2.3.3 PDF File Sizes and Page-on-Demand Download Times

Progressive rendering, enabled through byte-request-enabled servers and optimized PDF files, makes the page contents of even large PDF files (1M and more) display quickly. While the user is viewing the page, subsequent pages of the PDF file (in sequential order) are downloaded. When the user moves to the next page, it may be completely downloaded and appear instantly.

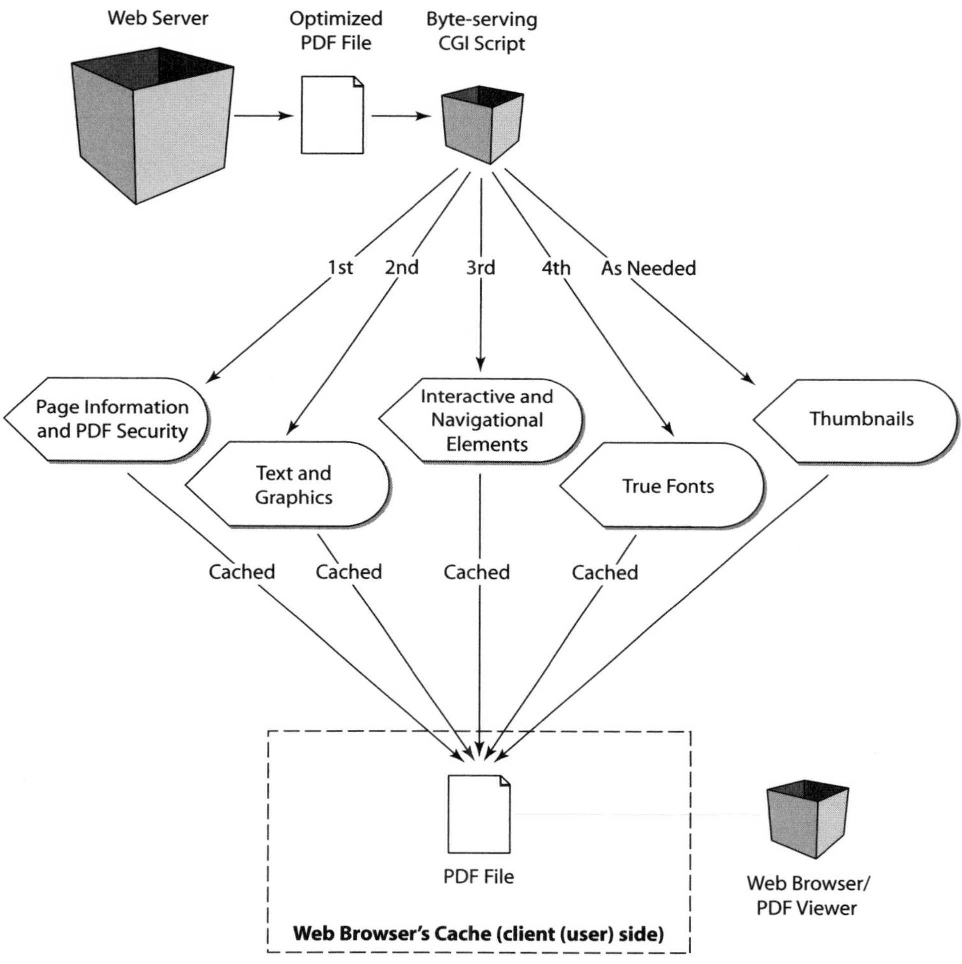

Figure 2.3—1 Progressive Rendering

The size and amount of text, graphics, images, and fonts of a single page determine the time required to download the page, not the PDF file's size. A single PDF page, similar in design to many HTML files found on the Web, is on average only 15 to 45K (kilobytes). Downloading a PDF document page this size takes approximately 13 seconds with a 28.8 kbps (kilobits per second) modem connection. However, PDF files with extensive use of images, fonts, and graphics—as PDF files should be used—can be between 100 to 250K per page, requiring just over a minute to wholly download at 28.8 kbps.

Acrobat 3.0's page-on-demand downloading enables users to navigate to any page of a multi-page PDF document. Choosing another page in the PDF document begins the progressive rendering of the selected page as the page's data is downloaded from the server. Downloaded data from previous pages is cached and read directly from the cache when a user navigates through previous pages. When the same image, graphic, or font is encountered again in subsequent pages of the document, the cached data is used (which is much quicker than downloading the elements again).

The combination of progressive rendering and page-on-demand downloading allows users to view and interact with a 100M PDF file with more than 100 pages just as quickly as a 100K PDF file with 10 pages. This makes it possible to combine and publish an entire site's-worth of PDF files in a single PDF document without affecting the time required to view any one page. However, the goal to integrate PDF files with other document types and the continual need to update and modify pages often make this practice ineffective.

2.3.4 Compatible with Server Software

HTML, PDF, and other Internet file formats can be served on the same site seamlessly. PDF files require no translation, compression, or special filters on any type of Internet server (FTP, Gopher, Web, etc.). Some older World Wide Web server software may require some basic configuration to recognize PDF files, display the proper icons (when viewed in an index), and allow page-on-demand downloading and progressive rendering of PDF files. These servers can easily add this capability for free by running a simple script to the server. Most servers today, however, come with this configuration built-in. (See Section 8.2, "Configuring Web Servers for PDF Files," for detailed information on configuring a Web server for PDF publishing.)

A number of companies support (or are planning to support) the full-text searching of PDF files via indexing, searching, and file management software running on a Web server.

2.3.5 Backward and Forward Compatibility of Viewers and Files

All versions of Acrobat viewers and PDF files are backward compatible. Some viewers, depending on the PDF file version, are forward compatible. This backward and forward compatibility enables older PDF files to be displayed in new viewers, or some older Acrobat viewers to display new PDF files (with the exception of Acrobat 3.0-generated files).

Acrobat 3.0 supports the Portable Document Format versions 1.0, 1.1, and 1.2. Features native to PDF version 1.2 and Acrobat 3.0 (e.g., compressed fonts, overprint settings, halftones, and transfer functions) are not compatible with Acrobat 2.1 and earlier versions. (See the Acrobat 3.0/2.1 compatibility chart in the Distiller 3.0 Online Guide for information on feature compatibility with previous versions of Acrobat software products.)

2.3.6 Interactivity and Linking

PDF documents share many of the same types of interactive features found in HTML documents and multimedia applications. PDF, like HTML, allows the basic level of interactivity—common lower level branching to other URLs through hyperlinks or context-based links called "hypertext."

PDF also has several content structures (such as bookmarks, magnification zooms, article threads, and notes) not found in HTML, which make interacting with PDF publications more compelling.

2.3.7 Searching PDF Files

PDF files can be searched at two levels, much like HTML documents. On one level, open PDF documents can be searched for specific words or text strings by using the Find command. This feature is accessible through the Find icon in the Acrobat toolbar when the PDF file is viewed in a Web browser.

Note: With the Find command, only the loaded text from either the PDF or HTML documents can be searched.

On another level, the entire contents of document files can be indexed—whether the documents utilize PDF, HTML, or other file formats such as text. The queries are requested of an Internet search engine, so documents don't need to be downloaded to be searchable. More and more Internet search engines are reporting that they intend to index PDF documents, thereby integrating searchable PDF documents with text, HTML, and other commonly indexed Internet file formats. A list of Internet server indexing and searching software can be found in Appendix B, "Internet Searching and Indexing Software."

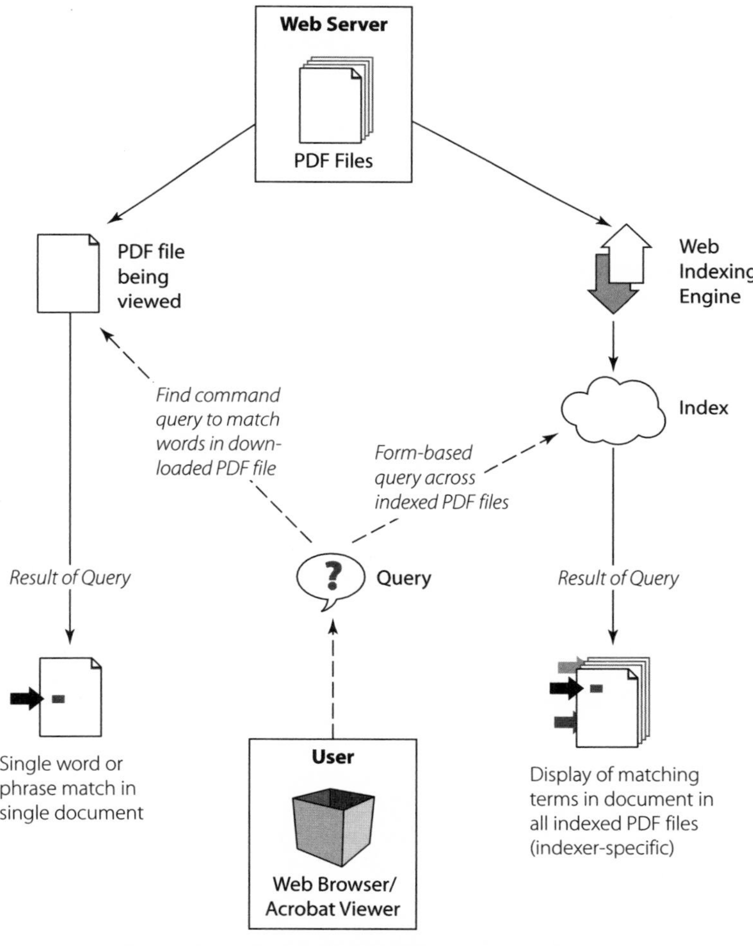

Figure 2.3—2 "Find" versus Searching

2.3.8 Security and PDF File Protection

As an option, PDF files can be encrypted with RSA Data Security Incorporated's RC4 Symmetric Stream Cipher. This very strong password protection scheme enables publishers to protect their documents at the client level, as a user is opening or downloading a document. Both off-line Acrobat viewers and viewers working with Acrobat 3.0-compatible Web browsers require the correct password to gain access. This additional security, which is supplemental to what the server can provide, helps publishers further protect their documents.

Web publishers will find that PDF provides a new level of document-level security. PDF supports a security feature that prevents the copying of text and graphics from a document. (This features does not prevent screen captures, however.) As an option, PDF files can be set to prevent users from making changes and printing a document. Password changes and preventive security options can be protected by requiring another unique password before changes can be made to the PDF file.

2.3.9 Extending the Capabilities of PDF Files and Software

The Portable Document Format is extensible. Through plug-ins or updates to Acrobat, PDF files can have additional capabilities. An example of an extension to the PDF file format is the Movie Plug-in, which enhances the list of PDF actions to allow publishers to link, open, and play multimedia files within a PDF document.

PDF files are flexible. They can be represented as binary data or ASCII text. PDF files can be updated incrementally, or have items removed without corrupting or affecting the file's overall structural integrity.

PDF files are dynamic. The Acrobat Form Plug-in (and other third-party plug-ins for Acrobat) permits user input, which allows the user to customize content.

2.3.10 PDF Is an Easy-to-Create, Publishable File Format

Generally, software packages that can print, can create PDF files through a PDF producer application. Some applications also have the resident capability to open PDF files (e.g., Adobe Illustrator, Transverter Pro, GhostView, etc.). Additionally, PDF files or portions of a PDF file can be exported or converted to other file formats (e.g., Rich Text Format (RTF), Encapsulated PostScript (EPS), PICT, etc.).

The Portable Document Format is a published specification maintained by Adobe Systems. Adobe holds no trademark to the Portable Document Format (or PDF)—only Adobe's Acrobat software is trademarked. Developers can refer to Adobe's Acrobat specification to create plug-ins, applications, and other tools that read, create, or modify PDF files without permission or licensing from Adobe Systems. By publishing the PDF specification, Adobe hopes to encourage users and developers to adopt the PDF file format as a file format standard for publishing graphically rich documents on the Internet and via other digital delivery options. The PDF specification (version 1.0) was first published in 1993 as the *Portable Document Format Reference Manual* by the Addison-Wesley Publishing Company. Notes regarding the update of the PDF specification from 1.0 to 1.1 are detailed in Adobe technical note #5156 available on Adobe's Web site. See the Adobe Developer's Association at http://www.adobe.com/supportservice/devrelations/ for information on PDF 1.2, and updates to the most current version of the PDF specification.

Acrobat Distiller 3.0 can create PDF files using either version 1.1 of the Portable Document Format (compatible with 2.1 and earlier), or version 1.2 (the version required for publishing progressively-rendered, page-on-demand downloading of PDF files on the Web). Version 1.2 of the Portable Document Format is compatible with Acrobat 3.0 and later.

2.3.11 The Look of a PDF File

PDF files maintain the look and feel of the original file format in the application that created them. Documents designed in Adobe PageMaker, QuarkXPress, Microsoft Word, CorelDRAW, and hundreds of other popular software applications can be converted to PDF files, thereby maintaining the way the document originally looked.

PDF's rich, visual integrity operates at several levels:

- The physical structure of the document is maintained, including the number of pages and its dimensions, margins, placement of text, graphics and images, and more.
- Information about each element's color and resolution is either preserved or represented so it can be reproduced in an Acrobat viewer or printer, independent of the installed software or hardware.
- At the character level, font data can be read from the user's machine (if the font is in residence), or read from the information embedded in the PDF file, or substituted by the Acrobat viewer.

Combined, each level works to produce a document that closely resembles the original document.

Acrobat software and the Portable Document Format bridge the gap between how the content should look and how it ends up looking, bringing the world of Internet publishing within reach. With no need to learn a complicated scripting or authoring language, the Web publisher can connect with an audience through interactive features built directly into Acrobat software and PDF files.

2.4 Where to Get Adobe Acrobat Software

The free Acrobat Reader and other free plug-ins, macros, and demos of Acrobat-related software can be found at the Adobe Acrobat Web site at http://www.adobe.com/acrobat/. Additionally, many of the commercial online services have Acrobat areas. Most Internet catalogs have listings for Adobe Acrobat and the companies that produce Acrobat-related products.

Note: Check http://www.adobe.com/ for more information and a list of locations that sell Adobe software. (See Section 10.6, "Acrobat-Compatible Viewer and Converter Applications" for a list of the companies that develop PDF viewing and conversion software, similar to Adobe's PDF viewers and producers.)

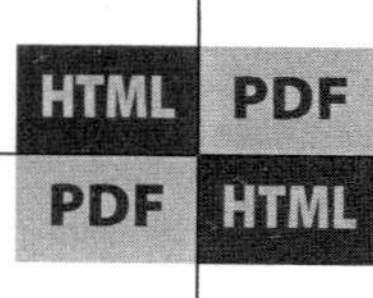

3

Selecting Content Strategies, Sources, Formats, and Service

Publishing content as Portable Document Format (PDF) files opens the powerful world of Internet publishing. Graphically rich PDF files transcend the limitations of computer platform-dependent file formats and enable Acrobat 3.0-compatible Web browsers to seamlessly display PDF documents quickly and easily. With Acrobat 3.0, PDF documents can be integrated with present HTML publishing efforts, ensuring that the appropriate file format matches the demands of the content.

The content and its use—either intended by the publisher or defined by the audience, not the technology—should determine the most suitable publishing file format. This chapter identifies strategies for content publishing and focuses on the types of content that is best published in HTML or PDF. How to serve these files and the tools that aid in the production of Internet content is discussed as well.

The following five points summarize the overall goals of this chapter:

- To effectively develop a strategy or strategies for publishing PDF files on the

Internet. Consider strategies that integrate HTML with PDF files that accommodate concurrent publishing on a variety of media and complement the publication of print-based documents.

- Collect content from any number of sources and use Acrobat to refine and adapt the content for the Internet. Sources include newly designed documents (specific for the Internet), existing electronic documents that require minimal modifications, repurposed content from other sources that require extensive design, or existing legacy documents in print that require conversion to electronic files.
- Given the publishing strategy and content, evaluate both HTML and PDF file formats in order to most effectively serve the content.
- With the most appropriate file format selected, develop a method to serve the content to best meet the needs of the audience.
- Given the publishing strategy, the content source, and the method the selected file format will be served, design the document to encourage interactivity, aid navigation, and facilitate general usability by the intended audience.

3.1 Content Development Strategies

The content strategies described herein—all specific to Internet publishing with PDF files using Adobe Acrobat—are development plans that identify potential content sources and ways to organize individual publication projects or entire Internet sites. Furthermore, these strategies establish a roadmap based on the content source and its development, which can assist the Internet publisher when selecting file formats and the modes of distribution (described in later sections in this chapter). Understanding the possible PDF publishing strategies aids in the entire process of publishing PDF files on the Internet.

Content sources include either existing documents or original content. Existing sources include corporate newsletters, magazines, data sheets, memoranda, videotapes, books, slide presentations, and many others. Original content sources are assembled for a specific publication or project. Existing content sources, which exist in other media formats, must be repurposed to be published as PDF files. Content in an electronic file format can be redesigned cooperatively with print-publishing creator applications and Acrobat software to take advantage of PDF navigational and interactive features. Content that is available only as "hard copy," those printed on paper, slides, transparencies, and other fixed media, is scanned and converted to PDF files with Acrobat Capture. For information on Acrobat Capture, see Section 2.1.6, "Adobe Acrobat Catalog." To convert other source media formats to PDF, see Appendix K, "Converting Other File Types to PDF," or Adobe's Acrobat Web site at http://www.adobe.com/acrobat/.

Note: Acrobat Capture and Capture Plug-in are the most efficient tools for digitizing printed pages to PDF files. Alternatively, optical character recognition or image digitization software may be a solution.

Table 3.1—1 outlines three common repurposed content design modifications. Source media should conform or be redesigned to meet these basic parameters. These summarized points are expanded in Chapter 4, "Designing Content for the Internet."

Item	Modification
Page dimensions	Redesign to fit well within a monitor 640 x 480 pixels (versus page sizes) and Web browser document windows. Remove extraneous margins and white space that are not needed for onscreen viewing.
Page elements	Remove page numbers, footnotes, and other items specific to print publications (and replicated in PDF).
Hypertext links	Add actions to navigate and provide interactivity between related content and context. These may correspond to features found in print documents (table of contents and cross-references, etc.).
Colors	Convert images and graphics that use CMYK colors (commonly used in print documents) to RGB[1]. The result is smaller files that display and print more quickly than those using CMYK colors.

Table 3.1—1 Common Physical Page Design Modifications for Web Publishing

[1] Acrobat Distiller converts CMYK colors to RGB by default. To change the default, Distiller's startup script must be reconfigured (see Appendix H, "Setting Options in Distiller's Startup Directory").

Note: PDF files served from on-demand print servers (see Section 3.3.1, "Using PDF Files on On-Demand Print Servers") may or may not need to be stripped of common page elements or have colors converted.

Repurposed content source strategies can include a concurrent strategy, where a single master file is used to generate a PDF version of the document and another exact copy for use on other media. Another strategy is the complementary strategy, where content sources produce two or more similar, but different publications (one in PDF, the others in other media formats). Original content strategies produce a single file, specifically design for publication as a PDF file. Finally, an integration strategy addresses methods for using existing or original content sources to produce both PDF and HTML files.

Note: It is recommended that PDF files be integrated with HTML files. Any of the existing or original content development strategies can be combined with integration. Through integration, publishers can achieve a greater potential audience and can exploit more of the Internet's publishing capabilities.

3.1.1 Concurrent Publishing of Content for Multiple Media

The resolution and color independence of PDF files and PDF support of interactive and navigational objects allow the publication of graphically rich and compelling print and electronic documents on the Internet from a single source file. This same source file can be used for professional, full-color magazines or much smaller in-house newsletters. PDF files are an optimal solution for publishing magazines, brochures, catalogs, product data sheets, reports, and other document types without the need to redesign the content before Internet publication.

Concurrent publishing, with the aid of Acrobat software, makes it possible to convert the same source file used for print reproduction (or reproduction to other media) to a PDF file. However, Internet publishers should carefully examine the online usability of a print-published document before adopting a concurrent publishing strategy. Generally, few print publications are as usable as they could be if they are simply converted to PDF files and uploaded to a Web site on the Internet. Converting a large amount of repurposed content to PDF files (referred to as "shovelware") hardly takes full advantage of PDF as a solution for Internet publishing.

Note: Publishers who create PostScript files from their files for traditional printing at a service bureau or commercial printer can convert this same PostScript file to a PDF file. Some modifications may be needed to make the file useful on the Internet. Most modifications can be accomplished with Distiller.

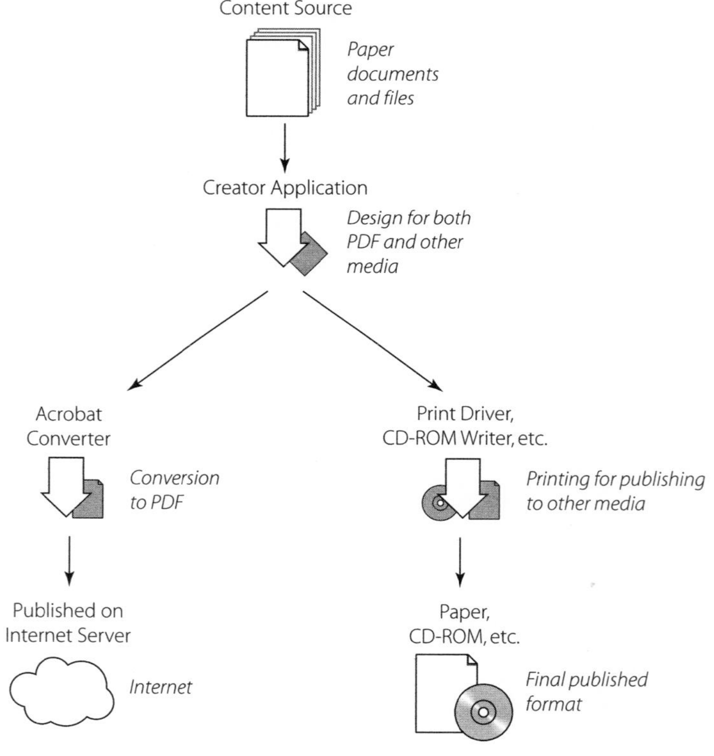

Figure 3.1—1 Concurrent Content Development Publishing Model

Web-savvy PDF files that offer the user a full range of interactive and navigational objects (bookmarks, hyperlinks, notes, etc.) can be as rich as PDF files published on other media (e.g., CD-ROM, intranets, and removable media), have very small file sizes, and fit well within a Web browser's document window. To automate the addition of PDF's interactive and navigational objects, which make interacting and viewing the file more compelling, the source file can be encoded with tags, called "pdfmarks." When converted to a PDF file with Acrobat Distiller, pdfmarks are converted to navigational and interactive objects such as links, notes, bookmarks, and more. The pdfmarks are inserted in files with a PDF-savvy creator application or by hand. Most commercial publishing creator applications support pdfmark to some degree. See Section 4.3, "PDF-Savvy Creator Applications," for more information on the capabilities of these applications. For information on manually inserting pdfmarks and pdfmark in general, refer to the *Portable Document Format Reference Manual*, in Section 10.1.2, "*Portable Document Format Reference.*"

Designing a document suitable for print and electronic media requires careful planning to maximize the capabilities of both media—without limiting those of either media. Professional printing issues (such as color separations, trapping, and resolution) are not as important to electronic publications as file size, interactivity, and portability. Acrobat Distiller aids in the conversion of a file designed for print use to electronic use by downsampling images, compressing images, and compressing or embedding fonts as it converts the file to a PDF file. Use Acrobat Exchange to further modify the converted PDF file and author interactive and navigational objects before publishing it on the Internet.

Note: Some creator applications (i.e., Adobe PageMaker) have a feature that enables publishers to assign a file print format (resolution, page size, use of color, etc.) for print-based publishing and another for electronic publishing.

The following table outlines many of the required attributes and the best Acrobat solutions for concurrently published PDF files. This table builds on the four basic parameters for repurposing content identified earlier in Table 3.1—1, "Common Physical Page Design Modifications for Web Publishing."

Print Requirements	Web Requirements	Acrobat Solution
High resolutions (600 to 2540 dpi)[1]	72 dpi maximum for screen	PostScript file resolution reduction when converting to a PDF file using Acrobat Distiller; no affect on the print-based job. Maximum resolution of Distiller versions 1.0 through 2.1 is 144 dpi. Acrobat 3.0 increases the maximum resolution to 1200 dpi.
Color separations	No separations required for screen use.	PDF supports color separations and can convert CMYK images to RGB images when converting a PostScript file to a PDF file. CMYK to RGB conversion (either off or on) is an advanced job option in Distiller 3.0. Distiller 2.1 converts CMYK to RGB by default to conserve file size and improve onscreen display. This 2.1 option can be disabled by modifying Distiller's startup script.
Custom page sizes	Page sizes limited by screen dimensions.	PDF viewers enable page zooming and custom scaling of pages to fit the dimensions of a monitor or Web browser; no effect on the print-based job. Supported by Acrobat 1.0 and later.

Table 3.1—2 Concurrent Publishing: Print versus Web Requirements

Print Requirements	Web Requirements	Acrobat Solution
No "size" limitations	Small file sizes (bytes)	PostScript file compression and image down-sampling when converting to a PDF file using Acrobat Distiller significantly reduces the data required to display the document, while not significantly reducing quality; no affect on the print-based job. Supported in Acrobat 1.0 and later.
Automated indexing, cross-referencing	Context and hypertext links	Solutions include third-party plug-ins, pdfmark, and some creator application macros that convert indices and cross-references to context and hypertext links. Supported in Acrobat 1.0 and later.
Margins (for footers, headers, page numbers, and binding)	Maximum screen use for content, print elements not needed.	Crop pages by configuring Distiller's startup script (see Appendix H, "Setting Options in Distiller's Startup Directory"); or crop pages in Acrobat Exchange after the file has been converted to PDF; or use Acrobat's interactive and navigational objects (e.g., article threads, zoom actions, fit visible page mode, etc.). Supported in Acrobat 1.0 and later. Article threads are supported in Distiller 2.0 and later.

Table 3.1—2 (continued)

[1] Resolution here is output, print-device resolution. Images 150 to 250 dpi are commonly processed by a PostScript RIP to generate an output image within the range of 600 to 2540 dpi.

Note: A concurrent content development strategy also may apply to the repurposing of other media formats (slides, video, electronic presentations, etc.).

3.1.2 Complementing Print-Based Publishing with PDF

The complementary content development strategy produces two or more different publications from existing, developed content sources. These publications can differ from their counterparts on other media formats with minor design or content modifications to make them usable on the Internet and other media; or, they can be substantially different with a new spin on content and design developed specifically for the publication's audience. With this strategy, publishers can leverage content sources into multiple publications, each with minor to major differences in content and design and each specific to an audience and media type.

Content modifications for PDF publishing include targeting audiences who have access to the Web (versus the target audience

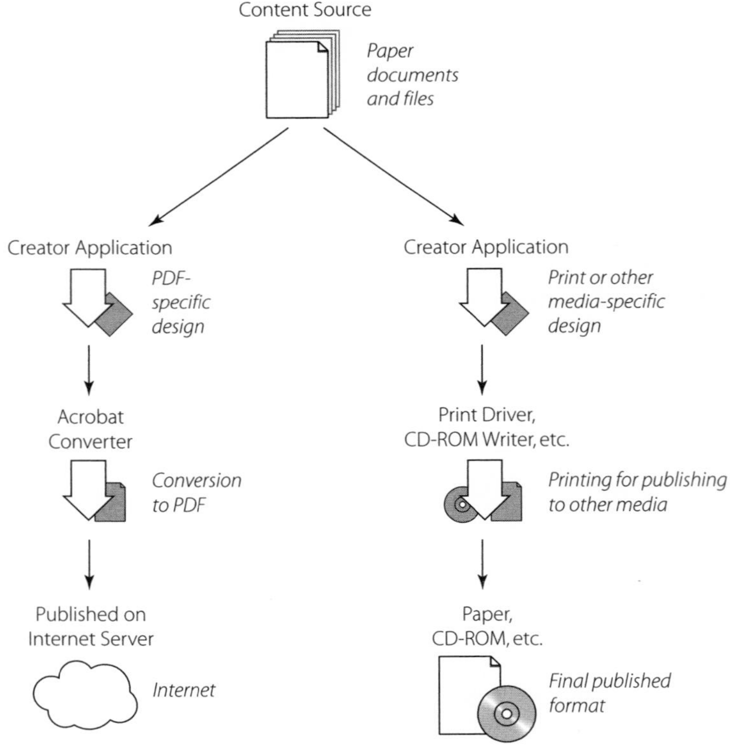

Figure 3.1—2 Complementary Content Development Publishing Model

of the other media publications), shortening and breaking up stories to facilitate onscreen reading, and changing the tone or writing style. Relative content links, connections between shorter bits, and progressively more focused and in-depth information are common in PDF and other electronic, hypertext-compliant publications. These content alterations require redesign to support the user's navigation and interaction with the content.

Design modifications affect the type and sizes of images, the publication's physical format, layout of text, use of fonts, and the types of objects (e.g., buttons, hypertext, and bookmarks) used to navigate and interact with the document. Design affects content organization, too. The process of updating timely chunks of content without radically altering the PDF file can be eased by separating information that frequently, occasionally, or never changes. Chunks of information may comprise two or more PDF files or may be integrated with HTML files (and other file formats), linked with hypertext, bookmarks, and other navigational objects.

The combination of a varied design and the target audience often can result in the production of PDF files much different from their print counterparts. They can, however, share the branding enjoyed by the dominant media publication. For example, *Wired* magazine's Web site, HotWired, often contains different, yet complementary content than that found in Wired magazine. Both publications target much the same audience, but chunk and select content appropriate to the medium and the file format in which content is delivered. Many print-based publishers, both large and small, have complementary Internet or Web-site versions of their publications including the *New York Times, Esquire,* and the *Wall Street Journal.*

Note: Some publishers have discontinued their print-based versions in favor of publishing over the Internet. Still other publishers are creating brand new Internet magazines without any paper ever being printed, such as Salon Magazine at http://www.salon1999.com.

3.1.3 PDF-Only Content Development

Using original content sources when creating PDF files for the Internet provides greater control over development of content and design. Rather than modifying existing content intended for another use, it can be organized and designed for a specific user, audience, and media. While greater control is advantageous, creating content to be published as PDF files requires the same skills as repurposing existing content. Usability, navigation, and interactivity apply to all PDF content development strategies, regardless if the publication's content source type is original or existing.

Original content sources may be stored in electronic file formats native to graphics, illustration, presentation, and word processing applications (among other software applications). Effectively converting these files to PDF files gives the user a richer, platform- and application-independent means of navigating and interacting with the content, previously only possible in the file's creator application. In some instances, the discrete files may be combined in a publishing application or combined when converted to PDF files to form a composite file, yielding a cohesive document.

This book details the development of both new and repurposed content to PDF publications. For detailed information on designing and creating PDF files from any type of electronic file

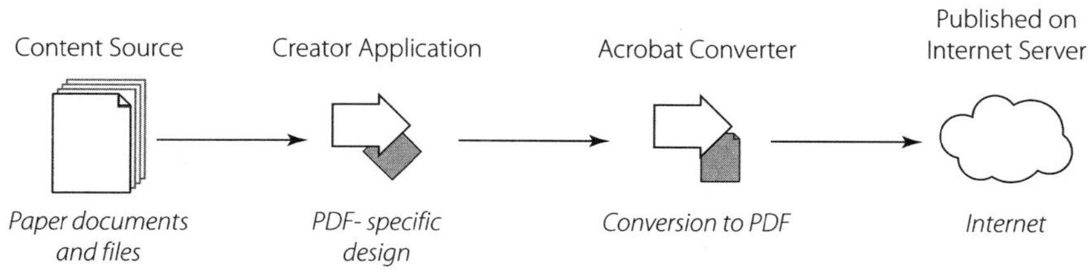

Figure 3.1—3 PDF-Only Content Development Publishing Model

(repurposed or original), refer to Chapter 4, "Designing Content for the Internet."

Note: Some PDF-savvy creator applications automate the process of adding interactive and navigational objects to a file when it is converted to a PDF file. (See Section 4.3, "PDF-Savvy Creator Applications.")

3.1.4 Integrating HTML with PDF Files

HTML, the content file type most commonly used on the Web, provides the underlying structure of an Internet site for most publishing efforts. However, integrating PDF with HTML results in the ability to publish both dynamic, flexible documents in HTML and visually rich, compelling documents as PDF files.

HTML is the accepted standard for Internet publishing. All Web browsers read HTML 2.0 (see ftp://ds.internic.net/rfc/rfc1866.txt for the specification as it presently stands); however, enhancements (such as those proposed by Netscape Communications at http://home.netscape.com), and custom file types (PDF, Shockwave, and RealAudio files) are viewable within fewer Web browsers. Therefore, publishing only in HTML allows the greatest potential reach. This exposure comes with limited design capabilities, which can minimize the graphic appeal of most publications when compared to PDF files.

Integration, at the most basic level, enables users browsing a Web site (or file server, CD-ROM, etc.) to alternate between content served as a PDF file or as an HTML file. The content is organized in such a way that following a link leads to a PDF file, which leads to an HTML file, which then leads to another HTML file or a PDF file, and so forth. Integration is also the inclusion of a PDF file within an HTML document, where the PDF file serves as a graphical item. From the user's perspective, there's little difference in the process of viewing an HTML or PDF file, only the file formats are different. Duplication, summarization, inclusion, and dynamic generation are other HTML and PDF integration methods that expand on the basic integration method.

For an integration strategy, content sources are typically documents already being published as either HTML or PDF files (or perhaps in both file formats). Content sources also may include documents designed specifically for online distribution, which require little modification when converted to either PDF or HTML file formats. This is because interactive and navigational features native to either format are automated and generated along with the document in the selected format or formats. Content sources that require modification before being published and integrated with PDF and HTML files are best conceived by using a complementary publishing strategy. Publishing content via multiple media—with the plan to integrate both PDF and HTML files—incorporates a concurrent publishing strategy. New content development strategies, for content which isn't designed for other media, also can wholly embrace the PDF and HTML integration strategy.

Note: Integrate content repurposed from existing sources by scanning and converting the documents to either PDF or HTML files with Acrobat Capture (see Section 2.1.7, "Adobe Acrobat Capture"), or optical character recognition software. Printed documents that are scanned and converted often require modifications to make the documents interactive and navigable—best managed first with a concurrent publishing strategy.

Duplication

Duplication, where a document is published in both PDF and HTML, is one solution to reach the most users while still allowing those who can view PDF files to experience the content in a more interactive and visually rich environment. Avoid publishing all documents as both PDF and HTML files. Serve HTML duplications of PDF files, not PDF duplications of HTML files. To determine which content is best served as a PDF file and which is best served as HTML, see Section 3.2, "Content Formats: PDF or HTML."

It is crucial that duplicated files contain the same information, because users may read the HTML version of the file online and download the PDF file for archival or print purposes.

Note: The process of developing a duplicate document is specific to each document. A number of PDF-savvy creator applications (see Section 4.3, "PDF-Savvy Creator Applications") are capable of publishing files as both HTML and PDF files, allowing greater control over the content, its version, and final file format. For existing PDF files, use the file as a master and extract the document's text (as a full Rich Text Format export of the PDF file) with the OLE Plug-in (see Appendix I, "Acrobat Plug-ins") and mark up the RTF export. Copy and paste images and graphics between a PDF viewer and a GIF-compatible application, saving the clipboard contents as GIF files (or JPEGs).

Summarization

Summarization presents the user with an executive summary, synopsis, or abstract of the PDF document in HTML. These summaries provide the user with a link to the complete PDF file or specific pages or page areas of the file. If interested in the entire document, users can view either the PDF files on the Web (if their Web browser supports this), or download the PDF file for off-line viewing.

Additionally, summarization can take the form of tables of contents, lists of figures, outlines, or other document navigational aids with hypertext links to specific pages or sections of the PDF file (most efficient as named destination).

Note: The summarization method is a useful alternative to duplicating files. Since all Web browsers support PDF file transfer, which allows the file to be downloaded and viewed with an installed PDF viewer application, users read the summary and if interested in the document, download the entire PDF file.

Inclusion

With HTML 2.0, the first page of a PDF file, not a defined first page, can be embedded within an HTML file as an image source (GIF, JPEG, etc.), or within a frame when viewed with a frames-compatible Web browser. An embedded PDF file's page dimensions may be scaled to fit. (The dimension need not be proportionate to the PDF page dimensions.) Embedding a PDF file within an HTML file limits many of the interactive and navigational features found in PDF files, effectively reducing the PDF file to a graphic. (The Acrobat viewer toolbar doesn't load, and any PDF objects such as links, buttons, and notes do not appear or function.) Clicking on the embedded PDF file either opens it in another of the Web browser's document windows or within the same document window, depending on the Web browser and platform. Opening the PDF file loads the Acrobat viewer's toolbar and the PDF file functions normally within the browser.

Within a frameset, PDF files retain their interactive and navigational features, allowing publishers to define frames that display both HTML (or other file formats) with PDF files. Users may interact with any of the documents displayed in the framesets.

Note: Depending on the PDF file's frame, some of the toolbar buttons may be hidden from view.

Dynamic Generation

Integration at a higher level uses scripts and applets; on the server side, it includes databases to generate user-specific content from queries, form data, and other user information. HTML or PDF form fields, filled-in by a user, are processed by CGI scripts or other applications running on the Web server (see Section 7.6, "Forms"). Query results take the form of either PDF or HTML files or, with some Acrobat-compatible search engines, a keyword search opens a PDF document, which highlights the matching term. Scripts and other applications process user input into HTML tables, generate graphic data as PDF files, or generate entirely customized PDF files based on data that users input. (For information on setting actions that link PDF files to CGI scripts, see Section 7.1.11, "World Wide Web Link Actions.") Plans to embed Java applets within PDF files have been announced, although not finalized as of this writing. (For current developments read the press releases at http://www.adobe.com/.)

3.2 Content Formats: PDF or HTML

Based on a content development strategy, the next step is to select the appropriate file format for publishing the content. The tables in the following sections help identify which types of documents and their attendant features are best published in either PDF or HTML.

Some of the issues that should be considered before making a decision are as follows:

- The application being used to develop the content (see Table 3.2—1, "Application Type").

- The content source's stage of development (see Table 3.2—2, "Document Creation Stages").
- The document's type (see Table 3.2—3, "Document Type").
- The intended use of the document and its interactive and navigational objects (see Table 3.2—4, "Document Activity and File Format Elements").
- Existing design features (see Table 3.2—5, "Design Attributes").
- Other considerations that focus on the audience and the publisher rather than the content itself.

For repurposed content, use the tables to identify whether the document is best published in HTML or PDF. The tables also can be used to help identify which design modifications, interactive and navigational objects, and other considerations will make the selected file format as usable and engaging as possible. For original content development, the tables help make basic design decisions. Use Table 3.2—1, "Application Type," to help determine the appropriate application to develop the content. Table 3.2—4, "Document Activity and File Format Elements," aids in the selection of the interactive and navigation features to be used. Table 3.2—3, "Document Type," helps define the best file format based on the common document design. Consult the hundreds of books on publishing Hypertext Markup Language files for information on publishing in HTML.

Note: For original content in the document development, stage it is assumed that the document has not been created.

These tables should be used as guides for identifying the best content format. Ideally, the combined results of all the tables and other considerations make selecting an optimal file format type simple and obvious. After consulting the tables, if an optimal file format isn't obvious, select a table that most effects the process of content development and select the file type based on the outcome of this table.

These tables also can help the Internet publisher make other publishing-related decisions, including the adoption of new PDF-savvy applications (for documents best served as PDF files). For example, a repurposed magazine based on a concurrent publishing strategy is best published as a PDF file (and integrated with HTML); however, the application used to publish the content works best with a selected application type that is best used to create HTML files; but the document type to be published with this application is best served as a PDF; both considerations determine that the file is best published as a PDF file with a better creator application—one that more fully embraces the creation of PDF files.

3.2.1 PDF or HTML by Application Type

The type of application used to create documents impacts the way content is best published on the Internet. For original content development, identify familiar applications that have the desired capabilities for a type of document (e.g., automated table of contents, the capability to import specific image file types, support for a particular plug-in, etc.). (Table 3.2—3, "Document Type," has a list of potential document types.) Repurposed content development uses the file's native application—unless it is possible to import or convert the file into another application without design or content modification.

Best as HTML files

HTML files that have been generated by print-publishing applications that are capable of marking up files with the Hypertext Markup Language can be converted to PDF files. However, publishing these files as PDF files rarely results in any significant advantage over publishing them as HTML files. Hence, they work best as HTML files (integrated with PDF files, if appropriate).

Note: A number of HTML markup and management applications (e.g., Adobe PageMill and Adobe SiteMill) support linked or embedded PDF files, easing the integration between HTML and PDF files.

Work well as either HTML or PDF files

Word processors and spreadsheet applications provide a middle ground with capabilities to markup text as HTML files and to create richer documents with custom formatting, images, fonts, charts, tables, and graphs. An application's capability to create complex documents and the realization that these documents cannot be effectively published as HTML files defines an application's appropriateness for creating PDF-published content. Applications capable of creating complex documents are also capable of creating simpler content, which is best published as an HTML file. See the tables below to determine the level of complexity (based on specific design attributes) and the type of document (based on common document types) to further advance the file format selection process.

Word processors can facilitate conversion to HTML with built-in support, macros, plug-ins, or templates. Spreadsheet applications typically support generation of HTML tables from spreadsheets through an export filter. As modifications or browser-specific features are added to HTML markup, these new features may not be supported by the applications thereby requiring code-level editing of the HTML file.

These same files can be converted to PDF by generating a PostScript file and converting the file to PDF with Acrobat Distiller. PDF-savvy creator applications (see Section 4.3, "PDF-Savvy Creator Applications") automatically add the interactive and navigational objects to the PostScript file, which become usable after conversion to a PDF file. Plug-ins for Acrobat Exchange also can convert typical document features (table of contents, index, cross-references, etc.) to interactive and navigational objects after the PostScript files have been converted to PDF.

Note: Since virtually all word processors can export files to text, they can be used to mark up HTML files.

Work well as PDF files

Files created with desktop publishing, image editing, illustration and presentation software—all of which are used to create complex, visually rich documents—work well when converted to PDF files. A number of desktop publishing applications can export documents as HTML files. Typically, these exported HTML files require modification and cannot preserve accurately all the document's design features, unless the document was designed with HTML's limitations in mind. (Unsupported HTML design features are listed in Table 3.2—5, "Design Attributes.") For this reason, most documents created by using desktop publishing applications work best as PDF files. An HTML export feature may ease the PDF and HTML integration process.

Neither PDF nor HTML files works well

Multimedia software organizes information more dynamically along a timeline making it difficult to represent the content as discrete pages. As a consequence, neither HTML nor PDF files is an effective means for repurposed multimedia content. It is possible to prototype or create effective "multimedia" productions from original content with PDF's interactive objects, such as buttons, forms, and with the Movie Plug-in; however, PDF files lack many of the higher levels of interactivity frequently demanded by most productions. In addition, the large file sizes of most movie files do not permit their efficient use over the Internet. Movie and animation files used in multimedia productions can be linked to or from within HTML and PDF files. (Movies may be played from within a PDF file with the Movie Plug-in. HTML files require a Web browser plug-in or a helper application.)

3.2.2 PDF or HTML by Document Creation Stages

The stages of document creation are important variables when choosing to publish content as a HTML or PDF file. In Table 3.2.2, "Document Creation Process, the document creation process begins with a straight text file; it then has a structure applied to it (either a simple hierarchy or a meta-language); next it is styled (based on a style sheet), put into production and published (either as an electronic file format such as HTML or on paper or other media).

HTML Works Best	Both Work Well	PDF Works Best	Neither Works Well
HTML WYSIWYG editors	Word processing programs	Desktop publishing programs	Multimedia authoring software
Text editors	Spreadsheet programs[1]	Illustration programs	
Database programs[2]		Presentation software	

Table 3.2—1 Application Type

[1] Spreadsheet programs that can export to HTML tables (e.g., Microsoft Excel with the Internet Publisher Wizard, see http://www.microsoft.com) work well as applications to create tabular content as either HTML or PDF files. Spreadsheets that cannot export to HTML tables are best published as PDF files.

[2] Database programs, used through proprietary database servers, interface nicely with HTML documents. HTML, as a document format alone, has no database functionality. Third-party developers have announced database connectivity functionality through PDF.

The stage at which a document functions in the creation process fits within the content development strategies described earlier (see Section 3.1, "Content Development Strategies"). Original content being developed for documents not yet created has the flexibility to be published as either PDF files or HTML files (or both). If a document has been published already as an HTML file, it is best left in that format—even if a concurrent publishing strategy is being employed. Existing electronic documents marked up with a structured language (e.g., SGML) work best as HTML files; documents styled with a style sheet work as both PDF and HTML files. Completed documents (depending on the document's type and features applied by the application in which it was created) work best as PDF files. Similarly, documents that exist only as hard copies work best as PDF files when the content's intended design needs to be represented exactly as it originally appeared.

Note: For applications that don't support HTML output, import styled documents into an HTML publishing application (e.g., PageMill or HoT MetaL Pro) to convert the document's style sheet to HTML heading tags and save the converted file as an HTML file.

Best with HTML	Both Work Well	Best with PDF
Document has been published in HTML.	Document has not been created.	Document has been designed and produced.
Document tagged with a structured language (SGML[1]).	Document has been styled based on a traditional heading 1 to heading x style sheet (commonly found in word processing files and RTF files).	Document has been published on paper (no digital file).[2]

Table 3.2—2 Document Creation Stages

1 SGML, a superset of HTML, is a meta-language for defining and standardizing the structure of documents.

2 Digitize using Capture or the Capture Plug-in.

3.2.3 PDF or HTML: Document Type

The structure and design of a certain document type (and the attributes that comprise design) work better as HTML or PDF documents (and as other file types as well). A document's type, based on design and the way content is presented (both physically, and the author's tone and writing style) are underlying features that aid (or add noise to) communication. Some of these features can be represented accurately in the HTML file format; other features require a PDF file's visual richness to preserve the document and its message.

Best with HTML

Documents that work best with HTML either have no defining formal structure, or can be represented well with HTML's design features. For example, email messages are MIME-encoded, ASCII text and are commonly devoid of design elements. (ASCII art and attached images enhance the message, but are not required to facilitate understanding.) Email messages, however, share a common organization that includes the recipient's name and address, sender, date, subject of the message, the message itself, and a closing. (Some messages can include and optionally display URLs, an attached file, information about the pathway and the server the message was sent through, etc.) The design requirements and organization common to email messages make them work best when published as HTML files. Publishing email messages in PDF yields no advantages over HTML. Other documents have similar organizational requirements, but with slightly greater design requirements. Memos, basic letters, simple reports, and other miscellaneous text-based documents combine text—usually without columns or custom formatting—with images and graphics placed strategically throughout the document (e.g., lines to separate sections, company letterhead logos, product illustrations, etc.). Both the design requirements and the organizational structure of these documents are best supported by the design features afforded HTML files.

Both HTML and PDF work well

Documents that require portions of the information in the document to be represented graphically work well as either HTML or PDF files. Additionally, both HTML and PDF files support interactive objects like user-fillable forms and navigational objects like hypertext. Home pages with no defined structure and varied designs work well as either PDF or HTML files; however, with PDF files, users must be able to view PDF files within their Web browser. (See Section 8.5, "Serving PDF Files as Home Pages.")

Graphical data can be represented by using HTML tables (for spreadsheets and tables), or as GIF files (for spreadsheets, tables, charts, and figures), or the entire document (including tables, charts, graphs, etc.) can be published as a PDF file. For data generated on-the-fly (e.g., up-to-date stock data, graphs based on user input and other content, or time sensitive information), HTML offers the greatest amount of flexibility (and software solutions to generate this data); however, PDF offers some interesting options for dynamic generation (see Section 8.13, "Dynamic PDF").

Note: Only PDF files allow users to print and see information within form fields. See Section 7.6, "Forms," for more information on creating forms within PDF files.

3.2.4 PDF or HTML by Document Activity and Items

PDF and HTML files allow users to navigate and interact with content through objects which include hypertext, buttons, and form fields. HTML and PDF files share some user-controllable actions, while each format supports a suite of other features specific to its file format. Based on how a document is used, either the HTML or PDF file format (or perhaps both) works best.

Best with HTML

HTML supports a number of areas (including meta-tags and

Best with HTML	Both Work Well	Best with PDF
Email[2]	Basic specification sheets and data represented graphically.	Newsletters
Memos	Web home pages	Magazines
Basic letters	Order forms	Posters
Simple reports		Annual reports
Miscellaneous text-based documents		Brochures, flyers, advertisements, books

Table 3.2—3 Document Type[1]

[1] The identified document types are common "names" for print documents, plus the home page. There are a number of document types not included in the list, and Internet publishing will likely give birth to other types of documents as it did with the home page. Use the document types as a general guide, basing content and design format on a document's structure, layout, use (online, off-line, and printed), timeliness, and other elements that affect content and its design.

[2] Email can be batch-converted to HTML pages (or simply text files).

server-push animation) that can be updated constantly upon connection to the server. HTML also provides access to user-controllable information such as databases and search engines. Publishers can format how the information is presented with frames (see http://home.netscape.com for pointers to frame tutorials) or enhance the interactive environment with JavaScript or applets.

Both HTML and PDF work well

PDF files share with HTML the capability to link to URLs and locations on the Internet through an Acrobat- or Acrobat 3.0-compatible Web browser. URLs shared between PDF and HTML files include standard hypertext (see Section 4.1.2, "Hypertext cues"), links (see Section 7.4, "Links"), mailto links (see "Setting World Wide Web Link actions that use other Internet protocols," under Section 7.1.11), and named destinations. The files also can send data to CGI scripts for processing either dynamically through a form or hard-coded into a URL (see "Setting World Wide Web Link actions to CGI scripts," under Section 7.1.11).

Best with PDF

PDF files have some activities that HTML files cannot do as elegantly as PDF files and are outside HTML's capabilities. PDF files, for example, can assign a single URL to images, graphics, and text (or any combination of the three). This can be done with HTML files, but each element of the HTML file must be tagged with the same URL. A PDF file's device- and resolution-independent output to printers is much cleaner and more efficient than most HTML files. Acrobat 3.0 adds enhancements that produce professional quality results from PDF files previously attainable only with PostScript files. Acrobat 3.0 PDF files also can receive data from a server and fill in the form's fields with the downloaded data. Finally, PDF files can be individually encrypted. HTML files are secured at the server level where PDF files can be locked—not at the file level. The security options for PDF files include several methods to limit user actions (see Section 7.11, "PDF Security Options"), when interacting with the file.

3.2.5 PDF or HTML by Design Attributes

PDF files support all print design attributes generated by popular publishing applications. HTML files support only some of these attributes, but have a set of HTML-specific (and sometimes

Best with HTML	Both Work Well	Best with PDF
Server side (and environment information)	Links to URLs	URLs place links over both text and graphics.
Server-push animation	mailto: links	Document-based security (client-level addition)
Index service (PDF, HTML, and other formats)	CGIs (imagemaps, URL redirection, and form processing)	Movie and sound playback
Database connectivity	Forms	High-resolution printing
Frames[1]		Form population
Java applets[2]		

Table 3.2—4 Document Activity and File Format Elements

[1] PDF files do not support frames, but can be the target of a frame.

[2] Support for Java has been announced.

browser-specific) design attributes not supported by either creator applications or PDF viewers.

For repurposed content, a printed document's design attributes can (almost) always be preserved in a PDF file. Through enhancing some attributes such as converting the document's table of contents to bookmarks, or removing other attributes such as page numbers and footers, the result is a more useful electronic document.

When creating original content to be published as PDF files, take advantage of special formatting attributes found only in PDF, which increase legibility and contribute to visually rich documents. Avoid relying on these attributes when creating documents to be published as HTML files or as both PDF and HTML files.

Table 3.2-5, "Design Attributes," includes many attributes that are found in PDF and not in HTML. Shared attributes in which one file format does a better job than the other, or where an attribute deserves special attention are noted. The table below describes only design elements found in either PDF or HTML. Features found in neither PDF or HTML are not listed, nor are features found in both. Consult the list to help decide if a particular layout technique is important (or not important) enough to justify the use of either HTML or PDF.

Design Attribute	HTML	PDF	Notes
Custom-sized text	Yes*	Yes	*Text size may be altered by defined user settings.
Custom text typefaces	No*	Yes	*Often done in HTML as a GIF graphic, not good for large text blocks. *Support for custom typefaces in HTML document has been announced.
Text leading	No*	Yes	*Only default leading
Type styles (bold, italic, outline, etc.)	Some	Yes	
Type width (condensed, normal, etc.)	Some	Yes	
Text alignment (center, left, right)	Yes	Yes	
Rules (lines)	Yes	Yes	
Hyphenation	No	Yes	
Expert fractions and type characters. and special characters and symbols	Some	Yes*	*For typefaces that support them.
Kerning and word spacing	No	Yes	
Text indents	No*	Yes	*Through the use of tables only.
Breakout (or pull quote, blurb)	Yes*	Yes	*Through use of tables.
Bleed art	No*	Yes	*No real page borders

continued

Table 3.2—5 Design Attributes

Design Attribute	HTML	PDF	Notes
Page numbers	No*	Yes	*No real pages
Columns	Yes	Yes	
Drop cap (initial cap)	Yes	Yes	
Margins	N/A*	Yes	*No defined edges
Wrapping text around images	Yes*	Yes	Browser window and screen sizes may not have text wrapped as intended.
Run text over images	No*	Yes	Possible with background GIFs, but not in-line images.
Image caption	Yes*	Yes	*Not a traditional caption, often used when image loading is turned off.
Bullet and numbered lists	Yes	Yes	
Created on the fly	Yes	No*	*Can be, but not widely used.

Table 3.2—5 (continued) Design Attributes

* Read the referenced text in the right-most column, for more information.

3.2.6 PDF or HTML: No Easy Conclusion

If after evaluating a particular document based on the tables, no obvious conclusion to use one file format over another can be made, consider the following issues.

Control

PDF documents allow precise control of text, graphics, and images through the many publishing software packages available. How much control over the placement of text, images, and graphics is required? Does text need to wrap around irregular shaped objects? Do graphics run over text? Is text rotated or run on a path?

Frequency of updates

For Web documents that are automatically updated (or automatically generated) via a database, script, magic cookie, or other method, HTML files are the best choice. For other documents that must be updated by hand, easy-to-use desktop applications and the ease of publishing PDF files from these applications, make PDF an attractive option.

Compare the PDF and HTML files

Which file format downloads the first page fastest? When an optimized PDF file downloads, is it quicker to view the file in HTML or PDF? During the download is the progressive rendering of the file compelling? Does it progress fast enough to keep a user interested? When the download is complete is the PDF file significantly more compelling than the HTML file?

Accessibility of audience to Acrobat viewers

Does the audience (and the computer platform they use) have access to Acrobat viewers and HTML browsers? If access to Acrobat 3.0-compatible Web browsers and the resources required to view PDF is in short supply, HTML is a better choice.

3.3 Content Service

Content defined as document type and published as PDF, HTML, or other file formats can be organized on an Internet server to meet the specific needs of users. The organization, the types of documents on the server, and the way in which users access the information define the site's approach to content service. In addition to serving content by using the general-use Web site model, a site can be organized to serve content that can be printed on demand, served over a limited access network, or used to store images and graphics for quick retrieval. These content service options may be combined or may be exclusive to a site (a site being defined by an individual domain name).

The files are organized within directories from a collection of hard-coded links, or generated dynamically via a search function connected to an index of the documents on the server (and potentially other servers). Files organized within folders are categorized with common topics and contextual connections. Links to files that are hard-coded into HTML documents provide access across a single server to other sites and documents that share commonalties. Dynamically generated links, generated from a query posted to a search engine, share commonalties based on the query. Documents that are retrieved based on a query may match the common keyword, phrase, or topic searched for and may match to some degree, or may not match at all.

Web sites are constantly evolving as more corporations add Web sites for their brands in addition to information about their companies. Content has been growing steadily in depth, appropriateness for the medium, and with increased interactivity. PDF publishing on the Web (and on other Internet servers) expands this trend by offering interactive documents well suited for the Internet from a much wider range of content sources including new and repurposed content. The Web site centers around goals of quick and focused information access and information dissemination, organized by corporate communications professionals, information professionals, and individuals. To reach these goals, alternative content service options have been developed.

3.3.1 Using PDF Files on On-Demand Print Servers

Some documents are designed to be read only on a computer monitor screen. Other documents are designed for viewing and printing, and still others are designed strictly for printing. PDF files print independently of the printer type or its resolution, thereby enabling a PDF file to be printed on almost every type of printer, at that particular printer's highest possible resolution.

A print-on-demand server can use the same server software as a common Web server, functioning as a repository so that files can be downloaded quickly and printed. Print-on-demand servers can be part of a Web site, or function independently. PDF files stored on an on-demand print server may have larger file sizes than those used on a general-use Web site. Therefore, an isolated server may perform quicker downloads when competing with everyday Web server traffic.

Note: While the main use of an on-demand print server is to print, documents can be viewed in a Web browser window or off-line in an Acrobat viewer.

The print-on-demand approach is often employed for what corporations call mission-critical documents: datasheets, specification sheets, brochures, and other sales materials. The PDF files need not be optimized to enable progressive rendering in an Acrobat 3.0-compatible Web browser, although page-on-demand downloading may be advantageous depending on the structure of each document. These documents are perfect items for Acrobat-compatible (not necessarily Acrobat 3.0-compatible) Web browsers and sites. Sales forces armed with laptops can have access to a virtual warehouse or distribution center. And rather than spending millions on printing, distribution, and recycling out-of-date, mission-critical documents, a print-on-demand PDF server can support thousands of road-warriors. For some companies or documents, there may be more than one version of a document: versions in different languages, with or without cost figures, and versions in color, or black and white.

Note: Adobe's PrintMill (see http://www.adobe.com/) provides desktop printing features from within the PrintMill browser interface to print documents from an application directly to a URL. A file also can be sent to printers and other print services available via an intranet or the Internet.

3.3.2 Using PDF on an Intranet

Many organizations are creating internal networks, or intranets, which use Web server software and Web browsers as client software. The platform-independent intranet solution is less costly than proprietary network software, and increases the usability of published documents through a single, simple interface.

PDF is excellent for exchanging documents and publications within a closed intranet site. Serving PDF files on intranets combines the geographical access of the Internet, the cross-platform benefits of HTML and PDF, graphic integrity, corporate branding, and the simplicity of printing PDF to paper.

Intranet users can customize PDF files and Acrobat software to suit their needs with the use of plug-ins. (Exchange is required for extensive plug-in use.) The extensible PDF file format allows corporations to easily write plug-ins that meet specific needs. These plug-ins could include a database lookup field, the use of forms, revision control, mark-up of documents in transition, or facilitate online presentations.

Intranet servers can be used as an organization's presentation server as well. Approved presentations are posted on the server for employees or field staff. With Acrobat Exchange's capability to import, export, and arrange page order, unique presentations can be created.

Another intranet use could be as an archive server, which could contain legal contacts, forms, and non-disclosure information. While not discussed broadly in this book, Acrobat Capture—the PDF-optical character recognition software and hardware solution—can change a static, paper-based archive into a dynamic digital library.

Note: PDF files may be integrated with more traditional networking and collaborative software such as NetWare and Lotus Notes.

3.3.3 Using PDF on an Image Archive Server

PDF files can be used as a universal graphic and image archive format. Graphic or image collections that are served on Web, FTP, or Gopher servers are compiled into an index that displays thumbnails of the images in the collection. Graphics can be converted from their original file format to PDF files, or can include an index with links from the thumbnail to the original file, facilitating the downloading of the selected image or graphic.

Converting common graphics and image formats into PDF files creates a smaller, more searchable and scaleable directory of files. The PDF version always will be smaller than the index—unless additional resolutions of some files are included. The images or graphics can be annotated with PDF notes or text captions. Graphics or images in the PDF index can be magnified to show greater detail. A number or a keyword in a caption under the graphic or image can help users search a file for graphics.

Note: Indices of graphics are compiled to show the images in the collection without the need to download each file in the collection. Many indices are larger than the average graphic file in the collection. Most graphics or images on the Internet are only suitable for 72 dpi screen display.

Converting graphic and image formats into PDF files enables users to browse a variety of images and graphics in one file type—without the need to switch among JPEG, GIF, TIFF, and EPS viewers.

To extract images and graphics from PDF files, a PDF viewer's cut-and-paste function serves the needs of most onscreen image or graphic uses. Alternatively, a PDF file's security features can prevent users from cutting and pasting and printing PDF pages, while still allowing them to browse the archive.

4

Designing Content for the Internet

The goal of this chapter is to outline parameters for the most efficient methods of Internet publishing with Acrobat. This chapter concentrates on the overall design of PDF files to be published on the Internet and optimized for the Web. This includes the selection and use of creator applications—from basic word processors to sophisticated publishing systems—which fully support the file features found in PDF. In addition, methods for creating PDF files to maximize the document's usability on the Internet, such as design parameters to decrease file sizes, improve readability, and decrease screen rendering times, will be discussed.

The most successful PDF documents combine interactivity with design—unifying layout with intuitive usability. Designing successful documents and publishing them on the Web is a result of efficient use of software design tools, a clear understanding of how PDF documents are used on the Web, and the designer's skill (in both aesthetics and interactivity).

The list below consists of design considerations that will help produce better PDF files for publishing on the Internet with Acrobat:

- Build navigational and interactive cues (buttons, hypertext cues, and form fields) directly into the design to encourage interactivity and content-specific navigation.
- Configure PDF files to open at the optimal page size or at a specified magnification to maximize text legibility on standard monitors. Offer links to other resolutions for uncommonly large or smaller monitor sizes (or Web-browser document windows).
- Make page sizes fit comfortably within popular screen sizes, or within a Web browser's document window.
- Remove extraneous white space and print-only items such as page numbers and footnotes.
- Use only essential fonts. However, don't omit fonts that lend to the design or branding of the PDF file simply to reduce file size.
- Ensure that the point size used for the majority of the document's text isn't Greeked when it is opened on standard monitors.
- Whenever possible, employ master pages and other techniques that reuse graphics and images to get visually interesting images, which when optimized for the Web result in lower-bandwidth overhead.
- Choose a creator application that is not only useful for content development, but also utilizes the skills and proficiencies of those working with the software.

- If one particular application isn't suitable for developing all content, combine the capabilities of several creator applications (word processors, illustration programs, spreadsheet programs, etc.) in addition to traditional print-publishing programs.
- Whenever possible, use creator applications that in some way support the PDF file format (which eventually make creating and working with PDF files easier).

4.1 Designing PDF Documents for the Web

The best designed PDF documents on the Web combine the interactive and navigational objects native to the PDF file format by using established models of interactivity. These interactive and navigational objects include hypertext cues, forward and back buttons, and other easily identifiable interactive objects and icons. All these objects take advantage of and complement the compelling and rich graphic design capabilities extended to the Web from print-publishing programs and graphic design software.

While modeling PDF interactive cues after established HTML Web interactive objects would contribute to intuitive, highly usable documents, using HTML Web-page layout as a defining model for PDF design would waste the capabilities PDF extends to a publisher. Likewise, applying the defined model of print publishing to an interactive, dynamic media would result in visually rich documents that are hard to use and navigate.

The design of a PDF document borrows from a number of design, navigational, and interaction ideas that originated in related fields such as desktop publishing, multimedia authoring, and

Web page design. Excellent Web-published PDF files are designed with an understanding of how these publishing fields interrelate and complement design.

Documents used on the Internet, or simply viewed on the Internet and potentially printed, need to conform to both onscreen and print design parameters dictated by hardware (e.g., common printer page dimensions and resolutions).

Note: Some may argue that design for the screen and for print are diametrically opposed; however, as onscreen design continues to meet the printed world, more designs will compliment both onscreen and printed output.

4.1.1 Selecting Page Dimensions

Based on a content publishing strategy, select a page dimension that is suitable exclusively for onscreen viewing or exclusively for printing; or select a dimension that may be viewed both onscreen and printed, given common hardware configurations. Most Internet users are accustomed to having documents fit within the document window. With HTML, non-formatted text and some graphic elements will reflow to fit within the Web browser window. PDF document dimensions do not scale. Users scale the document (zooming in or out) to view the page (or portions of the document page).

Onscreen document dimensions

A PDF page's dimensions may be set for viewing at 100%, or at a relative magnification to increase or decrease magnification to fit the whole page, the page width, or just visible portions of the page within the Web browser's document window (and within the monitor's dimensions). PDF page dimensions also may be set for viewing at an arbitrary dimension that requires user interaction and navigation to view all the content. Table 4.1—1, "Magnification Descriptions," outlines how documents are scaled to fit within a monitor or Web browser's document window. The magnifications may be applied to the entire document as an open preference (see Section 7.12, "Open Preferences"), or engaged via the Go To View action (see Section 7.1.2, "Go To View Action").

Magnification	Value	Description
Fixed	100%	Pages are sized to fit within a document window at 100% on small monitor sizes. The document's text must be easy to read and require no scrolling of the document window, or zooming to see the document's content.
Fit Page Fit Width Fit Visible	Magnification relative to the PDF page size and content	Pages are scaled (zoomed in or out) to fit as much of the page as possible (or visible page items), at the highest magnification possible within the document window.[1] The scaling is a function of the Acrobat viewer (even if viewed through a Web browser).
Arbitrary	Any (from 12% to 800%)	Pages are opened to no defined magnification. User must use interactive and navigational tools to view content. The amount of scrolling and zooming required to view the content depends on the user's document window size and monitor dimensions.

Table 4.1—1 Magnification Descriptions

[1] The document window may be that of either an Acrobat viewer or a Web browser displaying the PDF file.

Note: The monitor size (in pixels) is an important factor. A 13-inch monitor at 640 x 480 pixels yields substantially different results than a 21-inch monitor at 640 x 480 pixels.

Table 4.1—2, "Page Sizes at 100% for Monitors 640 x 480 Pixels in Netscape Browser," lists several different page dimensions that open at Actual Size (100% magnification) on monitors 640 x 480 pixels, regardless of the magnification view selected (Actual Size, Fit Page, or Fit Width while in Page Only, Bookmarks and Page, or Thumbnails and Page view). The page dimensions in the table work in the default Netscape Navigator document window (488 x 293 pixels), and text is Greeked if smaller than six pixels. Resizing the Web browser's document window, or disabling the Netscape Navigator toolbar items (Toolbar, Location, etc.), will scale the page to best fit within the document window.

Note: Six pixels is the default size at which text is Greeked in Acrobat viewers, but can be changed in the Acrobat viewer's preferences.

Page Dimension	Greeked Text	Magnification	View(s)
6.639 x 3.917 inches	No	100% Actual Size	Page Only
478 x 282 pixels		100% Fit Page	
39.83 x 23.5 picas		100% Fit Width	
4.555 x 3.917 inches	No	100% Actual Size	Page and Bookmarks
328 x 282 pixels		100% Fit Page	Page and Thumbnails
27.33 x 23.5 picas		100% Fit Width	

Table 4.1—2 Page Sizes at 100% for Monitors 640 x 480 Pixels in Netscape Browser

Note: Any document size that conforms to a 4:3 page-size ratio will generally work with Fit Page view on a monitor at 640 x 480 pixels.

Print page dimensions

Common print page dimensions can be used comfortably for both onscreen viewing and printing. Given the small Web browser document window in which most users view PDF files (on common monitors 640 x 480 pixels), a user must enlarge the Web browser document window, use Acrobat's zoom features, or make use of interactive and navigational objects (such as article threads, see Section 7.9, "Article Threads;" or the Go To View action, see Section 7.1.2, "Go To View Action"), to comfortably read text online. No common page sizes fit in a Web browser window at 100% (Fit Visible) on a monitor 640 x 480 pixels.

Most Web-browser document windows are only 488 x 293 pixels large—narrower and much shorter than a letter-size page (8.5 x 11 inches or 612 x 792 pixels). Enlarging a Web-browser document window to fit a page 8.5 x 11 inches within the window at 100% requires a 25-inch or larger monitor, or a portrait monitor.

Large page sizes can fit within a small document window by using Acrobat's view buttons to display the page area (e.g., Actual Size, Fit Page, and Fit Width); or page view can be used to display just the page or the page with bookmarks or thumbnails, thereby allowing common page sizes often used for printing to be viewed and read. The view and magnification at which a page opens can be predefined by the publisher by setting an open preference from within Acrobat Exchange. Users can select a magnification to view the page. (This can be accomplished by using the zoom tool from the Viewer's toolbar, or by selecting a magnification from the Zoom menu in the menubar to access the pop-up menu at the bottom of the document window in a Web browser and viewer.) Users also can choose to view only the page, the page with bookmarks, or the page with thumbnails. Additionally, each view and magnification can display a single page at a time,

Page Dimension	Greeked Text	Magnification[1]	View(s)
Letter (8.5 x 11 inches)	14-point and below	35% Fit Page	Page Only Page and Bookmarks Page and Thumbnails
Letter (8.5 x 11 inches)	No[2]	78% Fit Width	Page Only
Letter (8.5 x 11 inches)	11-point and below	54% Fit Width	Page and Bookmarks Page and Thumbnails
Letter (landscape: 11 x 8.5 inches)	11-point and below	46% Fit Page	Page Only
Letter (landscape: 11 x 8.5 inches)	12-point and below	41% Fit Page	Page and Bookmarks Page and Thumbnails
Letter (landscape: 11 x 8.5 inches)	No	60% Fit Width	Page Only
Letter (landscape: 11 x 8.5 inches)	12-point and below	41% Fit Width	Page and Bookmarks Page and Thumbnails
Tabloid (11 x 17 inches)	18-point and below	23% Fit Page	Page Only Page and Bookmarks Page and Thumbnails
Tabloid (11 x 17 inches)	No	69% Fit Page	Page Only
Tabloid (11 x 17 inches)	12-point and below	41% Fit Page	Page and Bookmarks Page and Thumbnails
640 x 480 pixels[3]	9-point and below	59% Fit Page	Page Only
640 x 480 pixels	10-point and below	51% Fit Page	Page and Bookmarks Page and Thumbnails
640 x 480 pixels	No	75% Fit Width	Page Only
640 x 480 pixels	10-point and below	51% Fit Width	Page and Bookmarks Page and Thumbnails

Table 4.1—3 Common Page-Size Magnification, View, and Greeked Text Comparisons

[1] Actual Size magnification not included.

[2] Nine-point is the minimum point size tested; smaller point sizes may be Greeked.

[3] 640 x 480 pixels is not a common print size. This size is included because it is common to presentation and multimedia publishers.

a single column of pages, or two columns of pages. Acrobat scales the page to fit within the Web-browser document window given the page size, magnification, and whether bookmarks or thumbnails are displayed.

Text can be read by magnifying the page (at the user's discretion), or by scaling to fit within a predefined area (a navigational feature added to PDF files to allow easier onscreen reading of text). (See Section 7.9, "Article Threads," for more information about Articles.) When scaled, text smaller than six pixels (the factory-set default in Acrobat viewers) is Greeked, or converted to gray lines. Six pixels is the default Greek text size for Acrobat viewers.

Print and onscreen page dimensions

Page sizes smaller than common print-page sizes (letter, legal, tabloid, etc.) can be printed on most printers. Any of the onscreen page dimensions and the common letter-size dimensions are suitable for the majority of users who will download and opt to print the PDF files.

Note: When printing, users may select the Shrink to Fit option that reduces (and if necessary rotates) oversized pages to fit on the paper size currently installed in the target printer. Shrink to Fit is always available directly within an Acrobat browser. However, if a PDF file is printed from within a Web browser, it may or may not have the Shrink to Fit option, depending on the capabilities of the selected print driver.

If a PDF file's page size is smaller than the target printer's page size, PostScript printer users (and those who have printers that support n-up printing), may take advantage of the unused page's real estate by printing several of the PDF file's pages on a single printed sheet. This is called n-up printing. Because screen font sizes are characteristically larger than those used for print-only documents, n-up print jobs can reduce these larger font sizes to legible, efficient font sizes for print reading.

4.1.2 Navigational Design

In Acrobat documents, much like HTML pages on the Web, the combination of a visual component and an action comprises an object that is used to navigate through a single PDF page, a PDF file, or the Internet. The most common navigational objects are hypertext, buttons, and bookmarks. Visual components include graphics, pictures, text, or any combination of these objects. These object's actions range from magnifying areas of the same page to linking to other sites on the Internet. The design of each visual component should indicate as clearly as possible the link's action.

Navigational objects are recognized by their apparent function—buttons are pressed, areas of a picture or hypertext are clicked. HTML files often use colored, underlined text as a hypertext cue. Likewise, graphics and images are sometimes displayed with a colored border (a cue that they are links). In a PDF file, navigational objects on a page added with Acrobat Exchange or PDF-savvy creator applications are limited to rectangular hot spots. These hot spots are indicated with a colored or transparent border in three varying line widths and in two styles (dotted or solid). A wide range of navigational objects can be created by combining transparent hot spots with visual components during the design stage, which greatly expands the navigational design possibilities.

The goal of document interface design is a document that is easily navigated by as many users as possible. Here, other resources focusing on document interface design will prove useful as a PDF publication is designed. Within the parameters of Internet publishing with Acrobat, particular navigational cues (and their actions) require advanced planning to maximize the opportunity to reach this goal.

PDF file navigation occurs at the viewer level and at the individual document level. In every PDF file, the Acrobat viewer's toolbar contains four buttons for navigating through pages of a PDF file, and another two buttons to "go to previous view" and "go to next view." These buttons enable the user to page backward and forward through pages in sequential order, or skip to the first or last page of a PDF file. If the components have been added, Acrobat viewers also allow navigation through bookmarks and thumbnails. (See Section 7.5, "Bookmarks," and Section 6.1.3, "Thumbnails.") As a document can be created with virtually any software (or combination of software) applications, a custom navigational design specific to the document's content can be created. More options are then extended to a user beyond the basic toolbar, thumbnail, and bookmark components built into Acrobat viewers.

Hypertext cues

The universal cue for a hypertext link is colored, underlined text. The hypertext link's color cue stands out from the majority of the document text. In most Web browsers, hypertext in HTML documents will change color after it has been followed (or selected). Presently, followed links in PDF files do not change color.

Action	Cues	PDF Action	Description
Links to Next Page, Previous Page.	Arrows, page curl, "Next," "Previous", "Back"	Links to page.	Links the user one page back or forward in the document. Pages need not be ordered sequentially. Most common in Acrobat files and multimedia applications.
Links to Home.	House icon, "Home"	Links to page.	Links the user to a central page, which may be the table of contents, main menu, etc.
Links to a description, related items, definition, etc. of a word or phrases.	Colored, italicized text (hypertext), icons near words	Links to page area.	Links the user to other content somehow related to the link, which is itself part of the content.
Links to magnified area.	Icons, "Click to Zoom In"	Magnifies area of a page.	Links to a greater magnification of a specified page area.

Table 4.1—4 Common Navigational Actions

Hypertext in PDF files may either conform to what is found (and used) on the Web, or it may be "styled" with PDF's navigational and interactive object cue—a colored rectangle around the word or phrase. Documents being published concurrently in print and on the Internet from a single source can add hypertext cues as colored rectangles in Acrobat Exchange to avoid hypertext-styled text in the print version of the document.

Note: pdfmarks embedded in PostScript files that are generated from PDF-savvy creator applications do not effect the output of printed jobs.

If the hypertext cue is to conform to the colored, underlined text found in HTML documents, the cues can be produced most easily by styling and coloring the text—which will be the link—as the document is in the designed stage. Later, in Acrobat Exchange (or added automatically with a PDF-savvy creator application through pdfmark), a transparent rectangle will be drawn over the hypertext and the hypertext action (e.g., a World Wide Web Link, Open File, or Go To View) will be assigned.

Within Acrobat Exchange, Adobe's Touch Up Plug-in and other third-party plug-ins can be used to style, color, or edit text in a PDF file to conform to the content's hypertext link cue designs. Use these plug-ins to reset outdated hypertext links to normal text.

Note: Layout-altering modifications, numerous hypertext changes, or changes to the hypertext link's cue style often are completed most efficiently in the software application in which the file was designed, rather than with the Tough Up Plug-in or other plug-ins.

Image and graphic cues

On the Web, graphic and image navigational objects (for example, visual components such as buttons and icons) often are identified with a colored border. In Acrobat Exchange, use the form tool to create a button field. Buttons can have a custom icon (imported from a PDF file) and name, which will change when clicked. Use the link tool to draw a colored, rectangular border around graphics or images in PDF files. If the graphic or image is irregularly shaped or circular, either add a colored border as the document is being designed in the creator application, or omit the colored border visual cue by adding a transparent rectangle over the navigational object. Links can have an action and no visual component, creating an invisible link. See Chapter 7, "Adding Interactive and Navigational Objects," for more information.

As in HTML files, when a user moves the arrow cursor over a link or bookmark in a PDF file, the cursor icon changes to a pointing hand. The cursor changes to a hand with an arrow in it when the user moves the cursor over an article thread. Moving the cursor over a link to a movie or sound file causes the cursor to change to the movie icon, which looks like a small segment of a film strip. All these visual cues help users better understand interactive objects in the document and what action they perform.

Use creator applications to create visual components and cues (if applicable); use Acrobat Exchange to add the actual interactive objects. Links added in Acrobat Exchange can be placed over any area of the page, but must be rectangular in shape. Form buttons, created in Exchange with the form tool, can have one or more actions that are triggered by user actions.

4.1.3 Selecting Fonts

Select fonts suited to the document's publishing strategy. For onscreen use, ensure that the font allows for easy reading at a variety of magnifications. Typefaces can lose legibility at various magnifications. Font selection is a balancing act between graphic design and the ability to read the font onscreen.

For fonts that are not embedded (see Section 6.1.11, "Checking Embedded Fonts"), check to see how the Acrobat viewer substitutes the fonts in a PDF file, or use fonts known to be installed on the user's system. The substitution font, combined with the width of the true typeface, may create a very readable hybrid, or a font that is more difficult to read.

See Appendix F, "Font Copyrights," for more information on the legal implications of embedding a typeface or font in a PDF file for publication on the Internet.

Note: When publishing for a specific audience that may use a particular computer platform to view the PDF files, check to see which fonts are standard and commonly used on the system. Often these fonts are tuned for efficient and effective onscreen reading (and are common to the user's onscreen reading).

Sans serif fonts such as Helvetica, Frutiger, and Ariel are generally more legible onscreen than serif typefaces such as Times, Palatino, and others.

Note: Acrobat 3.0's anti-aliasing of text, which applies soft edges to fonts to eliminate stair-stepping, increases legibility to allow type sizes as small as nine points to be read on most monitors.

Use	Typeface
Titles and headings	Choose fonts with clearly defined widths for best results. Increase kerning (or tracking) for greater onscreen legibility.
Body text	Choose fonts that are legible at 100% on a monitor 640 x 480 pixels. Additionally, see how the font looks at 200% (at 640 x 480 pixels), the magnification most users use to read body text in article threads.
Captions	Choose fonts that are displayed large enough not to be Greeked at 100% on most monitors. Typefaces with hint tables have better results for these typically smaller font sizes.
Display type	Choose fonts that render quickly on most machines and print well, as these typefaces will often be embedded to preserve their uniqueness.

Table 4.1—5 Typefaces

Font point sizes

Set font sizes at 10, 12, or 14 points—not fractional sizes such as 11.5 or 12.75 points. These incremental sizes can magnify oddly and stretch Acrobat's font substitution algorithms. Incremental sizes also require more memory for font substitution and result in slower page rendering and printing.

View the PDF file in a Web browser (on a monitor 640 x 480 pixels) at common magnifications (100%, fit view, fit page, etc.), to determine at what point size the text is Greeked. Smaller page sizes, large font point sizes, or strategically placed Articles and Go To View actions can minimize text Greeking on standard monitor sizes.

Font format selection

PDF files support TrueType, Type 1, Type 1C (compressed Type 1), Type 3, Multiple Master fonts, and Asian language (CID) double-byte fonts. Conversion to PDF files via PostScript Type 1 fonts yield smaller PDF files than other font formats and render more quickly in a PDF file than other fonts. Whenever possible, use Type 1 fonts or other fonts that may be easily converted to Type 1 (or TrueType) when designing a document. When printing the file to a PostScript printer, some drivers (e.g., the Windows 3.1 PS driver) convert other font formats to Type 1 fonts. See Table 4.1—6, "Font Format Issues," for additional font format information.

Note: Adobe's CID (Character Identifier) keyed font technology enables the supported Asian languages to be mixed on the same page.

Type 1C fonts, a Type 1 font compressed by Acrobat Distiller 3.0, decreases file size more than Type 1 and other embedded font formats. Additionally, using a compressed Type 1C font prevents users from illicitly removing Type 1 fonts from the PDF file. If Type 1C fonts are not used, it calls into question a number of licensing issues publishers should carefully consider.

Note: Only Acrobat 3.0 supports compressed Type 1 (Type 1C) fonts. PDF files with compressed Type 1 fonts can be used only with Acrobat 3.0 or later viewers.

Font Type	Issue
TrueType[1]	TrueType fonts are converted easily to Type 1 (Distiller 2.0 or 2.1) or Type 1C fonts (Distiller 3.0 and later).
	The Microsoft Windows 3.1 PostScript printer driver coverts TrueType fonts to PostScript Type 1 fonts by default when it creates a PostScript file for PostScript printing. Distiller 3.0 converts this font to a Type 1C font.
Bitmap fonts[2]	Bitmap fonts (Type 1 or 3) require considerable storage space and result in much larger PDF files as compared to Type 1 (or Type 1C) outline fonts and PDF files that use Type 1 outline fonts.
Type 3[2]	Documents converted to PDF files that contain Type 3 fonts have very large file sizes because a Type 1 font is created for each size of the typeface used and are slow to render onscreen.

Table 4.1—6 Font Format Issues

---

1 Special Type 1 font subsets are used and the names of these fonts may not be unique. This causes a problem for Acrobat Distiller 1.0. Use Acrobat Distiller 2.0 or later because the problem has been fixed.

2 Bitmap and Type 3 fonts are generally less legible onscreen than Type 1 fonts.

See Appendix G, "Font Embedding Information," for detailed, platform-by-platform information on how Acrobat Distiller and the Acrobat viewers process different font formats.

4.1.4 Adding Form Fields

PDF documents may be designed to solicit a user response. These solicitations are common in the print world in the form of business reply cards, order forms, subscription forms, surveys, and so on. Increasingly, more and more Web sites are including forms for user feedback, online ordering, searching, and other queries. Most Web servers, through server-based scripts or applications, allow automated compilation of these queries and return personalized results.

Form fields are authored with Acrobat Exchange. Reader and Exchange users may fill in the forms and submit the completed form to be processed by the Web server, print the form for their own use, or export data from the forms. The Web server, using a Common Gateway Interface (CGI) script, Java applet, or other scripting or programming language, then processes (and can respond to) the PDF file's fields in the same manner it processes HTML forms. Creating forms is detailed in Section 7.6, "Forms," and in the Acrobat Exchange 3.0 Online Guide.

Note: Documents should be designed to include form field areas during layout. Documents that are well designed reflect the existence of a form object onscreen and on paper. Design the PDF document with form field labels and give the user enough room in each field to complete the form online, or after it is printed.

Field Type	Description
Text field	Allows the entry of arbitrary text into the field.
Password Text field	
Combo box	Allows selection of an item from a drop-down list.
List box	Allows selection of an item from a displayed list of items.
Multiple-Selection List box	Allows selection of one or more items from a displayed list of items.
Checkbox	Allows the selection of one or multiple field items.
Radio button	Allows the selection of one or another field items.

Table 4.1—7 PDF Form Fields Types

4.1.5 Reusing Graphics and Images

The reuse of graphic and image bitmaps in an optimized PDF file decreases the overall file size and speeds the rendering of the bitmaps. Wherever a design permits, reuse is encouraged.

Optimizing PDF files in Acrobat Exchange deletes redundant images and graphic bitmaps. Only a single copy of the bitmap is stored in the PDF file. After a PDF file with an optimized graphic or image bitmap is downloaded, it is cached and its rendering on subsequent pages is greatly increased.

Note: Designers should take advantage of this feature for common interface parts, background textures, and images. Some creator applications, such as Adobe PageMaker, QuarkXPress, and Adobe FrameMaker, have a "master pages" feature. Master pages are a convenient location to store and keep track of shared graphic and image elements in a document. After the file is converted to a PDF file, optimization (see Section 7.14, "Optimizing PDF Files for the World Wide Web"), removes the redundant data that describes other occurrences of the reused image and graphics, reducing the overall size of the PDF file.

4.2 Choosing Creator Applications

Most software applications capable of printing can be used to create PDF files with the addition or selection of a PostScript printer driver. (See Section 5.1.1, "The PostScript Printer Driver," for more information about printer drivers.) PostScript files are converted to PDF files with Acrobat Distiller (see Chapter 5, "Converting PostScript Files to PDF Files").

Note: The process of creating a PDF file from a creator-application file can be accomplished easily—often in one step—by using Acrobat Distiller Assistant. See the Distiller 3.0 Online Guide.

A single creator application can be selected for the layout of documents and later for the conversion to PDF files. However, PostScript files or the resulting PDF files from any number of different applications (desktop publishing, spreadsheet, and graphics) can be combined into a single PDF file, allowing several creator applications to create a single PDF document.

Depending on individual documents and publishing strategies, consider the following issues when selecting the most appropriate creator application.

Issues	Description
Installed base creator applications	Applications that are used for other publishing efforts (and other purposes) allow PostScript-file (and some PDF files) creation with minimal staff training and expense. Concurrent publishing strategists often find this issue the most advantageous.
Support for HTML[1]	Allows HTML/PDF integration publishing efforts to standardize on a single creator application that can be used for the creation of both HTML and PDF files.
Support for PDF files and objects[1]	PDF-savvy creator applications automate the addition of interactive, navigational, and general PDF file-specific attributes (including conversion, for some applications). See Section 4.3, "PDF-Savvy Creator Applications."

Table 4.2—1 Creator Application Selection Issues

[1] Support may be either built into the creator application or extended through plug-ins, XTensions, filters, macros, and so on.

4.3 PDF-Savvy Creator Applications

PDF-savvy applications make the process of converting to PDF files more efficient by controlling and adding PDF file objects and attributes at the design stage. PDF file support is built either directly into the application or added to the application through plug-ins, XTensions, filters, macros, and so forth

PDF-savvy creator applications automate the addition of interactive and navigational objects (bookmarks, article threads, or notes, etc.) to PDF files by embedding commands (called "pdfmarks"), in the PostScript file. After the PostScript file is converted by Acrobat Distiller, the resulting PDF file exhibits the navigational and interactive features added originally in the creator application.

Some PDF-savvy creator applications also can control the process of converting from the creator application's file type to a PostScript file, and then to a PDF file through interapplication communication (IAC). These applications often use a limited-use "Private Edition" version of Acrobat Distiller to generate PDF files. Other applications can save files directly to the PDF file format, bypassing the PostScript file to PDF conversion process completely.

4.3.1 Using Adobe PageMaker 6.0, 5.0

PageMaker 6.0 includes support for PDF with Adobe's Create PDF Plug-in (included with PageMaker 6.0). Through this Plug-in, PageMaker embeds pdfmark operators within the PostScript file it generates to automatically add links, article threads, notes, bookmarks, document information, and other objects to a PDF file.

PageMaker also controls the PostScript file to PDF conversion process by printing or saving the document to a PostScript file, launching Acrobat Distiller, and then converting the PostScript file to PDF. The Plug-in controls Distiller's Job Options (see Section 5.2, "Using Acrobat Distiller"), which override Distiller's preset or default settings. Custom settings then can be sent without the need to preconfigure or intervene in the automated conversion process. For Acrobat Distiller 2.1 users, PageMaker has an optional Job Option item that converts CMYK images to RGB images. (This CMYK to RGB conversion is possible with 2.1 Distillers, but the option doesn't appear in the Distiller 2.1 user interface. It is only accessible by editing the startup script (described in Appendix H, "Setting Options in Distiller's Startup Directory").

Earlier versions of PageMaker also can produce PDF by outputting PostScript language files and then launching the Distiller. However, the direct, automated PDF linking features built into PageMaker 6.0 are not available. PageMaker 5.0 users can use xMan software's PDF Navigator to assist with link creation from a table of contents, with bookmark creation, and with PostScript file creation. (See Appendix I, "Acrobat Plug-ins," for more information about PDF Navigator from xMan software.)

For concurrent print and Internet publishing, PageMaker 6.0 can be configured with different printer styles (see the *Adobe PageMaker User Guide*) to allow settings specifically for PDF files, and other settings for traditional print output.

PageMaker 6.0 supports a PDF and HTML integration strategy using Adobe's HTML Plug-in (included with Adobe PageMaker 6.0 and later). The plug-in allows the creation and publication of print, PDF, and HTML files from PageMaker 6.0.

PDF Object	Description
Bookmarks[1]	Bookmarks are generated from a PageMaker file's automatically generated table of contents and index. To create bookmarks from a document's table of contents, select File > Create Adobe PDF > PDF Options > Create Bookmarks. Bookmark hierarchy is defined by the table of contents. To create bookmarks from a document's index, select File > Create Adobe PDF > PDF Options > Create Bookmarks. One bookmark appears for each occurrence of the indexed item on a page. A bookmark's Go To View action magnification may be set in the PDF Options dialog box. (See Section 7.1.2, "Go To View Action," for more information on Go To View magnifications.)

continued

Table 4.3—1 Interactive and Navigational Objects Supported by PageMaker 6.0

PDF Object	Description
Links[2]	Links are created from a PageMaker file's automatically generated table of contents and index. To create links from a document's table of contents, select File > Create Adobe PDF > PDF Options > Link table of contents Entries. Links are created from each line item in the table of contents to the appropriate page (the table of contents must be generated by PageMaker). To create links from a document's index, select File > Create Adobe PDF > PDF Options > Link Index. Links are created from index entries to their locations in the document. A link's Go To View magnification action may be set in the PDF Options dialog box. (See Section 7.1.2, "Go To View Action," for more information on Go To View magnifications.)
Article threads[3]	To create article threads, select File > Create Adobe PDF > PDF Options > Create Articles. Article threads follow the story's PageMaker-defined thread.
Notes[4]	To create a single note on the first page of the PDF file, select File > Create Adobe PDF > PDF Options > Add Note to First Page.
Thumbnails	To create thumbnails for either the first or all pages in a PDF file, select File > Create Adobe PDF > Edit... (overrides Distiller's Job Options).

Table 4.3—1 (continued) Interactive and Navigational Objects Supported by PageMaker 6.0

1 While the bookmark's hierarchy is set according to the table of content, the expanded or contracted nature of the hierarchy cannot be set from within PageMaker.

2 The link's style (line color, size, etc.) cannot be predefined, but can be changed in Acrobat Exchange. By default, PageMaker-created links appear as invisible rectangles that invert when clicked.

3 Applying threads to stories may be defined by a story's number of characters or selected manually from a list of all stories within the file (or book).

4 Some of a note's attributes including title, text within the note, and the note's opened or closed display status can be controlled. Note placement, font selection, color, dimensions, and information cannot be set from within PageMaker.

Document information—including the title, author, subject, and keywords—can be set from within PageMaker before converting the PageMaker file to a PDF file.

Note: The PageMaker user guide has further details on creating PDF files from PageMaker.

4.3.2 Using Adobe FrameMaker 5.0

FrameMaker 5.0 supports PDF navigational and interactive objects directly by selecting the Generate Acrobat Data option from the Print dialog box. Selecting the option embeds pdfmarks in the PostScript language file created for the document.

HTML markup is also supported by FrameMaker. (FrameMaker also has a run-time viewer for viewing native FrameMaker files for PDF and HTML integration strategies.)

FrameMaker includes partial automation of the FrameMaker-to-PDF file conversion process through its Generate Acrobat Data option. Selecting this option sets the file to print to a PostScript language file rather than a printer. (Additionally, the Skip Blank Pages option—the default—is deselected.)

PDF Object	Description
Bookmarks[1]	Bookmarks are generated from FrameMaker's style hierarchy. A dialog box for setting which paragraph styles should be included as bookmarks and the hierarchy of these selected styles is available by selecting Acrobat Setup from the Print dialog box.
Links	To automatically link from one text block to another, use FrameMaker's cross-reference feature. When converted to a PDF file, the cross-references become hypertext links. To manually designate a word or phrase as a link, select the text and change its character format to define the link's beginning and ending boundary. (FrameMaker ignores pair kerning, spread change bars, and case format changes.) Select Special > Marker > Hypertext (see Table 4.3—3, "FrameMaker Hypertext to PDF Objects" below).

continued

Table 4.3—2 Interactive and Navigational Objects Supported by FrameMaker 5.0

PDF Object	Description
	To designate an entire paragraph or text section as a link, make sure that there are no format changes in the paragraph. Select Special > Marker > Hypertext (see Table 4.3—3, "FrameMaker Hypertext to PDF Objects" below).
	To manually designate a word or phrase as a link without changing the appearance of the link area, selected the As Is character format option.
	To designate a graphic or image as a link, draw a text frame that covers the entire graphic. A text frame may be required to do this. Select Special > Marker > Hypertext (See Table 4.3—3, "FrameMaker Hypertext to PDF Objects" below).
	A link's Go To View action destination includes specific areas of a page, other pages in the same document, and other PDF files mounted locally. (World Wide Web Link actions are not supported.)
	To designate an area as a link that appears on every page, place a link on a master page, rather than a body page. (Disable the link by placing a graphic or text frame over the link on the document page.)
Article threads[2]	Article threads are created from a story's text frame. Article threads are created for all text frames.
	The article thread title will be the same as the title of the flow tag in the FrameMaker document.
Notes[3]	To set a note, set a point for the marker, select Special > Marker > Hypertext (see Table 4.3-3, "FrameMaker Hypertext to PDF Objects" below).
Thumbnails	FrameMaker has no options for automating the creation of thumbnails. To create thumbnails from FrameMaker-generated PostScript files, select the Create Thumbnails option in Acrobat Distiller's Job Options.

Table 4.3—2 (continued) Interactive and Navigational Objects Supported by FrameMaker 5.0

1 The expanded or contracted hierarchy cannot be set from within FrameMaker.

2 Article threads flow according to a document's page numbers from front to back. Change the progression of the thread in Acrobat Exchange.

3 Some of the note's attributes—including its opened or closed display status—can be controlled. Note that font selection, color, and dimensions cannot be set from within FrameMaker.

A link's action and the title and text of a note may be set from within FrameMaker by setting a coded hypertext marker. The following table lists the syntax and resulting PDF object.

Marker Syntax[1]	PDF Object	Description
gotopage n	Link using the Go To View action.	Links to a specific page number.
nextpage	Link using the Go To View action.	Links to the next page in the same document.
previouspage	Link using the Go To View action.	Links to the previous page in the same document.
gotolink firstpage	Link using the Go To View action.	Links to the first page in the same document.
gotolink lastpage	Link using the Go To View action.	Links to the last page in the same document.
Alert z (z = the text of the note, 255 characters maximum)	Note	Creates a note.
openpage y:n (y = filename, n = page number of the target document)	Link using the Open File action.	Opens a target PDF file to a defined page number.

Table 4.3—3 FrameMaker Hypertext to PDF Objects

[1] The following FrameMaker hypertext commands are not supported: alerttitle, exit, gotolinkfitwin, message openfile, message system, openlinkfitwin, opennew, popup, previouslink, previouslinkfitwin, quit, quitall, and winexec.

FrameMaker uses a number of other hypertext commands that perform specific tasks in the view-only mode of FrameMaker. These commands do not work in Acrobat, although they perform actions similar to the actions found in the toolbars of Acrobat viewers.

Note: The FrameMaker user guide, Using FrameMaker, has further details on creating PDF files with FrameMaker.

4.3.3 Using Adobe Illustrator

Adobe Illustrator 6.0 (Macintosh) or Illustrator 5.5 (Macintosh with the free PDF Plug-in available from Adobe's Web site) are PDF-savvy only in their capability to open and save to the PDF file format. Opening a PDF file allows editing of objects on single pages of a PDF file. However, when saving an Illustrator file as a PDF file, there are no compression options available. This results in considerably larger PDF files than those converted from PostScript files by Acrobat Distiller. Check Adobe's Web site at http://www.adobe.com/ for information on other versions of Adobe Illustrator (and which platforms) that support the PDF file format.

Note: For more compact PDF files, create a PostScript file of the Illustrator file and convert it to PDF with Acrobat Distiller.

Adobe has a tutorial on using Illustrator to create links. The EPS Links tutorial can be found on Adobe's Acrobat Web site at http://www.adobe.com/acrobat/.

4.3.4 Using QuarkXPress

Use QuarkXPress to create PDF files by converting Quark files to PostScript files through a PostScript printer driver. The PostScript files then can be converted to PDF files with Acrobat Distiller. Third-party XTensions for Quark add enhanced support for PDF files. Through these XTensions, pdfmark operators are embedded within the PostScript file generated from QuarkXPress, thereby automating the addition of PDF objects and document information. Third party developers offer several HTML markup XTensions, supporting PDF and HTML integration strategies. Third-party developers that provide PDF-specific XTensions for QuarkXPress are listed in Appendix J, "Acrobat-Related Creator Application Plug-ins."

For the best possible Quark-created PDF files (with or without third-party PDF file XTensions), use the Adobe Acrobat PostScript Printer Description (PPD). (A PPD file is a set of printer instructions.) It was specifically designed for QuarkXPress files to generate PostScript files for conversion to PDF files. On the Macintosh computer, Acrobat 3.0 installs the Acrobat Distiller PPD in the Printer Descriptions folder, which is in the Extensions folder, found in the System Folder. On Windows systems, the Acrobat 3.0 installer places the ACRODIST.PPD into the Windows/System directory. The installer for both Macintosh and Windows also places the PPD file within the Acrobat Distiller Xtras directory.

Note: Outline text created in QuarkXPress displays as white characters in Acrobat viewers, but prints correctly to PostScript printers. Quark updates may fix this bug.

4.3.5 Using Corel Ventura Publisher

Corel Ventura Publisher 5.0 and later versions support PDF navigational and interactive objects directly by converting the table of contents items, index, or cross-reference entries to PDF bookmarks and links via pdfmark.

To create a PDF file from Ventura, first set up the table of contents, indices, and cross-references. Renumber the publication and generate the table of contents. In the Print Dialog box, choose Print to File from the File/Print option and select Encapsulated PostScript driver in the Print/Setup/PostScript options. Select Acrobat in the Print/Options dialog box.

Ventura supports HTML markup as well as an option to view native Ventura files as electronic documents within Ventura. This is especially useful for HTML and PDF integration strategies.

PDF Object	Description
Bookmarks	Bookmarks are generated from Ventura's native table of contents and index.
Links	Create hypertext links with Ventura's cross-references.
Notes[1]	Create notes via Ventura's hidden text[2] commands (<$text>). Insert this hidden text code into the text to be loaded in the Ventura file. The text that is typed within the brackets is hidden within the Ventura document.

Table 4.3—4 Interactive and Navigational Objects Supported by Ventura 5.0 (and later versions)

1 <$!text> creates hidden text within Ventura and is converted to a note when Acrobat Distiller is used for conversion. <$!~text> will create hidden text within Ventura, but the tilde (~) suppresses the hidden code from being converted to a note when Distiller is used.

2 Hidden text will not convert properly to a PDF note if it is the first entry in a paragraph. Insert a space before inserting the hidden text code.

See the *Corel Ventura User's Guide* for more information on creating PDF files with Ventura.

4.3.6 Using Microsoft Word and Microsoft Excel

Microsoft Word and Excel have no built-in support for the automatic creation of interactive or navigational objects in PDF files. However, one-step PDF file creation can be added to Word and

Excel through a macro that adds a "Create Adobe PDF" option to the File menus of both applications (available in the retail version of Acrobat 3.0, for Windows 95 only). Choosing the Create Adobe PDF option automatically switches to the PDFWriter driver, creates the PDF file, and then switches back to the previously selected printer driver.

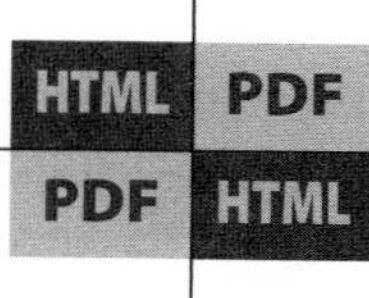

5

Converting PostScript Files to PDF Files

Optimal use of Acrobat Distiller's job options results in PDF files with the high onscreen quality and quick Internet download times. A wealth of information on preparing PostScript files and using Acrobat Distiller is available in the Acrobat Distiller Online Guide. This chapter covers the basic steps in the PostScript file generation process and focuses on using Acrobat Distiller to convert PostScript files to PDF files for Internet publishing.

When converting a PostScript file to a PDF file, consider the following items to ensure that the resulting PDF file is well suited to be published on the Internet:

- Always use the Acrobat Distiller PPD file when printing to a PostScript file.
- Use Distiller's default job options and examine the resulting PDF file. After examining the quality of the resulting PDF file, adjust the job options if necessary.

- For an image-heavy document, try the highest compression levels and work backward, reducing the level of compression until the image quality is satisfactory for the standard magnifications at which the images will be displayed.
- Convert a text-rich file first with font embedding on—then with it off. Remove the fonts used in the document from the computer on which the file is being viewed and compare the quality and rendering speed of the substituted fonts onscreen. When printed, compare the quality with that of the file containing the embedded fonts.
- Whenever possible, use substitute fonts to keep the PDF files as small as possible.
- As a general rule, don't use the high-quality print enhancements introduced with Acrobat 3.0 for PDF files to be published on the Internet. (Unless the PDF files will be available on a print server where this quality may be required.)
- Allow Distiller to compress text and graphics and to downsample images, rather than pre-compressing these items before saving to a PostScript file.
- Convert PDF files to binary files, not ASCII files. Binary files are 12 to 20% smaller than ASCII-encoded PDF files.
- For added flexibility and control, configure Distiller's Example.ps startup script to customize the conversion of PostScript files. (See Appendix H, "Setting Options in Distiller's Startup Directory," for more information on configuring the Example.ps file.)
- To conform to the file naming systems still being used by some users, use short names for PDF files (less than eight

characters) and always use the ".PDF" suffix. Consider making the file names ISO 9660 Interchange Level 1-compliant (see Section 5.2.5, "Naming the PDF File").

5.1 Generating PostScript Files

PostScript files are generated by saving the data normally sent to a printer to a file. Consult the Acrobat Distiller Online Guide for information on selecting printer drivers and generating PostScript files.

5.1.1 The PostScript Printer Driver

Use a PostScript printer driver that supports PostScript Level 2. PostScript Level 1 drivers do not support many of the features that are useful in making PDF files. Most applications (and system software) allow the selection of a PostScript Printer Description (PPD) as the printer driver.

For Macintosh, use LaserWriter 8.1 or later. For Windows 95, use the PostScript mini-driver (developed with Adobe Systems), which supports and uses both PPDs and Windows Printer Descriptions (WPD). For other operating systems, use the resident system's PostScript printer driver or install the Adobe PS Printer.

Adobe ships its own PostScript printer driver, PS Printer (Macintosh) or Adobe PS Driver (PC), for use with creator applications. With the PS Printer (and other PostScript printer drivers) installed, almost every software package capable of printing can be used to generate PostScript files.

Note: Acrobat 3.0 ships with the Adobe printer driver for Macintosh and Windows. Adobe recommends using this printer driver when generating PostScript files.

5.1.2 Selecting the Distiller PostScript Printer Description (PPD) File

Every operating system and application handles the selection of a PostScript Printer Description file differently. Check the operating system's documentation to learn how to select a PPD file.

Select the Acrobat Distiller PPD (Macintosh) or ACRODIST.PPD (PC/UNIX). The Acrobat Distiller PPD/ACRODIST.PPD is in the Xtras folder within the Acrobat directory. The Acrobat PPD includes special filtering to enhance PDF quality when converted by Acrobat Distiller.

Using other PPD files rather than the Acrobat PPD may affect the PDF differently. Using a black-and-white PPD file results in black-and-white PDF files (color elements are converted to grayscale). PPDs also may be configured for a specific paper size, print order, or color correction.

5.1.3 Printing a PostScript Language File to Disk

With a PostScript printer driver and the Acrobat Distiller PPD/ACRODIST.PPD file selected, choose the print command from the creator application to select the option to save as a PostScript file.

Within the PostScript print dialog box, indicate the document pages to be saved as a PostScript file (generally, the default is all pages). Next, choose the option to save the PostScript language file to the hard disk. Depending on system software, creator application, and the selected printer driver, a number of other

Item	Options	Description
File format	PostScript	Writes the file to a PostScript file format.
	EPS (with preview grades)[1]	Select Encapsulated PostScript file, which produces a file intended for embedding into other files.
Font inclusion	None	Includes none of the fonts in the PostScript file.
	All[2]	Select None if Distiller will have access to the fonts used in the file.
	All but Standard 13	Select All But Standard 13 if Distiller doesn't have access to the fonts used in the file.
	All but fonts in PPD	
PostScript Level	PostScript Level 1	Writes the PostScript file in one of the two PostScript language versions.
	PostScript Level 2	Select PostScript Level 2, which supports more features advantageous to PDF files.
Data mode	ASCII	Encodes the PostScript file in one of two data modes.
	Binary	Select binary which reduces the PostScript file's size by 20% or more.[3]

Table 5.1—1 Common Printer Driver Options

[1] By definition, EPS files cannot contain more than a single page.

[2] Acrobat installs the standard 13 fonts (plus one other), with all Acrobat viewers. Distiller never embeds these fonts in PDF files, so they may be used liberally. Use this option if TrueType fonts are used in the document.

[3] This depends on the types of elements in the document that is saved as a PostScript file.

Note: PostScript errors can include illegal instructions, corrupt code, or extraneous data used for specific printers that Distiller cannot convert. To troubleshoot PostScript errors: 1) Generate the PostScript file again; if the error still exists, 2) switch printer drivers and try again. If the problem still exists, 3) switch PPDs and try again; and finally, 4) break down the file by page and then by page element to identify the element causing the PostScript error. If this doesn't work, consult technical support when encountering reproducible errors during PostScript file generation. Also, consult the printer driver's error log for information and the cause of the error (if supported by the driver or creator application).

options may be available. Select either save or print and choose a location for the PostScript file.

5.2 Using Acrobat Distiller

Acrobat Distiller reads and interprets PostScript files, applies compression, downsamples graphics and images, embeds fonts, and converts the PostScript file's data to a PDF file.

Note: To convert PostScript files (or Encapsulated PostScript files), select File > Open..., select a PostScript file, and name the resulting PDF file. Distiller also converts PostScript files dropped into defined directories. See the Distiller user guide for information on naming the resulting PDF files converted from a watched folder.

Use Acrobat Distiller as the principal tool to compress text and to compress and downsample graphics and images when converting a PostScript file to a PDF file. Distiller's settings for job options control the downsampling, compression type, quality of images and graphics, and the compression of text. Distiller automatically applies whatever compression technology is specified in Job Options to all text, graphics, and images (unless overridden by Distiller-specific commands in the PostScript file). PDF files can be encoded as either ASCII or binary data file formats.

Note: Consult the Acrobat Distiller Online Guide for information on Distiller's general use in creating PDF files.

For many documents to be published on the Internet, Distiller's default job options yield reasonably well-compressed files with satisfactory image quality. (Evaluation of PDF file size and general attributes, PDF file pages, colors, and other document attributes after conversion to a PDF file is described in Section 6.1, "PDF File Evaluation.")

The original images and graphics in the creator application document can be compressed or downsampled before generating a PostScript file. However, since Distiller can downsample and compress images and graphics as it converts the PostScript file to a PDF file, it is a better choice for compressing and downsampling images and graphics than batch processing them—especially before importing them into a page layout program. Use the creator application's file as a master to allow concurrent publishing for other media.

Note: During conversion, Distiller downsamples and applies the defined method and level of compression to the various image types included in the PostScript file. To downsample one or more images at a lower resolution than what is being applied by Distiller, downsample the image during the design stage with an image editing program before converting the file to a PostScript file. Different levels of compression can be applied only to individual pages of a PDF file—not individual images. This can be accomplished by converting each page separately with custom compression and downsampling options and then combining the pages into the whole document later. Use either the RunFile procedure (see Appendix H, "Setting Options in Distiller's Startup Directory,") or Acrobat Exchange (see Section 6.2.1, "Inserting, Deleting, Extracting, and Replacing Document Pages").

To downsample one or more images to lower settings than those set for the other images in a PostScript file, use Adobe Photoshop. For most images, Photoshop's downsampling rivals and often surpasses Distiller's image-downsampling quality. However, using Distiller to downsample images is easier and often much quicker than downsampling images in Photoshop.

Unexpectedly large PDF files can be reduced by converting the PostScript file again with higher levels of compression. For JPEG files, higher compression results in lower image quality. Large PDF files also can be reduced by downsampling to lower resolutions, or using an entirely different compression technique (e.g., ZIP rather than Run Length or LZW).

5.2.1 Distiller's General Job Options

Taking advantage of Acrobat Distiller's job options results in PDF files that can be distributed to a wider audience with its compatibility feature; files that are binary-encoded thereby utilizing lower bandwidth than with ASCII encoding which yield faster download times and high-quality onscreen resolution.

Compatibility

Distiller's compatibility options can be set for Acrobat 2.1 (and earlier) compatibility to allow resulting PDF files to be view in all 2.1 and earlier Acrobat viewers. Acrobat 3.0 (and later) compatibility generates smaller, more efficient, and Web-suitable PDF files than with earlier viewers. Most Web publishers should choose Acrobat 3.0 compatibility. The Acrobat 3.0 Reader is free and widely available so there should be no need to serve two version of the same PDF file—one compatible with 3.0 and another with Acrobat 2.1. If an audience doesn't have access to an Acrobat 3.0-compatible viewer—perhaps a workgroup that has not yet upgraded from version 2.1 of Acrobat Exchange—provide that audience with only the 2.1-compatible file.

Note: See "Choosing a compatibility setting," in the Distiller 3.0 Online Guide for more information about specific feature compatibility.

ASCII format

Choosing the binary option (the alternative to checking the ASCII option), results in a smaller PDF file. A binary-encoded PDF file is between five percent (low) to 20% (high) smaller than the same file encoded as an ASCII PDF. The default for ASCII coding is off. Binary PDF files also work better as email attachments since ASCII PDF files can be corrupted by older email gateways.

Default resolution

Acrobat 3.0's default resolution is 600 dpi. For most device dependent resolution objects (such as images), this setting is acceptable. For image-heavy PDF files that will rarely or ever be printed, try a lower resolution to save additional file space (which sacrifices resolution).

Default page size

The Default Page Size job options allows the entry of a page size to be used for PostScript files that don't have a defined page size (e.g., Encapsulated PostScript files).

QuarkXPress or Adobe Illustrator users often save document pages as Encapsulated PostScript (EPS) files. EPS is a graphic format that allows single PostScript file pages from one program to be placed within another application's document for printing. EPS files do not contain information about the size or orientation of the page. EPS files converted to PDF files may get cropped or appear with the wrong orientation (landscape when the file should be portrait).

Note: To crop pages, use Acrobat Exchange. The Default Page Size option functions only when the PostScript file has no defined page dimensions. Distiller's startup script also can be configured to rotate or crop (or prevent cropping) EPS files when converting them to PDF files (see Appendix H, "Setting Options in Distiller's Startup Directory").

Job Option	**Best for Internet PDF files**
Compatibility	Acrobat 3.0 compatibility (unless the audience doesn't have access to the free Acrobat 3.0 Readers).
ASCII format	Binary (ASCII is unchecked).
Default resolution	600 dpi
Default page size	Depends on the page dimensions.

Table 5.2—1 Distiller Job Option Descriptions: General

Note: The Generate Thumbnails job option is available only in Acrobat Distiller 2.1 and earlier. Thumbnails may be created and deleted with Acrobat Exchange. Do not select the Generate Thumbnails job option for a PDF file that will be published on the Internet. The default for generating thumbnails is off. A thumbnail adds between one to three kilobytes per page, per thumbnail to the document's file size, depending on page size.

5.2.2 Distiller's Compression Job Options

Distiller's compression job options are factory-set to produce small, yet high-quality PDF files. Some understanding of resolution and image types may prove useful when experimenting with Distiller's manual compression options. Table 5.2—2 below lists the recommended Distiller compression settings for most files.

Job Option	Best for Internet PDF files
Compress text and line art	Checked (on)
Downsample or subsample color, grayscale, and monochrome images	Downsample 72 dpi for color and grayscale images, 300 for monochrome images
Automatic compression or manual compression	Automatic

Table 5.2—2 Distiller Job Option Descriptions: Compression

Compress text and line art

Compressing text and line art results in much smaller PDF files. The on-the-fly decompression performed by the Acrobat viewer has no significant affect on performance. Choose to compress text and line art for all PDF files to be published on the Internet.

Note: Acrobat Distiller compresses text and line art with ZIP compression (or LZW compression for Acrobat 2.1 compatibility).

Downsample or subsample color, grayscale, and monochrome images

Downsampling reduces the size of an image by averaging the pixel color or sample area with a pixel of the averaged color. The number of pixels averaged together is determined by the defined dpi.

Subsampling reduces the resolution (and therefore the image's size in kilobytes) by randomly choosing a pixel in a sample area. It then replaces that area with the chosen pixel. Compared to downsampling, subsampling requires significantly less time to process the same image.

For most PDF files to be published on the Internet, Distiller's factory-set 72 dpi downsampling option works well. Downsample monochrome images to 300 dpi. Downsampling is generally a better option when converting image-heavy PostScript files unless processing time is a concern. Printing color graphics and images downsampled to 72 dpi on a 300 or even 600 dpi printer will result in satisfactory results. Documents intended to be printed at high resolutions should not be downsampled, or should be downsampled to the intended print level at most.

Note: Most Macintosh monitors display a maximum of 72 to 75 dpi; Windows and UNIX monitors display 96 dpi.

To squeeze a few extra kilobytes from the file, try downsampling color or grayscale images to 70 dpi or a slightly lower. Drop monochrome images down to 270 to save a few kilobytes. Be sure to view the file's images to see if the below-recommended compression settings significantly affect the quality of the images.

Automatic compression

The automatic compression options work well in most cases. Increase the compression settings (which switches to manual compression) to squeeze a few extra kilobytes from the file.

Note: For detailed information about which compression algorithm is used for various types of images, refer to "Using Automatic Compression" in the Distiller 3.0 Online Guide.

Manual compression

With the manual compression option, color, grayscale, and monochrome images can be compressed via a specific algorithm. Various compression algorithms affect individual images and whole documents differently. Experiment to discover which configuration offers the best image quality with the smallest file size. Also consider the time required to draw the image on the screen.

Compression	Type	Application	Description
JPEG	Lossy	Color or grayscale images (8-, 16-, and 24-bit color)	JPEG is a cross-platform photographic file format designed by the Joint Photographers Expert Group (JPEG).
		Continuous-tone images (e.g. photographs, or paint program graphics)	The degree of JPEG compression applied affects file size (reduced by discarding data from the image). Different JPEG images hold up differently under various quality levels. Files compressed too much may exhibit artifacts (seen as rectangular splotches in the image).

continued

Table 5.2—3 Distiller Compression Options

Compression	Type	Application	Description
ZIP	Lossless	Text Line art Screen shots (color or grayscale) Monochrome images with large areas of repeating patterns	ZIP compresses data with no loss of information. Decompression of ZIP-compressed items may take slightly longer to display on slower systems. ZIP compression is only available in Acrobat 3.0 and later. ZIP-compressed documents cannot be opened in Acrobat 2.1 or earlier viewers.
LZW	Lossless	Text Line art Screen shots (color or grayscale) Monochrome images with large areas of repeating patterns	This compression method compresses data with no loss of information. Decompression of LZW-compressed items may take slightly longer to display on slower systems. LZW usually is not the best compression method for continuous-tone images, such as photographs.[1]
LZW 4-bit	Lossless	4- or 8-bit images created in paint programs	LZW (4-bit) applies LZW compression and converts 8-bit image data to 4-bit; whereas LZW applies LZW compression, but does not change the bit depth.
CCITT[2] Group 3	Lossless	Monochrome[3] images (e.g., line art)	Group 3 compression is used for compressing monochrome images one-line-at-a-time. This compression technology was invented for, and is commonly used in, facsimile machines to speed transmission. The results of this type of CCITT compression are often less than desirable.
CCITT Group 4	Lossless	Most monochrome images	CCITT Group 4 is a general-purpose method. CCITT Group 4 produces good compression for most types of monochrome images.
Run Length	Lossy	Monochrome images with large areas of black and white	A redundancy-reduction technique (often used in facsimiles).

Table 5.2—3 (continued) Distiller Compression Options

[1] Photographs, commonly in the form of continuous-tone images, can grow in file size if LZW-compressed.

[2] Consultative Committee on International Telephony and Telegraphy

[3] Monochrome images can be compressed by CCITT Group 3, CCITT Group 4, LZW, or Run Length.

5.2.3 Distiller's Font Embedding Job Options

Embedding a font in a PDF file adds the actual font metrics that most systems and applications use to display and print a typeface to the PDF file. Embedded font data is used by Acrobat to display and print type and fonts. Acrobat Distiller 3.0 can embed all popular font formats. (See the Acrobat Distiller Online Guide for a list of supported font formats by platform.)

Overall, embedding a font contributes significantly to the look and feel of a document, especially with documents that contain ornate fonts. Unique typefaces may need to be embedded to preserve the font's unique characters.

Acrobat uses Multiple Master font technology to emulate the look of a font. This technology also substitutes another font for fonts not embedded in the PDF file or available on the user's machine.

Note: Capitalize on the Acrobat viewer's font substituting capability to avoid the need to embed a font, which keeps PDF files small. However, substitute fonts increase screen drawing and printing times. The viewer can only substitute normal text fonts (Times, Gill Sans, etc.) and cannot substitute symbol fonts that include musical notes, Zapf Dingbats, or mathematical symbols. Symbol fonts (or fonts with symbols), if available, are automatically embedded in PDF files. If they are not embedded (the PDF file may have been created with an application that saves to the PDF file format, like Adobe Illustrator), then the symbol font must be installed on the user's system, or the symbol will not be rendered.

Job Option	Best for Internet PDF files
Embed All Fonts	Checked (On)
Subset Fonts below n	25%
User Fonts List	Displays user's font lists, if set.
Always Embed List	Displays fonts set to always be embedded, if set.
Never Embed List	Displays fonts set to never be embedded, if set.

Table 5.2—4 Distiller Job Option Descriptions: Font Embedding[1]

[1] Acrobat uses a font that is very close to Adobe's Minion and Myriad Multiple Master typefaces to substitute serif and sans serif fonts. If Minion or Myriad is in a document, there's no real advantage in embedding those fonts.

Embed All Fonts

Embedding an average font increases the PDF file size from 20 to 30 kilobytes per font (average), or as high as 70 kilobytes for Type 1 fonts (common to most systems and embedded with Acrobat Distiller 2.1 and 2.0). Embedding a Type 1C (Type 1 Compressed fonts, used when Acrobat 3.0 compatibility is selected) increases the PDF file seven to 20 kilobytes per font. Embedding double-byte Asian language fonts can add several megabytes to a PDF file. Selecting the Make Font Subsets in Distiller's job options and choosing to compress fonts substantially reduces the size of the embedded font data.

Note: When embedding fonts in a document, consider any related legal issues. (See Appendix F, "Font Copyrights.")

Make font subsets

Always select the Make Font Subsets job option to keep PDF files as small as possible. A font subset is comprised of only the font's glyphs (characters, numbers, and symbols like the underscore or dollar sign) used in a particular document. When embedding a font, Distiller embeds only the glyphs used, rather than the whole font (which includes all the glyphs).

If less than the defined percentage (25% is the default) of glyphs are used in a PDF file, the font is subset; if more than the defined percentage is used, the entire font is embedded. In previous versions of Acrobat Distiller (versions 1.0 to 2.1), if more than 10% of a font's glyphs were used, the entire font—not a subset of the font—was embedded in the PDF file. (This option can be controlled by setting the option in the startup script.)

5.2.4 Distiller's Advanced Job Options

The advanced job options extend a number of features that are useful for publishers who use PDF as a file format for print publication, rather than as a publishing file format for the Internet. Distiller's default advanced job options produce PDF files that are more than suitable for the Internet—and in most cases, suitable for most print servers (which may or may not be Internet-based).

Note: These options are best suited for print publishing and are thoroughly covered in "Choosing Advanced Options settings" in the Distiller 3.0 Online Guide. Refer to the Online Guide for more information.

Job Option	Best for the Internet
Distill with prologure.ps/ epilogue.psd	Depends if PostScript file has a PostScript prologue or epilogue. This option, which requires some knowledge of the PostScript language, can process two or more PostScript files into a single PDF file, insert watermarks, create global links, and more.
Convert CMYK Images to RGB	Checked (on) Converting CMYK images to RGB images typically results in a smaller image. CMYK images are useful for high-end print jobs, but have little use for Internet-published PDF files.
Preserve OPI Comments	Checked (on)
Preserve Overprint Settings	Checked (on)
Preserve Halftone Screen Information	Checked (on)
Transfer Functions	Preserve selected
Under Color Removal/ Black Generation	Preserve selected
Color Conversion	Depends on use of color and audience.

Table 5.2—5 Distiller Job Option Descriptions: Advanced

5.2.5 Naming the PDF File

Facilitate file management on a variety of computer platforms (DOS, UNIX, Macintosh, OS/2, etc.) and computer media formats (hard drives, CD-ROMs, LANs, etc.) by naming PDF files according to the ISO 9660 file naming convention. ISO 9660 is a subset of the MS-DOS file naming convention that allows the use of only the uppercase English letters A through Z, the digits 0 through 9, plus the underscore and period characters. Filenames are formed with any of these valid characters, a period, and a three-character extension, generally used to identify the file type. Use "PDF" as the three-character file extension. An ISO 9660 file hierarchy is limited to eight folder levels.

Note: Using other file naming conventions (often platform specific) may result in a truncated filename, which removes the ".PDF" filename extension. This causes some Web browsers to read the PDF file as text or to return an error.

To better identify the content and purpose of the file, use the PDF file's title, subject, author, and keywords fields. Optionally, the PDF file can be integrated with other PDF or HTML files which provide information about the nature and contents of the PDF file.

Note: Some PDF file indexing software requires certain naming conventions (usually based on conventions dictated by the platforms or operating system). Most, however, support 8.3 or ISO 9660 naming conventions.

Web browsers, email clients, and other network software identifies files with the three-character .PDF extension as PDF files and launches an Acrobat viewer as a helper application. Most Web browsers come preconfigured to launch PDF viewers when downloading or opening files with the .PDF file extension. Other Web browsers that don't support Acrobat 3.0 require users to select the PDF viewer as a helper application.

Off-line, removing the .PDF extension prevents Windows versions of an Acrobat viewer from launching when a locally-mounted file is double-clicked. UNIX users may not see PDF files without the .PDF extension in the Open dialog box (if the filter pattern is <directory>/*.pdf).

Note: For Macintosh, Windows 95, Windows NT, and UNIX files, rename the often longer filenames to meet the ISO 9660 naming convention before publishing the file on the Internet.

6

Fine-Tuning PDF Documents

After converting a PostScript file to a PDF file, there are two steps Internet publishers should take before adding interactive and navigational objects. The first step is to evaluate the quality of the PDF file to determine if—in its present form—it is suitable for publishing on the Internet (see Section 6.1, "PDF File Evaluation"). Second, the publisher should make any whole-page or single-line text changes to delete outdated or incorrect pages or to import new pages into the PDF document (see Section 6.2, "Modifying PDF Documents"). Additionally, the publisher should correct spelling errors, modify the style of text, or replace words. Making small text changes or replacing whole pages of a PDF document can be easily done with Acrobat Exchange.

Note: The order of the steps in assessing a PDF file's suitability for the Internet is important. It is advised that publishers first evaluate how suitable a PDF file is for the Internet, and then make any text or whole-page changes. Making text and page changes only to find out the PDF file is too large and needs to be reconverted with a higher level of compression results in the loss of valuable editorial time.

When evaluating the quality of a file converted to PDF, use the following guidelines to fine-tune a PDF file for publication on the Internet.

- Check the PDF file's size and each page (in bytes). Do most pages render quickly (between 10 and 20 seconds) at a typical user's modem speed?
- Examine the quality of images. Can they be viewed at reasonable magnifications without losing significant quality or resolution?
- Check the embedded font list. Are the proper fonts—and only the proper fonts—embedded and subset?
- Is the PDF file's document information correct? Make modifications with Acrobat Exchange if necessary.
- Do the colors in the original document match the PDF file (with reasonable variances)?
- Are the orientation and dimensions of each page in the PDF file correct?
- Can the dimensions of the PDF document be reduced to eliminate excess white space (margins, headers, footers, etc.)?
- Is the page order correct? Do the Acrobat page numbers match the page numbers that appear on the original document's pages?

- Are there spelling errors, or words which need to be edited or replaced? Do some words need to be styled with a different font, size, style, or color?

6.1 PDF File Evaluation

After conversion from PostScript, open the PDF file in Acrobat Exchange, inspect the file, and make any required changes. Adobe Acrobat Exchange allows the modification of whole pages or portions of text in a PDF file.

As the content, circumstances, and use of the PDF file change, the file may need to be re-evaluated and other changes made.

Examine the attributes of the entire PDF file. For Internet publishing, the goal is the smallest PDF file possible—to allow speedy downloads and page rendering—without sacrificing overall quality and design elements (fonts, color, interactivity, and navigation).

Note: Don't use Exchange like a desktop publishing application; the PDF file format isn't designed to have major revisions made to it. If extensive editing is required, make the edits in the creator application's file. PDF files can be updated incrementally to replace older pages with modified pages.

Item	Evaluate
Whole file	File size (in bytes) Approximate per-page download and rendering time Page count Thumbnails Document information (Creator, General Info fields, etc.) File name Security settings
Image quality	Color saturation and quality Clarity (check for blotchy areas) Render time Print quality
Embedded fonts	Inclusion Legibility Subsets
Substitute fonts	Substitution quality Legibility Print quality
Color	Color matching
Document pages	Dimensions Orientation Page order
Automatically generated interactive and navigational objects	Actions Attributes (color, style, title, text, etc.) Position/Location

Table 6.1—1 PDF File Evaluation and Modification Checklist

6.1.1 File Size and Approximate Per-Page Downloading and Rendering Times

After conversion, evaluate the resulting size of the PDF file. Given the bandwidth capabilities of the average or intended user, evaluate the approximate time required to download the first page, and then the time required to download subsequent pages. Also examine the time required by slower machines to render the images, graphics, and text on each page.

With page-on-demand downloading of PDF files, PDF file size is rarely a factor. (Users wait only for each page—not for the whole file—and may not see all the pages in the PDF file.) The whole PDF file's size is a factor if the file is being served on FTP or Gopher servers (which do not support page-on-demand downloading of individual pages from a PDF file), or if the PDF file is being distributed via email.

Note: Generally, it is not recommended that both a high- and low-bandwidth version of a single PDF file be produced. (This is a common practice with HTML files.) Produce the PDF file with all the attributes and advantages the file format affords. If most user's bandwidth limitations make the file unusable, use another file format (such as HTML or text).

Table 6.1—2, "File Size Reduction Options," lists a number of elements and options to reduce the overall size of a PDF file. Some of these elements include converting the file again, resetting Distiller's job options, or selecting other options based on the reduction options listed below.

6.1.2 Page Count

After conversion, check the total number of pages in the PDF file. Delete extraneous pages or import pages from other PDF files with Acrobat Exchange. Combining a number of PostScript files together by using the RunFile command in Acrobat Distiller, or creating a PDF file from a number of other files with a publishing application (such as PageMaker's Print Book option), may

Item	Options	Size-Reduction Solutions
Compatibility	Acrobat 3.0 or Acrobat 2.1	Acrobat 3.0 compatibility creates smaller PDF files than 2.1 compatibility. Users of Acrobat 2.1 and earlier viewers cannot use the PDF file.
ASCII	Binary (by default) or ASCII (if selected)	ASCII-encoded PDF files are 12 to 20% larger than binary PDF files.
Page	None[1]	Delete non-essential pages.
		Break the file up into multiple files.
Convert color images to grayscale	None[2]	Use grayscale rather than color, or use color judiciously.
Embedded fonts	Change font embedding options	Don't embed fonts—or embed only essential fonts. Use Type 1C (Acrobat 3.0-compatible).
Notes	None	Condense and edit notes (note text is not compressed).
Images	Compression	Use a higher manual compression setting for ZIP- or JPEG-compressed images, or try other compression options.
	Downsample	Downsample the image to 72 dpi.
	Convert CMYK images to RGB (on by default)	Convert CMYK images to RGB, which reduces image sizes and increases onscreen rendering times.

Table 6.1—2 File Size Reduction Options

1 Delete pages with Acrobat Exchange.

2 Make this change by using a black-and-white PostScript printer driver to set the images to grayscale from within the original file

---

Note: The first page of a PDF file, as a general rule, should be relatively small so it downloads as quickly as possible, especially when this page contains the navigational links to the rest of the content.

result in missing or extraneous pages. These errors are often caused by blank pages in the original file or application errors. How to use the RunFile command, which combines two or more

PostScript files into a single PDF file, is described in Distiller's help file procedure (see Appendix H, "Setting Options in Distiller's Startup Directory").

Note: The quickest route to delete extraneous pages is with Acrobat Exchange (see Section 6.2.1, "Inserting, Deleting, Extracting, and Replacing Document Pages"). However, avoid importing pages into a file by using Acrobat Exchange because the addition of subset fonts to the whole file can greatly increase file size.

6.1.3 Thumbnails

Thumbnails add about 3.5 kilobytes per page, per thumbnail to a PDF file. This calls into question their usefulness in most Internet-published documents.

Note: Thumbnails may be created with Acrobat Exchange, or with Acrobat Distiller when the PostScript file is converted to a PDF file (Distiller versions 1.0, 2.0 or 2.1).

6.1.4 Document Information

During conversion, Distiller compiles and includes information about the document. This information includes the application in which the file was created originally, the application that converted the PostScript file to a PDF file, the date and time the file was converted (creation date), and the date and time the file was saved after modifications were made (modified date). The creation and modification dates are useful for document management. Some PDF indexing applications use these fields to list files chronologically or to respond to date-based queries.

Additionally, some PDF-savvy creator applications automatically insert information into the document's title, author, subject, and keywords fields. Acrobat 3.0 automatically includes Document Structuring Comments (DSC) from the PostScript file in the PDF file's document fields. DSC inserts the PostScript file's "For field" in the PDF file's "Title field," the DSC's "Title field" in the PDF file's "Title field," and the "Author field" in the PDF file's "Author field." These fields can be edited in Acrobat Exchange.

Viewing these fields also displays the document's filename. Examine the PDF file's name. Ensure that the name conforms to other PDF filenames if the file is part of a series (especially those linked to a specific file via a URL). Also make sure that the filename ends with the .pdf file extension. Many Internet and Web servers are case sensitive, so make note of capitalization (.pdf versus .PDF). The document's filename is limited by the maximum number (and type) of characters imposed by each operating system, so the document's title is often different. Change a PDF filename by choosing File > Save As... and enter a new name for the file, or edit the filename with the operating system's file editing procedures. These fields can be viewed by selecting File > Document Info > General... .

Note: To add custom creator and producer names to a PDF file, add a pdfmark command within the PostScript file prior to converting the file to a PDF file. See the Portable Document Format Reference Manual for more information.

Attribute	Example	Description
Filename	/Documents/FILENAME.PDF	The file's name and relative path. This can be changed using Exchange, and by selecting File > Save As... or renaming the file via the operating system.
Title	Distiller Online Guide	The title is used by searching and indexing software. The title is comparable to an HTML document's title (e.g.,"Adobe's Home page") versus the document title (e.g., index.html).
Subject	Help	Useful for document management. Indexing and searching software can use this field when creating a searchable index of the file.
Author	Adobe Systems	Useful for document management. Could be a name, department, and so forth.
Keyword	Help, user guide	Useful for document management. Indexing and searching software can use this field when creating a searchable index of the file.
Creator	PageMaker 6.0 for Macintosh	The application that generated the PostScript file, which was then converted to a PDF file. Presumably, this is the application in which the original file was created. Not all applications pass this information.
Producer	Acrobat Distiller 3.0	The Acrobat (or third-party) PostScript-to-PDF conversion application.
Creation date	3/28/96 9:35:45 PM	The date the PDF file was created. The Acrobat producer inserts the date conversion began—not the date and time conversion was completed.
Modified date	5/5/96 10:27:18 AM	The last date and time some part of the document was modified and saved. This does not apply to user interaction such as viewing bookmarks or opening notes (unless they are saved that way). Only viewers capable of saving changes to a PDF file can alter the modified date.
File size	638490 Bytes	The file size (in bytes).
Optimized	Yes (or No)	Indicates if the file has been optimized for Web publishing.

Table 6.1—3 File Attributes

6.1.5 Filename

The name of the file should—at the very least—include the period (.) and "PDF" file extension. Also consider adopting an accepted standard naming convention (e.g., ISO 9660). Ensure that the PDF file's name is unique from other PDF files on the Internet server.

Note: For more information about PDF file naming conventions see Section 5.2.5, "Naming the PDF File."

6.1.6 Checking Security

Check a PDF file's conditional security options by choosing File > Document Info > Security. In most cases, the security method is either None or Standard. The Standard security mode uses the RSA data security algorithm. Algorithms and other security features (added by other PDF software or plug-ins) not supported by Adobe Acrobat viewers, may make the PDF file inaccessible when opened with an Acrobat viewer. However, these PDF files will work with the PDF application that set the security option.

Note: The Blowfish block-encryption algorithm by Bruce Scheiener is found in PDF files secured with Zenon's epPlus.

6.1.7 Checking Image Color Saturation and Quality

For Internet publishing, the goal of applying compression to images, line art, and graphics is to arrive at the smallest file size possible while maintaining satisfactory onscreen and print (optional) quality. The type of compression chosen, the degree of compression versus quality (for ZIP, JPEG, and LZW 4-bit reduction), and the display and print quality of downsampled images should be examined relative to the quality of the original image or graphic.

Test the image's onscreen quality by viewing the image at its intended magnification, and then test again at (at least) one-and-one-half times the intended resolution. The image quality should not be degraded considerably when magnified.

Variances in an image's color saturation can be a result of the output device (printer, monitor, etc.), the color matching or management software used by the system on which the PDF file is being viewed, the image itself, or a combination of any or all three possible causes. To troubleshoot the color saturation problem, reconvert the PostScript file by using device-independent color matching (one of Distiller's advanced job options). Also try viewing the troublesome PDF document on other platforms that use other color matching systems (a Macintosh using ColorSync, for example). Also try viewing the file with the MonitorSetup plug-in (see Appendix I, "Acrobat Plug-ins," for more information about the MonitorSetup Plug-in).

6.1.8 Checking Image Clarity

Overcompressed, low-quality images exhibit color banding (large areas of blotchy color) and other image artifacts. If the image lacks the required quality for onscreen display, convert the PostScript file again, but use a higher quality level (a lower level of compression). Also, use Distiller's default 600 dpi default resolution for images and other resolution-dependent objects. If 600 dpi yields unsatisfactory results when printed, consider increasing this resolution.

Symptom	Solution
Color bands	The resolution of the image is too low as a result of downsampling. Increase the resolution incrementally until the banding is less pronounced.
Color blotches	High-lossy compression exhibits artifacts from the compression (elimination) of data. Decrease the level of compression (by increasing the quality settings).
Lost pixels	Resolution downsampling reduces the number of pixels used to describe an object. Set a higher resolution than the level currently set to preserve the quality.

Table 6.1—4 Common Print and Onscreen Overcompression Symptoms

6.1.9 Checking an Image's Rendering Time

Some images, especially CMYK images, can take longer to render onscreen than RGB images. Depending on the selected compression, downsampling, and color matching options selected when the file was converted to a PDF file, some images may take longer than others to render. Evaluate the rendering times for images from the perspective of the intended user.

Note: Take into account the time it takes to render the image to the printer or off-line (perhaps when the image is read from the Acrobat viewer's cache). The printer and CPU's processor speed, as well as the color bit depth of the user monitor also affect the rendering time of images. Consider increasing the compression or decreasing the resolution of particularly slow rendering and printing images.

Slow-rendering EPS graphics

Complex EPS graphics often require significantly more time to render than bitmap images. Each vector of the EPS must be drawn individually: the more vectors—the longer the rendering time. To decrease the time required to render especially complex and thus slow-rendering EPS graphics, convert them to bitmap images in an image editing application before printing the original source file that contains the images to a PostScript file.

Note: Image editors that can parse EPS files (e.g., Adobe Photoshop 3.0), can save open EPS images as bitmap images. When EPS files are converted to bitmap files, the time required to render the graphic is decreased. However, the resolution (to whatever resolution to which images are downsampled) also is decreased.

6.1.10 Print Quality

Test the print quality of images and graphics by printing the PDF file on a standard 300 or 600 dpi printer (use a color printer if available and applicable to the document's use). If the print quality is higher than required, alter the default resolution in Distiller's general job options (the default is 600 dpi, good for most PDF files that will be published on the Internet). If the print quality of the images is less than expected, consider increasing the default resolution in Distiller's job options.

Note: The default resolution can be used only to reduce an image's resolution. It cannot increase the resolution of an image. If an image had a low resolution when it was imported into a document during the creation stages, the resulting PDF file will render the same image at the same or lower resolution.

6.1.11 Checking Embedded Fonts

Check the result of font embedding to ensure that the selected fonts have been embedded and that these fonts, if selected, have been subset. Open the PDF file on a system that doesn't have the embedded fonts installed (or temporarily disable them). Select File > Document Info > Fonts... in an Acrobat viewer to display the list of fonts embedded in the PDF file's first page. Click the List All Fonts button to see the embedded fonts in the subsequent pages of the PDF file.

Note: Checking embedded fonts on a system that has the embedded fonts installed will not identify the fonts as embedded fonts. (The fonts are used from the system rather than from the fonts embedded in the PDF file.)

Embedded fonts cannot be removed from the PDF file. To remove the embedded fonts from the PDF file, it must be reprocessed. Choose Never Embed the font and convert the PostScript file again. Accidental embedding can happen when an unintended font is included in a PostScript file and Distiller's Embed All option is selected. Move the erroneously embedded font to the Do Not Embed font list in Distiller's font embedding dialog box, or deselect the Embed All option and manually add the fonts to be embedded in the PDF file to the Always Embed list.

Note: Embedded and even subset fonts add data to a PDF file. Embed a font only when there is a noticeable difference between the original font's onscreen and print resolution.

Identifying embedded fonts

Embedded fonts are displayed in the Font Information dialog box by font name. The Original and Used font names match and the encoding is listed as "embedded." (See Table 6.1—5, "Checking which Fonts Are Embedded in a PDF File," for some examples.)

Note: If a font manage application such as SuitCase II for Macintosh is used (as long as the "suitcase" is located in the same folder and at the same level at which the outline fonts is open), Acrobat will find these outlines and indicate that the font is not embedded.

6.1.12 Checking Subset Fonts

Font subsets are created when the percentage of font characters used in a PDF file exceeds the threshold (a defined percentage) set in Distiller's Font Embedding job options. For publishing PDF files on the Internet, Distiller's default setting of 25% works well. Subset fonts include the font data for only the characters used in the PDF file—not the entire font—thus allowing the PDF file size to remain smaller than it would if the whole font were embedded.

Subset font names are preceded by a random set of six letters. Distiller appends the font name with the random six-letter prefix. This prevents font conflicts when downloading the font to printers or displaying the font on systems with the actual font installed.

Original Font	Used Font	Embedding
GillSans	DKGPKA+GillSans	Subset, Embedded
GillSans	GillSans	Embedded
Symbol	Symbol	Installed[1]
Arial, Bold	Helvetica-Bold	Substituted[2]

Table 6.1—5 Checking which Fonts Are Embedded in a PDF File

[1] Installed base-14 fonts cannot be embedded; here the "true" Symbol font is used as if it were embedded in the PDF file because it is installed on the user's system.

[2] Substituted fonts are not embedded.

6.1.13 Checking Font Legibility

Check the onscreen and print quality of substitute fonts. To display a list of substitute fonts (if any), select Select File > Document Info > Fonts. Substitute fonts are fonts that are used when names or font type (e.g., TrueType, Type 1, or Multiple Master fonts) don't match the original font.

If a substitute font differs substantially—either onscreen or when printed—the font may be embedded. Convert the PostScript file again and embed the poorly substituted font. Distinctive fonts used conservatively or as initial caps within the document can be subset—adding marginally to the PDF's final file size. Embedding the font increases the final PDF file size, but with the benefit of exact font matching.

Adobe Sans Serif and Adobe Serif typefaces are used to substitute for unavailable sans serif and serif fonts (respectively). However, a few specific TrueType fonts (Arial and Times New Roman) have been special-cased as other substitution fonts.

6.1.14 Checking Document Colors

Check the PDF document to ensure that the colors match the original colors as closely as possible. Acrobat—through PostScript Level 2's support of device-independent color—is based on RGB and CMYK colors and the international standard CIE 1931 (Commission International de l'Eclairage). CIE is a system for specifying color values based on human visual perception of color rather than technical color production. This allows more predictable color output on monitors and from color printers.

If color matching differs significantly with CMYK images and graphics, consider converting the CMYK images to RGB by selecting the Convert CMYK Images to RGB in Distiller's Advanced Job Options (on, by default), and then converting the PostScript file to PDF again. For Distiller 2.1, consult the Distiller Help file that describes how to edit the Example.ps script to convert CMYK to RGB.

Note: Other high-level color matching Distiller job options—added to meet the advanced needs of print publishers—also may contribute to better color matching. Most of these options are overkill for Internet publishing, which often requires onscreen color matching only.

Generating PostScript files on systems using a Color Management System (e.g., ColorSync, Kodak, etc.) yields the most accurate color display and print results on other computers using a color management system.

8-Bit color shifts

Some documents viewed on 8-bit (256 colors) monitors may appear to have shifted colors. PageMaker documents viewed in 8-bit colors often exhibit these color shifts. While the colors from the PageMaker document window and the Acrobat PDF document don't match up, the colors are correct. PageMaker includes a script that adds all the 8-bit colors to PageMaker's color library, providing a palette of non-shifting colors from which to choose.

6.1.15 Checking a Document's Page Orientation

All PDF files that will be viewed within a Web browser (and even those to be viewed from FTP and Gopher servers) should be oriented so that the text doesn't require rotation to be read. See Section 6.2.3, "Changing a Document's Page Orientation," for information on rotating the page, if necessary.

6.1.16 Checking a Document's Page Order

When using document page numbers (page numbers that appear on the pages themselves), be sure that these page numbers match the page numbers assigned by an Acrobat viewer. If they do not match, consider either removing the document page numbers or reordering the pages (perhaps by adding blank pages). Also see Section 6.2.4, "Changing a Document's Page Order."

6.1.17 Checking Automatically Generated Interactive and Navigational Objects

PDF-savvy creator applications often automatically create interactive and navigational objects (links, bookmarks, notes, etc.). Often these creator applications don't provide total control over the actions, attributes, and positioning of the objects they create. Before publishing a PDF file on the Internet, examine these objects and make any necessary changes. Attributes to look for include the object's action (World Wide Web Link, Go To View, etc.), general attributes (such as color, line style, title, etc.), and the position of these objects in the PDF document. For more information about modifying these objects, see Chapter 7, "Adding Interactive and Navigational Objects."

6.2 Modifying PDF Documents

After a balance between file size and document quality is reached, the PDF document may be further modified to make corrections to the document. These corrections can be accomplished either by modifying whole pages or single lines of text. If a document requires modifications that would affect the flow of text, such as deleting a paragraph or moving an image, it is best to make these modifications in the original creator application's file, and then convert the file (via a PostScript file) to a PDF file.

Item	Modify
Whole pages	Importing, extracting, deleting, replacing pages Dimensions (cropping pages) Orientation (rotating pages)
Page order (reordering pages)	
Lines of text	Words and phrases Text style and color Text size and other attributes
Automatically generated interactive and navigational objects.	Actions Attributes Position/location

Table 6.2—1 Modifying PDF Documents

6.2.1 Inserting, Deleting, Extracting, and Replacing Document Pages

Making major modifications in a PDF document is often best accomplished by inserting, deleting, extracting, or replacing a PDF page. These functions have a number of applications for Internet publishers. See the table below for some sample uses.

6.2.2 Cropping Document Pages

Margins and extraneous white space should be cropped to reduce the size of the page. Use Exchange to crop a page, several pages, or all the pages in the PDF file. Alternatively, crop all the pages of a PDF file when converting an Encapsulated PostScript file (or other page without a defined page dimension), to a PDF file by modifying Distiller's default page size (Acrobat 3.0 and later only). All PostScript files can be cropped when they are converted to PDF files by editing Distiller's Example.ps script (supported by all versions of Distiller).

Action	Internet Publishing Application
Insert page(s)	Adding pages from one PDF file into another creates composite PDF files. Potentially, this function could be used to create one single PDF file for an entire Web site from other PDF file content sources.[2]
Delete page(s)	Removing outdated, extraneous, or incorrect content pages keeps the content current and correct.
Extract page(s)[3]	Extracting pages is a useful way to reduce the overall file size of larger, multi-page documents—especially when the PDF files are served on Gopher, FTP, and other servers where progressive rendering and page-on-demand downloading is not available.[4] Use the Go To File or World Wide Web Link actions to connect the extracted page sections (see Section 6.2.1, "Inserting, Deleting, Extracting, and Replacing Document Pages").
Replace page(s)	Replacing pages adds flexibility to continually changing Internet documents, without the need to edit and update the interactive and navigational structure.
	When a page is replaced, the page's interactive and navigational objects remain. Resize or delete objects that no longer correspond to the replaced page's design.

Table 6.2—2 Inserting, Deleting, Extracting, and Replacing Pages in a PDF File[1]

1 A page's interactive and navigational objects are inserted, extracted, duplicated, or moved with the page. Ensure that the objects have an action. Replicate any page changes made with Exchange in the creator application's file to ensure a correct master file.

2 Inserting pages into a PDF file that uses subset fonts can add the font data from the inserted pages, resulting in a larger PDF file than anticipated. Inserting pages by converting PostScript files together by using the RunFile procedure (see Appendix H, "Setting Options in Distiller's Startup Directory"), can result in smaller PDF files.

3 Extraction saves the extracted pages as a separate file entitled, "Pages from [the original file]." Save any extracted pages before closing, or the new document is deleted.

4 Downloading a multi-page document's subsequent pages may result in faster downloads because font data and redundant images and graphics—often the largest part of a PDF document—already may be cached. In effect, breaking a multi-page document into separate documents and serving the documents when page-on-demand and progressive rendering is available, may actually increase the total time needed to download the total document's data.

Note: Always select File > Save As... after completing changes, particularly after deleting pages or objects from a PDF file. Save As... conserves file space by removing deleted objects (which remain inside a PDF document until a Save As... is performed).

To allow more efficient use of screen real estate, crop the page to remove white space, and print-based information such as page numbers and footers and headers. Page numbers are based on the order of the pages in the PDF file and are displayed in the document window. Information listed in headers and footers can be added in the PDF file's document information. Cropping page dimensions from a PDF file does not reduce its file size (in bytes). Cropping (and deleting) page elements (such as the text of footers or margin graphics) in Exchange may result in some reduction in the file size.

Note: The SuperCrop Plug-in (available for free from Adobe at http://www.adobe.com/acrobat/) for Acrobat Exchange adds a crop tool to the toolbar. Similar to the crop tools found in popular image and desktop publishing software, the crop tool allows for the selection of an area to crop rather than entering cropping dimensions in a dialog box (which is how a page is cropped in Exchange).

6.2.3 Changing a Document's Page Orientation

Use Acrobat Exchange to rotate the content of the page and the page dimensions simultaneously. Exchange allows rotation of pages in 90° increments. Single pages, a range of pages, or entire documents can be rotated.

Note: For print-only applications, pages of PDF documents can be oriented so the text isn't upright (for example, rotated 90 or -90 degrees).

6.2.4 Changing a Document's Page Order

Move particular pages to the beginning of the PDF file to emphasize new or timely items. This ensures that the user sees the pages when the document is opened, rather than leaving to chance that the pages are visited.

Change the page order in a document by using Exchange or by switching to Thumbnail and Page view (from the View menu or click on the icon in the toolbar). Click on the page number below each thumbnail to move it. There is no need to render the thumbnails to move them around. However, it may be easier to render the thumbnails if the pages being moved can be seen. Delete the thumbnails when done.

6.2.5 Changing Text

The Touch Up Plug-in, included with Acrobat 3.0, enables minor text changes such as spelling corrections, replacing words, changing text styles and fonts, correcting suspect words from PDF files converted with Acrobat Capture, and many other uses.

Note: The Touch Up Plug-in should be used only for single-line modifications to text. For layout changes or more extensive edits, make the changes in the original creator application's file and convert it to a PDF file again.

For Internet publishing, use the Touch Up Plug-in to make simple text modifications such as changing hypertext link names and altering the style of text to make it a cue for a hypertext link (colored, underlined text, etc.).

Note: The Acrobat Exchange Online Guide has detailed information about using the Touch Up Plug-in.

6.2.6 Changing Interactive and Navigational Objects

Making changes to automatically generated interactive and navigational objects (as well as adding new objects) is covered in Chapter 7, "Adding Interactive and Navigational Objects."

7

Adding Interactive and Navigational Objects

Navigational and interactive objects can be added to PDF files to make the content more usable and dynamic. From the user's perspective, navigational objects enable quick, easy access to specific information. Interactivity allows a customizable, personal experience with the content. The best documents combine content (for a specific audience) with excellent interactive and navigational features to access the content.

The navigational and interactive objects that are added to PDF documents transcend the capabilities of most paper-based documents. This allows the concept of design to move to a higher level—where the design fits the use, as well as the content and aesthetics.

Considerations for creating interactive, navigable PDF files include the following:

- Develop or use a standard visual cue for hypertext links. Apply the standard throughout the document, perhaps extending (or adopting) the visual cue as a standard for all similar electronic publishing efforts.

- Use a Base URL to allow global updates of the PDF file's relative URLs.
- Use the World Wide Web Link action to allow navigation from the PDF file to other sites, files, CGI scripts, and other URLs and Internet protocols (FTP, Gopher, etc.).
- Use bookmarks to define the structure of the document and to provide a means of navigation.
- Use thumbnails sparingly—or don't use them at all. Thumbnails increase PDF file size and require additional connections to the server.
- Create article threads for page- or column-long text blocks; use them where reading an area requires magnification, or when a story jumps to another page or file.
- Make use of notes to append or update information. However, use notes sparingly as the text within the note is not compressed, which adds to the size of a PDF file.
- Secure PDF files to prevent unauthorized access or actions, or both.
- Set an open preference for PDF files to control the view, page number, and magnification at which the page opens.
- Optimize PDF files before posting them on Web servers.

7.1 Actions

Interactive and navigational objects, which can include links, bookmarks, PDF pages, form fields, and buttons, can be assigned actions. These actions include World Wide Web Links, links to other files, links to specific pages or views, links for the submission of data, and more.

Links and bookmarks perform their assigned actions whenever they are clicked. Form fields and buttons have actions that are triggered whenever a user performs the specified form action. (A list of these actions can be found in Table 7.6—16, "Field Properties: Actions"). PDF pages can be assigned actions based on the page that is opened or closed by the user.

Plug-ins add specific actions. The Weblink Plug-in, introduced with Acrobat 2.1, adds the World Wide Web Link action, which allows a PDF file to link to a URL on the Internet via a Web browser. The Movie Plug-in, also introduced with Acrobat 2.1, opens and plays back movie and sound files within the Acrobat document. If the plug-in is not present, the action is unavailable.

Action Effect	Interactive/ Navigational Object	Required Plug-in	Description
Go To View	Links, bookmarks	None	Links to another page or another PDF file and a defined (or default) view magnification. The defined (or default) view magnification is based on either the pop-up menu options selected for view magnification, or a custom view defined by the magnification when the link is set.
Import Form Data	Form fields and buttons Links and bookmarks Pages	AcroForm	Imports a FDF file to populate a PDF form.

continued

Table 7.1—1 Actions

Action Effect	Interactive/ Navigational Object	Required Plug-in	Description
Movie[1]	Form fields and buttons Links and bookmarks Pages	Movie (released with Acrobat 2.1). No sound helper application required.	Opens and plays back a movie file within the PDF file (or in a window that floats above the document). Users can control the playback of the movie (including play, stop, pause, resume, and go to, which scans through the movie for a specific time). The movie files are not embedded within the PDF file—they must be linked to (streamed playback from the Internet is not currently supported).
None	Form fields and buttons Links and bookmarks Pages	None	No action
Open File	Form fields and buttons Links and bookmarks Pages	None	Opens a PDF file. If the selected file is not a PDF file, the Acrobat Reader attempts to launch the application in which the target file was created.
Read Article	Form fields and buttons Links and bookmarks Pages	None	Begins the process of following a selected article thread.
Reset Form	Form fields and buttons Links and bookmarks Pages	AcroForm	Resets the values of all form fields to their defaults (or to empty if no default is set).
Sound[1]	Form fields and buttons Links and bookmarks Pages	Movie (released with Acrobat 2.1). No movie helper application required.	Opens and plays back a sound file from within the PDF file. The sound files are embedded in the PDF file and are platform independent.
Submit Form	Form fields and buttons Links and bookmarks Pages	AcroForm	Submits the form as either a FDF file or HTML form data to a URL (often a script or application on a server). The submit action can accept a response from the server's script or application if the response is in FDF and ends in #FDF. See Section 8.9, "Processing PDF Forms."

Table 7.1—1 (continued) Actions

[1] The movie and sound actions are supported by Macintosh and Windows systems only.

7.1.1 Execute Menu Item Action

An Acrobat viewer's menu items can be controlled by embedding a menu command within an interactive object (links, bookmarks, form fields, etc.). This enables CD-ROM and multimedia developers greater flexibility and control over the way users interact with a document. For Web publishers, the action has less application. The execute menu item action controls only the Acrobat viewer, and not the Web browser. Setting an object to execute the Quit or Exit command when clicked, will quit or exit the Acrobat viewer—not the Web browser. However, any of the Web browser's Acrobat toolbar actions are supported. (The commands are sent to the Acrobat viewer—not the Web browser.) For example, actions such as changing the page mode, setting a page view, and selecting a magnification do work. When viewing a PDF file in a Web browser's document window, if an object that is used to execute a menu action tries to execute the menu item that is not supported by the Web browser's Acrobat toolbar, the result is either no action or some action within the Acrobat viewer (which is transparent to the viewing of the PDF file in the Web browser).

Note: Exchange-specific menu actions will not work with Acrobat Reader.

7.1.2 Go To View Action

Links and bookmarks can be defined to open a specified page at a defined (or default) magnification, or display the current page at a different magnification. The action can be set to zoom in, zoom out, or to view a single page. The magnification is set from the Go To View action's pop-up menu options, called the Handler Information. For a list of Go To View options, see Table 7.1—2.

View Options	Descriptions
Fixed	Uses the zoom magnification and position of the current page in the document window as the destination magnification.
Fit View	Fits the visible portion of the destination page in the window.
Fit Page	Fits the entire page in the destination window.
Fit Height	Fits the height of the page in the destination window.
Fit Width	Fits the width of the page in the destination window.
Fit Visible	Fits the width of the visible contents of the page in the destination window.
Inherent Zoom	Uses the zoom level in effect when the action is activated.

Table 7.1—2 Go To View Options[1]

1 The Go To View action can be set to common magnification percentages from the Magnification menu, or to custom magnifications by selecting the Custom option at the bottom of the Magnification pop-up menu.

Setting the Go To View Action to change magnification of the present page

The capability to zoom in on text and graphics is an option no Web browser supports. Use the Go To View action to enlarge or reduce text, graphics, images, or areas on the page. The action can emphasize, or call attention to, specific areas of the page, or simply be used to increase legibility. Alternatively, create Articles for larger areas of text, rather than using the Go To View action to magnify text.

Note: Zooming in on an image requires that an image redraw, which may take several seconds with a high resolution image or on slow processor machines. If the image is being viewed in a Web browser, it need not be downloaded again to be viewed at higher magnifications.

Setting the Go To View action to change pages and magnifications (optional)

Setting Go To View actions, which open other pages, provides an alternative to Acrobat's linear toolbar navigation. This allows Web publishers to set context-related links (such as hypertext found in Web documents). The Go To View action, used with links or bookmarks, can create a document interface that allows users to navigate a document more easily. Additionally, this navigation lets publishers call attention to sections of a page by opening specific pages or zooming in on a specific area.

A link or bookmark can be set to open a specified page within the same PDF document. The destination page can be assigned a view (Fit Page, Fit Visible, etc.), or magnification (25%, 100%, etc.). Clicking a link not only opens the destination page, but displays the page at the defined view of the link.

Links and bookmarks set to other pages use the same Go To View action in their Handler Information pop-up menu. To set another page to be opened by the action (and optionally, another magnification), move to the target page, select the desired (or default) magnification, and click the Set Action (or Set Link) button.

7.1.3 Import Form Data Action

The Import Form Data action imports and populates a PDF file with form data from a FDF file. With Acrobat 3.0, Web publishers can use relative links to import form data. A better alternative for importing form data into a PDF file is the Submit Form Data option, which imports data (as either FDF or HTML) from the script or application's response. See Section 8.9.2, "Populating PDF Forms with FDF files," for more details about populating PDFs with the Submit Data action.

Note: The Import Data action is essential for users who want to import form data from locally-mounted drives and networks or when working off-line. To import data, simply select the FDF file to import to the form.

7.1.4 Movie Action

The Movie Plug-in adds the capability to play back movie files in a defined area of the PDF document, or in a modeless floating window within an Acrobat viewer or Acrobat 3.0-compatible Web browser. Supported movie formats include QuickTime (Macintosh and Windows) and AVI (Windows only). Choose the QuickTime movie format which, when flattened, provides the most cross-platform compatibility. The Movie Plug-in, available with the full retail version of Acrobat and from the Adobe Web site at http://www.adobe.com/acrobat/, is required for playback of media files. To play the movie files, Windows users need Apple's QuickTime 2.0 or later, or the Microsoft Video for Windows software. Macintosh users need QuickTime 2.0 or later. No additional helper applications are required for movie playback.

Movie actions open and play an external movie file. Setting a Movie action and selecting a file for playback does not copy the movie's data into the PDF file. Acrobat 3.0 doesn't support the streaming of video data for real-time playback over the Internet.

As a result, the movie file designated in the Movie action must be entirely downloaded before playback begins.

Movies are added easily by using the movie tool (or by selecting Tools > Movie). Select playback options for the movie in the Properties dialog box. Select a movie file using a relative URL. The file must be located somewhere on a local hard drive or network node for selection. It is best to keep the movie file in the same directory (or a lower directory that remains on the same local drive, CD-ROM, or Internet), as the PDF file that will play it back. After the source media file is set, only the movie's preferences may be changed. To replace the media file with a new movie or sound, the movie must be deleted and a new movie added in order to reselect a media source file.

Note: With the popularity of hybrid, integrated CD-ROM/Websites, be sure to save the movie file on the CD-ROM at the same level in the directory structure as the PDF file, which may be either on the Web server or CD-ROM. The movie's relative-link action will search for the locally-mounted movie file first. Then try to locate the file on the server if it cannot be found.

Setting a World Wide Web Link action from a PDF file to a movie file will not open the movie in the PDF file. Instead it will pass off the action to the Web browser that will respond appropriately—most likely launching a helper application to play back the movie.

Selecting a movie file flattens the data in the media file for cross-platform playback. A flattened movie combines all the data required to play the file into the data fork, thus enabling playback on either a Macintosh or a PC running Windows. When the

Movie Plug-in flattens the media file, the original file may be over-written, or saved with another name to preserve the original.

When a user positions the cursor over a link that uses the Movie action, the cursor icon changes to a movie frame to represent its action. Clicking opens the media file in the document window or in a modeless window. If the path to the media file has been broken, a dialog box will open in which the media file—or another media file—may be selected for playback (with the properties set for the movie link, regardless of the media file selected).

7.1.5 None

Interactive and navigational objects that use the None action maintain all the attributes of objects that have actions—including changes in appearance when clicked. Bookmarks with no assigned actions function as spacers, notes, or headings. Select a single bookmark and choose Edit > Properties and select None. Objects with an assigned action of None do nothing when clicked by a user.

7.1.6 Open File Action

Links, bookmarks, pages, form fields, and buttons can all be set to open another PDF or other file types. To open specific URLs (including PDF files on other sites), or to open other Web-based file formats known as absolute URLs, which contain the transport protocol, site name, path, and filename use the World Wide Web Link action.

For PDF files that will be served on the Web, use the World Wide Web Link action, which allows the most efficient method of passing PDF files through the server's byte-range request CGI script. PDF files must be routed via the server's byte-range request CGI script to enable page-on-demand downloads and progressive rendering. (Other Web servers, such as WebSTAR for the Macintosh operating system, use a different procedure for byte-serving PDFs.) See Section 7.1.11, "World Wide Web Link Action," for more information about configuring URLs in PDF files.

Acrobat 3.0 viewers use relative URLs to open files linked via the Open File action. The relative URL function is built into the Acrobat 3.0 viewer, so PDF files created with Acrobat 2.1 or earlier can use relative URLs without modification. A relative URL doesn't include the protocol and preserves the link to the targeted file (within the same path structure) across the Web, CD-ROM, wide area networks, and local drives. This allows collections of PDF files to be published on a variety of media formats and networks without the need to update the links or modify the network protocols. For example, a collection of PDF files on CD-ROM with the path E:Acro_CD/DOCS/TOC.pdf has a relative URL of ../Acro_CD/DOCS/TOC.pdf, and would be resolved as http://www.sitename.com/Acro_CD/DOCS/TOC.pdf by the Web browser and Acrobat viewer. When transferred between media formats or networks, the path's hierarchy must remain consistent. Do not rename directories, files, or move files between directories. Changing the directory or file names, or modifications in the file path result in the target file being lost. On Web servers, this results in a 404 error (file not found).

Note: Relative links first try to find the target file to be opened as a local file. If the file cannot be found, it treats the link as an http-

based URL. However, if the path to the target file includes the site name, it generally will not be possible to locate the file locally.

Using the Open File action to open other file formats

The Open File action can be set to open file formats other than PDF files. The action opens the target file by launching the application that created (or can read) the selected file. Which application is called upon to open the target file is platform-dependent and varies on individual computers.

For Web-based Open File actions, if the target file type (text, HTML files, etc.), or plug-in (QuickTime movies, RealAudio files, and PDF files, etc.) is supported directly by the Web browser, the browser replaces the PDF file in the document window with the target file. If the file type is not supported, the browser downloads the file and launches a helper application to read the file (if one is available).

The Open File action is set by clicking the Select File button, which opens a dialog box from which to select the target file. If the selected file is a local file (on a CD-ROM or hard disk), be sure that the path to the selected file remains constant when the PDF files and the selected target file are moved to other media formats or networks.

7.1.7 Read Article

The Read Article action opens and begins to follow a selected article thread. This action is most useful for bookmarks—where subsequent clicks on the page move the user through the article thread. However, it also can be used with most other navigational and interactive objects. To select an article from those in a PDF file, click Select Article, choose an article from the list, and click OK.

7.1.8 Reset Form Action

Clicking the Reset button clears all values from a form field and resets the fields to display the default value, if any. Radio and checkbox buttons are reset to their checked or selected defaults. List and combo-box field contents are not deleted; however, the default selection is shown or selected in the field.

7.1.9 Sound Action

The Sound action enables links, buttons, bookmarks, and other interactive and navigational objects to play back sound files. For the Web, choose AIFF sound files, which can be played on both Macintosh and PC systems running Microsoft Windows. The sound files are stored within the PDF file, which can make PDF files much larger than normal and take longer to download. To minimize the bandwidth requirements of sound files, use them sparingly for Web-based documents.

Note: Supported sound file types include AIFF and .sfl on Macintosh, and AIFF and WAV on Windows systems.

7.1.10 Submit Form Action

Choosing the Submit Form action opens the URL and Field Selection dialog box. Enter the destination URL of the script or application that will be processing the form data. In the Export Format section of the dialog box, select either the Forms Data

Format (FDF) or HTML (URL encoded). The Field Selection area of the dialog box presents the following options for the exporting of form data: export all fields in the form, all fields except a select list, or only a selected list of fields. To export empty fields (those with no values), select the Include Empty Fields option.

The target script or application can send data back in the FDF format during processing to effect changes to the form. The response coming back from the server (via the processing script or application) must be a URL that ends with "#FDF." These changes could include populating form fields with processed data, changing the appearance, action, and other attributes of the field or form, and a wide variety of other actions. See Section 7.1.3, "Import Form Data Action," for more information on importing FDF data to make modifications in a form.

Note: To simply export form data as an FDF file, rather than submitting the data for processing, use Acrobat Exchange 3.0 (or later) and choose File > Export Form. The exported form data is saved as an FDF file on a local volume.

7.1.11 World Wide Web Link Action

World Wide Web Link actions use the Weblink Plug-in to connect to servers and files on the Internet. The location of these servers and files are expressed as Uniform Resource Locators (URLs), used extensively by Web browsers and other Internet client software. PDF file World Wide Web Link URLs support all common transport protocols including Hypertext Transfer Protocol (HTTP), Gopher, or File Transport Protocol (FTP).

World Wide Web Link actions are set by clicking the Edit URL button in the action's handler information and entering a valid URL. Enter the full URL, which includes the transport protocol, site name, path, and file name. Or enter only the relative path and assign the document a base URL (see Section 7.2, "Setting a Base URL in a PDF File"). The URL may be a site or a specific file on the site.

World Wide Web Link actions open a URL via a Web browser. Acrobat 3.0-savvy Web browsers process this information directly through a Web browser's application programming interface through interapplication communication (see Appendix D, "Interapplication Communication and Web Browsers"). Other Web browsers use platform-dependent interapplication communication to open the URL and switch between the Acrobat viewer and a Web browser—depending on the format type of document being viewed.

Viewing PDF files a page-at-a-time as they download and progressively render onscreen requires a connection to a Web server capable of serving byte-range requests, an optimized PDF file, an Acrobat 3.0 or later viewer, and an Acrobat 3.0-savvy Web browser. The minimum requirements for following a World Wide Web Link action are a connection to the Internet, an Acrobat Viewer (version 2.1 or later) with the Weblink Plug-in installed, and a Web browser that supports the Acrobat Weblink Plug-in. The minimum configuration doesn't support progressive rendering or page-on-demand downloads of PDF files. Instead, it downloads the PDF file entirely, launches the Acrobat viewer, and then opens the PDF file. The Weblink Plug-in is included with the free Acrobat Reader (2.1 and later).

Users can identify World Wide Web Links (when used as an action for links) by moving the cursor over the link, which then changes from the arrow cursor icon to a pointing finger with a small "w" in it.

Note: When viewing a PDF file within an Acrobat viewer, the viewer's preferences can be set to display the destination of the URL. Presently, there are no Web browsers that support the display of World Wide Web Links as they do HTML links.

Setting a World Wide Web Link to a site's home page or directory listing

A World Wide Web Link set to a Web server's URL (e.g., http: //www.adobe.com) without specifying a file, loads the site's home page from the server—a default file configured in the Web site's server software (e.g., default.html, index.html). A World Wide Web Link with a URL set to FTP or Gopher servers without specifying a file often displays the site's directory file list.

Setting the World Wide Web Link's URL to a site rather than a specific file reduces the chance that the URL is incorrect (often

World Wide Web Link	Opens....
http://www.adobe.com(/)	Adobe's home page
http://www.adobe.com/new.html	The specific file "new.html"
http://www.adobe.com/acrobat	The home page for the Adobe Acrobat area
ftp://ftp.adobe.com	The file list for the Adobe FTP site

Table 7.1—3 Link URL to Home Page or Directory Listing Syntax

files are changed more frequently than paths). If the file name or server's path has changed (or was incorrectly entered in the URL), the Web browser displays an error. See Section 9.4.1, "Server Errors," and Section 9.4.2, "Client Errors," for a short description of the most commonly displayed client or server errors.

Setting a World Wide Web Link Action to a server's file

A World Wide Web Link action to a specific URL—upon connection with the server by the Web browser—initiates the viewing of the PDF file. If the requested PDF file is optimized and the Web server is capable of sending requested bytes (through the byte-range request CGI script), the Web browser will begin the page-at-a-time downloading and progressive rendering of the PDF file. If the requested file is of another file type (such as HTML, RealAudio, or text), the Web browser responds appropriately by launching another in-line viewer (e.g., Acrobat 3.0 viewers), or a helper application (defined in most Web browser's preferences); or, the Web browsers reads the file directly into its document window (as Web browser do with HTML, text, and GIFs).

Setting World Wide Web Links actions to optimized, byte-served PDF files

On most Web servers, enabling Acrobat 3.0-optimized PDF files to download a page-at-a-time and progressively render in a Web browser's document window requires that the byteserver script be reflected in the World Wide Web Link's URL. Most servers store the script in the cgi-bin directory. For more information about installing the CGI script, see "Installing the Byteserver Script," under Section 8.2.2, "Serving PDF Pages on Demand."

World Wide Web Link	Configuration	Action
http://www.adobe.com/cgi-bin/byteserver/TechNotes/1404.pdf	Web browser and Acrobat Reader 3.0	Downloads the PDF file, loads the Acrobat viewer to handle the PDF information, and progressively renders text, graphics, images, and fonts on the first page of the PDF file in the browser's document window.
http://www.adobe.com/TechNotes/1404.pdf	Web browser and Acrobat Reader 2.1 (or earlier)	Downloads the PDF file and then launches the Acrobat Reader (or other Acrobat viewer) as a helper application to view the PDF file.
http://www.emrg.com/pdf_sw.html	Web browser only	Downloads the HTML file "pdf_sw.html".
ftp://ftp.adobe.com	Web browser only	Opens the file list for the Adobe FTP site (in HTML).

Table 7.1—4 World Wide Web Link Action to File Syntax[1]

1 If the PDF file is not optimized, or the Web browser is not Acrobat 3.0-savvy, or if the file is not a PDF file and can be rendered in-line, the browser will download the file completely and launch a helper application to open the file.

The URL syntax for byte-serving a PDF file located at http://www.servername.com/path/pdf_file.pdf uses the script byte-server.pl. (A Perl script would be http://www.servername.com/cgi-bin/byteserver/path/pdf_file.pdf.)

Note: PDF files presently not byte-served—but available on the Web—that use base URLs can be globally changed by modifying the PDF files' base URLs to reflect the path through the cgi-bin directory and byte-server script.

Setting World Wide Web Link actions to CGI scripts

Set a World Wide Web Link action to a CGI (common gateway interface) script by entering the URL of the CGI script, together with the data that the CGI script will process. Data (a <search-part>), combined with the URL, is processed by the CGI script. (See RFC 1738 on Uniform Resource Locators at ftp://ds.internic.net/rfc/rcf1738.txt.) A result is issued—commonly in HTML, but it could be configured to respond with a Forms Data Format (FDF) file—based on the submitted data. Note that the data submitted to the script with the URL is not dynamic, but embedded in the PDF file's object's action and cannot be altered by the user.

Since World Wide Web Link actions to CGI scripts are static, they work best with CGI scripts that don't require data to process a result, or those which take data submitted with the URL. If the script requires dynamic input from the user, either a PDF or HTML form often works best. See Section 7.6, "Forms," for more information on submitting user-entered data for processing. For on-the-fly generation of information based on dynamic factors (such as a counter that displays the number of users who have accessed a site), HTML works best. (Although it is possible to generate PDF dynamically, see Section 8.13, "Dynamic PDF.")

URL	Data	Type	Result
http://search.yahoo.com/bin/search?p=Adobe+Acrobat	p=Adobe+Acrobat	HTML-based search engine	Displays in HTML, all matching links to the requested terms.
http://www.hotwired.com/cgi-bin/users/imagemap/Tools/Maps/front.map?175,115	175,115	Imagemap	Opens a URL corresponding to the area clicked in the imagemap.
http://www.fedex.com/cgi-bin/track_it?trk_num=PVD000000&dest_cntry=U.S.A.	trk_num=PVD000000&dest_cntry=U.S.A.	Proprietary search engine	Accesses a database to find the requested airbill number.
http://quote.pathfinder.com/money/quote/qc?NAS-DAQ:ADBE	NASDAQ:ADBE	Proprietary search engine	Accesses a database of stock quotes and generates a report.
http://random.yahoo.com/bin/ryl	none (ryl))	Random URL lookup	Displays a random page based on a directory of possible URLs.

Table 7.1—5 World Wide Web Link Actions to a CGI Data Result Examples

Setting World Wide Web Link actions that use other Internet protocols

PDF World Wide Web Link actions enable access (via a Web browser and helper applications, such as Telnet, if needed) to other types of servers and services on the Internet. Set the World Wide Web Link action by entering a URL that uses other Internet protocols (other than the HTTP protocol used for Web documents). Table 7.1—6, "World Wide Web Link Action Syntax for Other Internet Protocols," lists the URL syntax for the most common Internet protocols.

Other supported, but less commonly used protocols include NNTP (Usenet news using NNTP access), prospero (Prospero

Transport Protocol	Syntax/Sample URL	Notes
Gopher	gopher://veronica.scs.unr.edu/00/veronica/how-to-query-veronica	URL for a document on a Gopher server. Most Web browsers can display Gopher directories, so no Gopher helper application is required.
Telnet	telnet://djnr.dowjones.com/	URL that starts a Telnet session on the Dow Jones Telnet site. The Web browser launches a Telnet application (required) as a helper application.
Telnet (with password)	telnet://<username>:<password>@djnr.dowjones.com/	Appends the username and password that is required for access and activation of the Dow Jones Telnet session.
FTP	ftp://ftp.adobe.com/	URL address of a FTP server. Most Web browsers can display FTP directories, so no FTP helper application is required.
FTP (with password)	ftp://<username>:<password>@ftp.adobe.com/	Appends the username and password that is required for access to the FTP server.
News (Usenet news)	news:comp.text.pdf	Opens a Usenet newsgroup. If the Web browser cannot display newsgroups, a helper application is launched to read news in the selected group (comp.text.pdf).
mailto (electronic mail address)	mailto:president@whitehouse.gov	Opens a new email message document in the Web browser with the address—president@whitehouse.gov—where the message will be sent. Most Web browsers support the mailto command (enabling email to be sent from a Web browser).
WAIS (Wide Area Information Servers)	wais://cnidr.org/directory-of-servers?	Opens a WAIS session. (This URL includes a query for a list of WAIS servers.)

Table 7.1—6 World Wide Web Link Action Syntax for Other Internet Protocols

Directory Service), and file (links to a specific locally-mounted files such as a PDF link to a file). Some Web browsers also support the passing of commands via a URL. Netscape Navigator 2.x, for example, displays a wealth of information about a document if about:document is entered as the URL.

Note: about:document is not a true URL and is available only in Netscape Navigator 2.x and later versions.

7.1.12 Show/Hide Annotation Action

The Show/Hide Annotation action shows or hides a bookmark, link, or button in the PDF file.

7.1.13 Third-Party Supported Actions

Third-party developers have extended the PDF file format by adding object actions that play media files, connect to databases, display information, and other actions. Most object actions require that the user have the plug-in installed in order to engage the object's action. Therefore, many action-extended objects are not useful for Internet-based documents. A list of plug-ins, some which have custom actions, are listed in Appendix I, "Acrobat Plug-ins."

7.2 Setting a Base URL in a PDF File

A base URL is the highest level, common directory path for a set of URLs. If a PDF file has a base URL, clicking an interactive or navigational object that uses a World Wide Web Link action appends the entry in the action's URL with the base URL to form the full URL. This full URL is then opened via the Web browser. Only World Wide Web Link actions without a transport protocol are appended. (Relative Open File actions remain unaffected.) Base URLs defined in Acrobat Exchange work like base URLs set in HTML documents.

For PDF files that will be served via the byte-server CGI script, a base URL offers the capability to set an absolute link that can pass the PDF files through the CGI script (http://www.sitename.com/cgi-bin/byteserver/pdf_file.pdf). This allows them to be downloaded a page-at-a-time and to render progressively. The relative linking feature used by the Open File option cannot be set to pass PDF files through the CGI script. Relative file links are a better choice for linking to movie files, for moving collections of PDF files across various media and network protocols, for PDF files that need not be byte-served, or for PDF files that are served on FTP and Gopher sites.

The URL text string entered in a World Wide Web Link action is uncompressed. A single World Wide Web Link with a URL of http://www.adobe.com, adds 313 bytes (not kilobytes) for the link. A base URL can save space by eliminating the need to enter the most frequently occurring part of the URL in the document.

A base URL is set in the Document Info dialog box. The base URL must include the transfer protocol (HTTP, FTP, etc.). When setting a World Wide Web Link action, the base URL will be displayed in the Edit URL dialog box.

World Wide Web Link URL	Base URL	Full URL
/acrobat/acro.hqx	http://www.adobe.com	http://www.adobe.com/acrobat/ acro.hqx
/acro.hqx	http://www.adobe.com	http://www.adobe.com/ acro.hqx
ftp.adobe.com	ftp://	ftp://ftp./adobe.com
http://www.adobe.com/Apps	None	http://www.adobe.com/Appshttp:// www.adobe.com/ acro.hqx

Table 7.2—1 Base URL (and World Wide Web Link Action) Syntax

The base URLs allow the development and testing of links locally, and they can be globally updated when the PDF files are uploaded to the Internet server. A base URL helps minimize the possibility of typographical errors and saves time when entering links because only a portion of the full URL is entered.

To set a World Wide Web Link action to a site that is the base URL for a PDF file, edit the base URL so that it does not end in a "/", (for example, http://www.adobe.com, instead of http://www.adobe.com/). Set the link and enter "/" for the link's URL, or enter the base URL as the link's URL. World Wide Web Link actions using the base URL should begin with a "/".

Base URL	World Wide Web Link Action URL	Full URL sent to Web browser
http://www.adobe.com	/	http://www.adobe.com/
http://www.adobe.com/	/	http://www.adobe.com//[1]
http://www.adobe.com/	(blank)	http://www.adobe.com/[2]
http://www.adobe.com	/acrobat	http://www.adobe.com/acrobat[3]

Table 7.2—2 World Wide Web Link to Base URL Syntax

1 Results in a 404 error from the Web browser.

2 Acrobat displays the message,"There is no URL specified. Please enter a valid URL," (regardless if a base URL has been defined).

3 This example shows how World Wide Web Link actions should be configured when the base URL uses a configuration that doesn't end in a "/".

7.2.1 Using a Base URL to Set Up a Local Internet Site

With a base URL, links between HTML and PDF files—and some other files types—that reside locally on a laptop, office, or home computer can be set up and tested. Setting the base URL to the file path of the local drive allows a fully functioning Internet site (without any server-supported actions) to be constructed. This locally mounted, working version of the Internet site then can be published globally by revising the base URL to the server's transport protocol (commonly HTTP for Web sites), the server's domain name (e.g., www.adobe.com), and subdirectories (e.g., /acrobat), and uploading the files to the appropriate directories on the Internet server.

Here's how to create a base URL to a file path:

1. Create a directory or folder in which to place all the Web documents. For Macintosh, create a folder on the Desktop called WWW_Site. PC or UNIX machine users should create a directory at the root level named WWW_Site (C:/WWW_Site, for example).
2. Place the PDF files and HTML pages within the directory. Note that any files linked to another file not in the WWW_Site directory will result in an error now and after the files are uploaded to a Web server.
3. Additional folders or directories can be created within the WWW_Site directory.
   - For Macintosh users, the base URL to WWW_Site is file:///Hard%20Drive/Desktop%20Folder/WWW_Site/. Use the "%20" instead of a blank space. Note that "Hard Drive" is the name of the computer's hard drive.

If the volume WWW_Site on which the file is mounted has another name, replace "Hard Drive" with the name of the volume.

- For PC Users, the base URL to WWW_Site is file:///C|WWW_Site/. Use "|" instead of a colon. If WWW_Site is on a different letter drive (or named volume), replace the "C" drive with the correct letter or volume name.

7.2.2 Testing a Local Base URL and World Wide Web Link Actions with an Acrobat-Compatible Web Browser

Launch an Acrobat-compatible Web browser and open an HTML or PDF file within the WWW_Site directory folder. Click the World Wide Web Link actions in the PDF files to engage the integrated viewing of PDF files, HTML files, and other file types to test the action and base URL.

7.2.3 Testing a Local Base URL and World Wide Web Link Actions with a Non-PDF-Savvy Web Browser

Launch an Acrobat 2.1 or earlier compatible browser (one that supports the Weblink Plug-in, but not progressive rendering within a Web browser's document window). Open a PDF file within the WWW_Site directory folder with an Acrobat viewer. Click the object by using the World Wide Web Link action in the PDF files to test the links and base URL.

7.3 Setting Page Actions

Individual PDF pages can be set to perform one or more actions when opened or closed by a user (see Section 7.1, "Actions"). Use these page actions to perform multimedia-like actions. Some of these multimedia-like actions can include the importation of form data from a Web server, the magnification of part of a page, followed by other actions.

7.4 Links

Links are "hot spots" users interact with to view other areas of a single PDF file, to open other documents (including HTML, PDF, and others file types on the Internet), other actions, or invisible areas. Create links with Acrobat Exchange, or have a PDF-savvy creator application create the links automatically.

Note: Links can be generated automatically by manually inserting pdfmark commands into a PostScript file. However, this is usually too time consuming for more than a few links. Automatic link creation is done most efficiently by a PDF-savvy creator application.

Create links in Acrobat Exchange by drawing a boundary around an area of the PDF page with the link tool and setting an action for the link. Clicking on the link initiates its defined action. Links are capable of all the possible PDF actions. (See Section 7.1, "Actions," for a complete list and description.) Links can be drawn around a single object or several objects. The area drawn defines the link area or "hot spot" with which the user interacts.

PDF-savvy creator applications (see Section 4.3, "PDF-Savvy Creator Applications"), can create links and other interactive and navigational objects within the original file before the file is distilled into a PDF file. A PostScript file can have pdfmark operators inserted into it, which then create interactive and navigational objects when the PostScript file is converted to a PDF file. For more information on pdfmark and its uses, see Adobe's technical notes (http://www.adobe.com/) and the *Portable Document Format Reference Manual,* included with Acrobat (or available on Adobe's Web site).

7.4.1 Link Sizes

When creating a link, the text entered for the link's action (e.g., World Wide Web Link actions) destination URL, or path is not compressed (unlike text in the body of the PDF file). Additionally, the data that defines the link itself (or other objects) adds a few bytes to the overall PDF file's size.

URL text	Size (in bytes)	Description
Untitled	192	Links to the location "none".
Adobe's Home Page	284	Links to the Adobe WWW site via a Web browser.

Table 7.4—1 Sample Link Byte Sizes

7.4.2 Link Appearance

Links can be either visible or invisible rectangles. Select a visible rectangle's color from any of the eight defined colors (white, black, red, green, blue, cyan, yellow, and magenta), or select a custom color. Link line widths may be thin (the default), medium, thick, and have a solid (the default), dashed, or "None" style. When clicked by the user, the link's highlight options—a visible cue to the user—include "None," invert, outline, or inset. Links can be resized or moved elsewhere on the page. However, links cannot be copied or pasted; nor can links be created, edited, or moved by using drag-and-drop techniques.

When viewing a PDF document, the user identifies a link by common cues, such as text that has been colored and underlined (using an invisible rectangle), a colored rectangle, or by changes in the cursor icon (either visible or invisible rectangles). Unlike many Web browsers, the Acrobat viewer does not change the color of previously selected links.

The design or look of a link may conform to traditional Web design, or may be innovative and unique by using the design tools available in Acrobat Exchange. Web design uses colored, underlined text (or hypertext) to cue the user to the existence of a link. Graphics and images may have colored borders, but many Web page designers rely on the change in the cursor icon—from an arrow to a pointing finger—to indicate the existence of a link. Some link actions, such as World Wide Web Links or movie or sound actions, use other cursor icons to indicate the action of the object. Acrobat Exchange can add visible, colored, or invisible boundaries around both text and graphics. PDF links function in the same way as hypertext links, but the text selected as the link is not formatted automatically as colored, underlined text.

Note: The Capture Plug-in can import images and graphics for use in a PDF file. Use these imported images as icons and other interactive cues. See the Acrobat Online User guide for information on using the Capture Plug-in to import images into PDF files.

For consistent Web hypertext design, text may be either in a creator application as the document is being designed, or styled later in Exchange using the Touch Up Plug-in. Add an invisible link over the hypertext. The styled text and invisible link combination results in the same functionality of hypertext found in HTML documents.

7.5 Bookmarks

PDF bookmarks, which often function like an electronic table of contents, are words or phrases that can perform any of the interactive and navigational actions of the PDF file. In a PDF file, when Document view is set to Bookmarks and Page view, bookmarks appear in a user-resizable margin left of the Document window, which is called the Overview window.

In Exchange, bookmarks can be created by selecting text and choosing Document > New Bookmark (for Acrobat 3.0 or later). The selected text is used as the bookmark text. Alternatively, bookmarks can be created manually by copying and pasting text from the document into the newly created bookmark. (Select the text, choose Document > New Bookmark, and then paste in the text.) Plug-ins can automate the creation of bookmarks as the PostScript file is converted to a PDF file, or later within Acrobat Exchange. Compose, xTools, and other third-party plug-ins can be used with Exchange to generate bookmarks.

Go To View is the bookmark's default action. When created, the bookmark's Go To View action is automatically set to the page and its magnification. Another action can be set (or reset), by selecting a single bookmark and choosing Edit > Properties.

Reset a destination for a bookmark (both magnification and page), by selecting the bookmark and choosing Edit > Properties to select another action. Alternatively, a page can be set as an example of the new destination by selecting the bookmark (clicking the bookmark icon only), and choosing Document > Reset Bookmark Destination.

7.5.1 Bookmark Appearance

Bookmarks appear as a page icon (with a dog-eared left corner) and a word to paraphrase text. Hierarchically, bookmarks that have subservient bookmarks appear with an arrow left of the page icon. Nested, hierarchical bookmarks—like the structure of an outline—can be expanded or collapsed by the user.

Hierarchically nested bookmarks are identified by an arrow that appears to the left of the bookmark's icon and text. When expanded, the arrow points down to display all subordinate bookmarks. When collapsed, the arrow points to the left and displays only the title text of the superior bookmark.

In an Adobe Acrobat viewer, bookmark text appears in black, 12-point Helvetica type. Bookmarks have a maximum length of

interact with form buttons; however, only Acrobat Exchange is capable of saving changes made in the form's fields (text additions, checkbox selections, etc.) and exporting or importing FDF files. Acrobat Reader 3.0 and later can submit form data to a CGI script or applet via the World Wide Web Link action with a URL embedded in a link, bookmark, form button, or other objects. Users can interact with form fields and buttons within Acrobat 3.0-compatible Web browsers or directly in Acrobat viewer applications. To submit form data to a Web server, the PDF file must be viewed in a Web browser (see Section 7.1.10, "Submit Form Action").

Note: Netscape 3.0 or later is required to send FDF data to a URL. See the Adobe Acrobat Web site at http://www.adobe.com/acrobat/ for a list of other Web browsers that can send FDF form data.

Most of the characteristics of form fields and buttons share similarities with HTML form fields and buttons. Forms in Acrobat documents can be constructed for online submission of form data (such as HTML forms), as forms that users fill out and print, or both. Unlike HTML forms, data can be imported into a PDF form to populate the form's fields. Only FDF files can populate PDF form fields. PDF forms can extend the interactive nature of form fields with one or more actions dependent on mouse location, action, and other states. See Section 7.6.6, "Form Field Actions," for a listing of these definable actions.

Note: Forms discussed here should not be confused with the PDF Language Reference Manual's XObject Form.

7.6.1 Forms: HTML or PDF

PDF forms use the same field types as HTML 2.0 forms (as defined by RFC 1866 ftp://ds.internic.net/rfc/1866). In contrast, PDF forms have a number of features that make them a better choice for user-specific queries, information processing, and printing. However, before choosing a form format (PDF or HTML), consult Section 3.2, "Content Formats: PDF or HTML," to decide which file format is best for the document. If it is clear that the form is best served as a PDF form, while the rest of the document pages are best served in HTML, integrate the two file formats by linking the HTML document with the PDF form.

There are several strategies a Web publisher might employ when adopting PDF forms. These strategies explain some of the better ways to work with PDF forms and how to fully integrate PDF with HTML.

Replacing HTML forms with PDF forms

Generally, if a form works well in HTML, it may not need to be replaced. Replace HTML forms with PDF forms to refine the features and appearance of the forms. PDF forms can have the same fields and functionality as the original HTML forms, or be entirely reworked to take advantage of specific PDF form features. Table 7.6—1, "HTML versus PDF Forms Features," lists a number of features and appearance options available to PDF forms that HTML 2.0 forms don't support.

Note: When replacing HTML forms with PDF forms, remember to verify connecting links as the named destination of the form as the file suffix of the form must be changed from HTML to .pdf.

Duplicate forms in PDF and HTML

Like the duplicate publishing strategy described in Section 3.1.4, "Integrating HTML with PDF Files," forms can be published as both PDF and HTML. If the PDF form is set to export URL-encoded HTML data (see Appendix C, "The Forms Data Format"), the submitted form data can be processed by the same server script or application that processes the HTML form data. Duplicate forms also can be used for different purposes. The PDF version could be the best option for users who want to complete the form off-line, print it, and submit it by mail. The HTML version can be designated as the form to use for online submission. (Although the PDF form also could be used for this purpose.)

New PDF forms

New forms created specifically for print or Web use, should capitalize on the features that make PDF forms more compelling than HTML forms. Rather than using present HTML forms as a template when creating forms in PDF, utilize the rich graphic and interactive features found in PDF.

Feature	PDF Forms	HTML Forms
Can be printed.	Yes. Form values are resolution-independent like the rest of the PDF file.	Most Web browsers cannot print the contents of form fields.
Can be processed by a script or application running on a server.	Yes. Scripts and applications used for processing standard HTML form data also can process PDF form data. (Use the HTML encoded export option.) Scripts and applications also can be written to process FDF files such as HTML data.	Yes.

continued

Table 7.6—1[1] HTML versus PDF Forms Features

Feature	PDF Forms	HTML Forms
Form can have values sent to a script or application on the server.	Yes. Form data can be sent as either Forms Data Format (FDF files) or URL-encoded HTML forms.	Yes. Data can only be sent as URL-encoded HTML forms.
Form can have values sent from a script or application on the server.	Yes. PDF forms can be populated with FDF form data. This can be in response to a user's action or simply to populate the form with default form data.	Only through a script or application. Scripts and applications could generate a new form, identical to the original, but with the user's processed or entered data as the default field values.
Form fields can have one or more actions associated with mouse location.	Yes. Form fields can perform actions when a user's mouse enters a field, leaves a field, or when the user clicks down on a field and releases the mouse button. Additional form field actions are described in Section 7.6.6, "Form Field Actions."	No. Only basic actions are supported (e.g., clicking a field to enter information, or clicking a button).
Button labels can change label and icon when clicked.	Yes. A form field button can have two states: 1) a text label and icon when dormant; and 2) another text label and icon when clicked down (optional).	No. Buttons may have custom icons, but they only become highlighted when clicked.
Form fields can have colored borders.	Yes. PDF form field can have a custom-colored border. A form's border also can have width and style.	No. Form field borders are black.
Form fields can have colored backgrounds.	Yes.	No. Form field backgrounds are white.
Form field buttons and text can be set to a custom color.	Yes.	No.
Form field buttons can have custom highlight options.	Yes. They can be depressed, inverted, outlined, or have no visible action when clicked.	No. The only highlight option is invert.
Form field buttons and text can be set to a font.	Yes. (Only the base-14 fonts.)	No. The user selected font is used.
Form fields and buttons can be set so they don't print.	Yes.	No.

continued

Table 7.6—1[1] (continued) HTML versus PDF Forms Features

Feature	PDF Forms	HTML Forms
Form fields and buttons can be set so users can read the fields, but cannot make changes.	Yes.	No.
Form fields and buttons can be hidden.	Yes.	Yes.
A form field can be set to require the user to enter a value.	Yes.	Yes.

Table 7.6—1[1] (continued) HTML versus PDF Forms Features

1 This table reflects the comparison of PDF forms and HTML 2.0 forms as described in RFC 1866 (ftp://ds.internic.net/rfc/1866). Plug-ins, Web browser-specific enhancements, Java applets, and later versions of HTML may have different features than those listed here.

7.6.2 Comparing HTML and PDF Form Field Objects

HTML and PDF forms and form fields have a number of similarities. Undoubtedly, Web publishers may want to replace or duplicate existing HTML forms with PDF forms. Web publishers also may want to compare the form features, specific to individual form object options, with those found in PDF forms. The following tables define the similarities between HTML form and field objects, including field values and tags.

Note: This chapter section is ordered (but somewhat restructured for comparison), like HTML 2.0 RFC 1866 to facilitate easy comparison between PDF form objects and HTML 2.0 forms.

HTML Forms	PDF Forms	Notes
<Form>...</Form>	Adding a form field to a PDF file creates a PDF form.	Unlike HTML files, PDF files can only have one form per file, although there are a number of ways to submit selected fields by allowing the appearance of more than one form field.
ACTION	See Section 7.6.6, "Form Field Actions," for a list of PDF form actions.	An HTML form's ACTION is limited to a URL. PDF forms can be configured to produce a number of actions based on user interaction with a form field or button.
METHOD	PDF forms that use the Submit Form action and the HTML export option use the POST method.	PDF forms, unlike HTML forms, cannot use the GET method for form submission.
ENCTYPE	PDF forms can submit data to a URL as either HTML data or FDF data.	HTML data is submitted as application/x-www-from-urlencoded). FDF data is exported and submitted as the FDF file type, which is registered as the PDF MIME type on most platforms.
INPUT	The PDF form types.	See Tables 7.6—3 through Table 7.6—12 below to compare the HTML/PDF form types.

Table 7.6—2 HTML and PDF Form Comparisons: Form

HTML Form	PDF Forms
LABEL	PDF forms don't add labels like HTML forms. Add the labeled as the form is designed in the creator application. See Section 7.7,"Form Design," for more information.
INPUT TYPE="n"	Select the Text field type in the Field Properties dialog box.
NAME="n"	Enter the name in the Field Properties dialog box.
VALUE="n"	Enter a default value in the Default Value field by clicking the Text Options tab in the Field Properties dialog box.
SIZE=n	The field size is determined by the field's border size.
MAXLENGTH=n	In the Field Properties dialog box, click the Limit of n Characters button in the Text Options field and enter the maximum number of characters a user can enter in the field.

Table 7.6—3 HTML and PDF Form Comparisons: Text Field and Password Field[1]

[1] PDF text fields have a password field option just like the HTML password text field input type (<INPUT TYPE="password">). In the Field Properties dialog box, click Password button in the Text Options field. When a user enters text in the field, the text will appear as asterisks.

HTML Form	PDF Forms
LABEL	PDF forms don't add labels like HTML forms. Add the label as the form is designed in the creator application. See Section 7.7,"Form Design," for more information.
INPUT TYPE="checkbox"	Select the Checkbox field type in the Field Properties dialog box,
NAME="n"	Enter the name in the Field Properties dialog box,
VALUE="ON"	By default, "On" is entered in the Export Value field found in the Checkbox Options tab in the Field Properties dialog box.
CHECKED	Click the Default is Checked box in the Checkbox Options tab in the Field Properties dialog box.

Table 7.6—4 HTML and PDF Form Comparisons: Checkbox[1]

[1] PDF forms have an option to select a custom check mark (check, circle, cross, diamond, square, or star), rather than the standard HTML check mark.

HTML Form	PDF Forms
LABEL	PDF forms don't add labels like HTML forms. Add the label as the form is designed in the creator application. See Section 7.7, "Form Design," for more information.
INPUT TYPE="radio"	Select the Radio Button field type in the Field Properties dialog box,
NAME="n"	Enter the name in the Field Properties dialog box,
VALUE="ON"	By default, "On" is entered in the Export Value field found in Radio Button Options tab in the Field Properties dialog box,
CHECKED	Click the Default is Checked box in the Radio Button Options tab in the Field Properties dialog box,

Table 7.6—5 HTML and PDF Form Comparisons: Radio Button[1]

[1] PDF forms have an option to select a custom radio button mark (check, circle, cross, diamond, square, or star), rather than the standard HTML bullet.

HTML Form	PDF Forms
LABEL	PDF forms don't add labels like HTML forms. Add the label as the form is designed in the creator application. See Section 7.7, "Form Design," for more information.
INPUT TYPE=IMAGE	A link or form field button may be used to simulate the HTML action. The Button form field option enables the direct import of an image specific to the button (see Table 7.6—14, "PDF Field Properties: Field Options"). Unlike the HTML IMAGE type action, which implies TYPE=SUBMIT, a PDF button's action can be any PDF file action type. Use any part of the PDF page. Icons can be imported for use as PDF form buttons.
ALIGN	This feature is simulated in PDF forms by the placement of the button in the PDF document (or is dictated by the document's layout).

Table 7.6—6 HTML and PDF Form Comparisons: Image

HTML Form	PDF Forms
LABEL	PDF forms don't add labels like HTML forms. Add the label as the form is designed in the creator application. See Section 7.7, "Form Design." for more information.
INPUT TYPE=HIDDEN	Set the Hidden option by selecting the General tab in the Field Properties dialog box.
	Form field with the Hidden option selected. Any PDF form field type can be hidden.
	The submitted value varies by field type. For fields with export values, the export value is submitted.
NAME="n"	Enter the name in the Field Properties dialog box.
VALUE="n"	Enter a default value in the Default Value field by clicking the field type's Options tab in the Field Properties dialog box

Table 7.6—7 HTML and PDF Form Comparisons: Hidden[1]

[1] In addition to the Hidden value, which every PDF form field type has available, there are three other attributes that are available: read-only, required, and don't print.

HTML Form	PDF Forms
LABEL	PDF forms don't add labels like HTML forms. The label should be added as the form is designed in the creator application. See Section 7.7, "Form Design," for more information.
INPUT TYPE=SUBMIT	Submit PDF forms data to a URL as either FDF or URL-encoded HTML data.
	Buttons, fields, links, or bookmarks can be set to perform submit form actions.
	All the fields in a PDF form may be submitted, or only specific fields.
	(See Section 7.6.6, "Form Field Actions," for a discussion of the various ways to trigger a submission of form data.)
NAME="n"	Enter the name in the Field Properties dialog box.
VALUE="n"	Enter a default value in the Default Value field by clicking the field type's Options tab in the Field Properties dialog box.

Table 7.6—8 HTML and PDF Form Comparisons: Submit

HTML Form	PDF Forms
LABEL	PDF forms don't add labels like HTML forms. Add the label as the form is designed in the creator application. See Section 7.7, "Form Design," for more information.
INPUT TYPE=RESET	Like HTML forms, the Reset Form action removes any user-entered text and resets the fields and choices to the defaults. Buttons, fields, links, or bookmarks can be set to perform Reset Form action. All the fields in a PDF form may be submitted, or only specific fields. Field values can be submitted through form actions. (See Section 7.6.6, "Form Field Actions," for a discussion of the various ways to reset a form.)
NAME="n"	Enter the name in the Field Properties dialog box.
VALUE="n"	Enter a default value in the Default Value field by clicking the field type's Options tab in the Field Properties dialog box.

Table 7.6—9 HTML and PDF Form Comparisons: Reset

HTML Form	PDF Forms
LABEL	PDF forms don't add labels like HTML forms. Add the label as the form is designed in the creator application. See Section 7.7, "Form Design," for more information.
SELECT.. </SELECT>	The combination of this value and MULTIPLE defines what PDF forms describe as a list box. For a PDF list box, select the List Box field type in the Field Properties dialog box.
NAME="n"	Enter the name in the Field Properties dialog box.
SIZE=n	The field size is determined by the field's border size.
MULTIPLE	The combination of this value and SELECT defines what PDF forms describe as a list box. See SELECT above.
<OPTION SELECTED>	PDF forms don't support this feature.
<OPTION>	The name of the list item. PDF forms allow a separate Export Value for list items (see Section 7.6.5, "Export Values").

Table 7.6—10 HTML <SELECT> MULTIPLE and PDF Form List Box Field Comparisons[1]

1 PDF form field list boxes have a Sort Items option that automatically sorts the list items alphabetically.

HTML Form	PDF Forms
LABEL	PDF forms don't add labels like HTML forms. Add the label as the form is designed in the creator application. See Section 7.7,"Form Design." for more information.
SELECT.. </SELECT>	For a PDF list box (sometimes called a pop-up menu), select the Combo Box field type in the Field Properties dialog box.
NAME="n"	Enter the name in the Field Properties dialog box.
<OPTION SELECTED>	This HTML feature is accomplished by placing the selected item at the top of the Combo Box Options list in the Field Properties dialog box.
<OPTION>	The name of the items in the Combo Box. PDF forms allow a separate Export Value for list items (see Section 7.6.5,"Export Values").

Table 7.6—11 HTML <SELECT> and PDF Form Combo Box Field Comparisons[1]

[1] PDF form field combo boxes have a Sort items option that automatically sorts the list items alphabetically. Additionally, an Editable option allows users to edit the item selected from the pop-up list. These edits are temporary additions—like text added to a text field—and are not added as items in the pop-up list.

HTML Form	PDF Forms
LABEL	PDF forms don't add labels like HTML forms. Add the label as the form is designed in the creator application. See Section 7.7,"Form Design," for more information.
TEXTAREA </TEXTAREA>	Select the Text field type in the Field Properties dialog box. PDF forms don't define text areas. Create a large field to mimic the space accomplished with the ROWS and COLS HTML form tags.
NAME="n"	Enter the name in the Field Properties dialog box.
ROWS=n	The field size (width) is determined by the field's border size.
COLS=n	The field size (columns) is determined by the field's border size.

Table 7.6—12 HTML and PDF Form Comparisons: Text Area Field

7.6.3 Form Data: HTML or FDF

PDF forms can be exported and submitted as either URL-encoded HTML data (application/x-www-form-urlencoded), or as Forms Data Format files. FDF files and HTML data can be processed by server scripts or applications, although most scripts don't process both data formats. Creating scripts and applications to process form data (either FDF or HTML data) requires more resources, expertise, and is more time consuming than creating a form. Given the number of pre-package and existing scripts and applications that process URL-encoded HTML form data, setting a PDF form's export option to submit data as HTML form data reduces the need to create new scripts for PDF forms.

FDF data includes much more information about the form than URL-encoded HTML data. This additional data within the FDF file can be used to modify the appearance and action of the form. For this reason, the FDF data format offers a number of new features not possible with HTML forms. For more information on FDF, see Appendix C, "The Forms Data Format."

Note: Most HTML forms submit form data as URL-encoded HTML form data and have no way of exporting data directly to a standalone file type such as the FDF file format. (Although the HTML form data can be written to a file, including FDF files, by a server script or application.)

7.6.4 Form Field Types

Each of the five types of fill-in form fields can have text, known as a value, associated with them. Button fields have no value. Combo boxes and list boxes also have one or more items users may select.

Each combo or list item has an export value. Radio buttons also can have an export value associated with them. When a PDF form is submitted or exported, either as a FDF or HTML form, the export values are transferred with the form data.

Field Names

All form fields can have a name. Use field names to identify one field from another. (Although PDF files allow fields to have the same name.) The form name is displayed in the PDF file only when the form tool is selected. When a script or application is processing a submitted form, in either FDF or HTML, the field name is often used to identify the value of the data being passed. Additionally, when importing a FDF file into a PDF form, the form name in the FDF file is matched with the form name of the PDF file, and matching fields are populated with the data in the FDF file.

Note: Field names cannot include periods. Periods interfere with the processing of the form.

Selecting Form Field types to match information types

Web designers have adopted a number of uses for forms, which include entering search requests, submitting personal information, ordering products, and logging-in to Web sites. PDF forms can be used exactly like HTML forms in every respect. See Table 7.6—13, "PDF Form Field Types," for a listing of the various types of PDF form fields and descriptions of possible uses.

File Type[1]	Use
Text field	Users enter arbitrary text into the field. The field's options allow the entry of passwords and can limit the number of characters a user can enter in the field. Useful for a variety of text input from name and password data to the entry of free-form comments.
Combo box	Users select a single item from a drop-down list. Selecting the Sort List option automatically sorts the list items in alphabetical order. Useful when the user must choose just one selection from a list (e.g., choosing one's favorite color or payment option). The pop-up feature requires less area in the form than the list box. For long lists (more than six items), use a list box.
List box	Users select an item from a displayed list of items. Selecting the Sort List option automatically sorts the list items in alphabetical order. Useful for longer lists where a user may choose from a number of items in the list.
Button	Used to perform a selected option or chain of actions. See Section 7.6.6, "Form Field Actions," for the list of action options. Useful as a visual cue. Can be used within a form, or for other interactive features. The button can be configured to have a different name and icon when depressed by the user.
Radio button	Users select one or another field item. Useful when the user has just a few choices and an option must be chosen. Radio buttons can be placed near icons and other visual objects, but the items need not be placed next to one another.
Checkbox	Users select one or multiple field items. Useful for the selection of one or more items. Like the radio button, it can be placed near icons and other visual objects, but the items need not be placed next to one another.

Table 7.6—13 PDF Form Field Types

[1] Text can be copied and pasted from field-to-field.

Form Field Options

Each form field type has a unique set of options associated with it. Table 7.6—14, "PDF Field Properties: Field Options," presents a list and related notes for each field type. In addition to each field's option, an appearance of a field can be customized. See Section 7.6.8, "Form Field Appearance," for the available form field appearance options.

Field Type	Options	Option Notes
Text field	alignment (left, right, centered) multi-line default value character length limit password	Displays the full contents of the field (rather than a single line) within the field. If the text in the field extends beyond the boundaries of the field, the text field scrolls horizontally to accommodate the lines of text. The default value is text displayed in the field prior to modification. Password text fields display the field's content as a series of asterisk (*) characters.
Combo box	Item Item's export value Sort items	When Sort is selected, items in the combo box are sorted alphabetically.
List box	Item Item's export value Sort items	If the number of items in the list extends beyond the vertical boundary of the field, a vertical scrollbar is displayed. When Sort items is selected, items in the list box are sorted alphabetically. Multiple selection allows the selection of a range of items, or disjoining a selection of items. (For example, in Windows a range can be selected by Shift-click; disjoin items by using Control-click.)
Button	Highlight (Invert, None, Outline, Push) Layout (Text only, Icon only, Icon over text, text over icon, Icon left -text right, Icon right-text left, text in icon) Appearance when up (with or without icon) Appearance when pushed (with or without icon)	The appearance when up and appearance when pushed options each allow an individual text entry that is displayed when the button is in the respective state (up or pushed). Additionally, these two button states can have individual icons assigned to them that change with the button state. Import icons for form field buttons by clicking browse and selecting an image or graphic from a PDF file.

continued

Table 7.6—14 PDF Field Properties: Field Options

Field Type	Options	Option Notes
Checkbox	Export value	The export value of a checkbox is "On" by default. (The value typically used by HTML forms.)
	Check mark (check, circle, cross, diamond, square or star)	
	Default is Checked	The Default is Checked option checks the checkbox.
Radio button	Export value	The export value of a checkbox is "On", by default. (The value typically used by HTML forms.)
	Button mark (check, circle, cross, diamond, square or star)	
	Default is Checked	The Default is Checked option checks the checkbox.

Table 7.6—14 (continued) PDF Field Properties: Field Options

7.6.5 Form Field Values

Assign a value to a form field or use the default value associated with the field. Depending on the field type, a value of a field is displayed in the field. In Acrobat Exchange, set or change a field's value by selecting the form tool and double-clicking the field. The Field Properties dialog box displays the value and property options for the selected type of field.

Field values can be a combination of alphanumerical characters or symbols that are based on the symbol set of the font used in the field (or by setting the font property field to Symbol). Field values may include a default value, or no value. Default values appear when the form is first opened or if the form field values are reset via the Reset button. Fields without values are blank. Adding values to a field in Exchange and saving the values redefines the value of each field as the default.

Export values

Export values that are associated with list items. They are not displayed to the user. Export values enable the user to interact and choose from a list of context-based items, while the processing application or script uses the selected or entered export value of the list item. An export value could be a simple number or some other data. For example, a user can choose a favorite color from a list of red, green, or blue, with the export values 1, 2, and 3, respectively. When the form is submitted, the processing script or application can generate a response to the user's input based on the numerical export value of the selected list item and it need not process the contextual list items.

Radio and checkbox form fields use the default export value of "on." This value is commonly assigned to radio and checkbox HTML forms. "On" indicates that the button is checked or select-

Field Type	Value	Exported Value(s)
Text field	Contents of the field	Contents of the field
Combo box	Selected list item	The selected list items are assigned value. If no export value is assigned, the selected value is exported.
List box	Selected list item	The selected list items are assigned value. If no export value is assigned, the selected value is exported.
Button	None	None
Radio button	Check button (check, circle, cross, diamond, square, or star)	Default export value is "On" for selected radio button(s).
Checkbox	Check mark (check, circle, cross, diamond, square, or star)	Default export value is "On" for selected checkbox(es).

Table 7.6—15 Field Value and Export Value Comparisons for FDF and HTML Forms

ed. Use this value, or the alternate "off" value, when submitting HTML form data to CGI scripts.

7.6.6 Form Field Actions

Unlike links or bookmarks, form fields have two actions. The first action is the form action. It is triggered by how the user interacts with the form field (see Table 7.6—16, "Field Properties: Actions"). When triggered, the second action, which is common to links and bookmarks, is initiated (see Section 7.1, "Actions"). One form field can have several actions, each with a different, secondary action associated with it.

Form field actions make highly interactive multimedia-like documents. Web publishers, whenever possible, should capitalize on the dynamic, interactive objects to further enrich content. The possible applications of combined forms and other actions are limitless.

Action Cause	Description
Mouse Up	Selected action occurs when mouse button (usually the left button) is released (after being depressed).
Mouse Down	Selected action occurs when mouse button (usually the left button) is depressed.
Mouse Enter	Selected action occurs when the mouse cursor enters the area of the form field or button.
Mouse Exit	Selected action occurs when the mouse cursor leaves the area of the form field or button after entering it.

Table 7.6—16 Field Properties: Actions

7.6.7 Form Field Sizes

A form field value, title text, and some interface features are not compressed (unlike text in the body of the PDF file). Each of the form fields (or other object) in a document adds a few bytes to the overall size of the PDF file. Imported form-field button icons also add to the PDF file size, although these images and graphics are often compressed.

For print-only use, forms fields don't need export values. Only the real values or field states (checked checkbox, selected list item) print.

To keep the size of online-only forms as small as possible, (especially if the default form data changes often), populate PDF forms with FDF data after the file has been read into an Acrobat 3.0-compatible Web browser document window. Entering the data directly in the form fields, or populating fields with the default values and saving this data with the PDF file, makes the size of the PDF file unnecessarily large. To populate the form with the default data, use a trigger or other interface feature to import the FDF data into the form when the user opens the page, or clicks a particular form field (see Section 7.3, "Setting Page Actions"). This approach keeps PDF files that use forms both as small as possible (there's no data in the form fields) and flexible (only the FDF files need updating, which can be generated on-the-fly by a script or application on the server).

Note: PDF files with form fields used for printing may be completed by the user off-line. Off-line users won't have access to the default data. If it is likely the form may be completed off-line, use the minimum default fields and values for the form.

7.6.8 Form Field Appearance

Form fields have three main components that affect their appearance and, to some degree, their action. Field borders have an assigned color, width, and style. These fields also can have a background color. Text appears in various point sizes in any color, in any of the base-14 fonts. Colors are selected from a system-dependent color picker.

Form field attributes mimic some of HTML forms attributes and values. The Hidden Form field attribute can be used like the hidden value tag for HTML forms, or simply to store hidden data within a document. Similarly, the Required field attribute functions much like its HTML form counterpart—both require the user to enter data in the defined field before it can be submitted. Read Only prevents users from making changes to the form field, although it can be viewed and printed. To prevent a form field from printing, assign it the don't print attribute. The form field can be interacted with, submitted, exported, etc.; however, when the PDF file is printed, the form field will not print.

Border	Text	Attributes
Border color (from color picker)	Text color (from color picker)	Read Only[1]
Background color (from color picker)	Text font (base-14 fonts)	Hidden
Border Width (Thin, Medium, Thick)	Text point size (auto, 6, 8, 9, 10, 12, 14, 16, 18)	Required[1]
Border Style (Solid, Dashed, Inset)		Don't Print

Table 7.6—17 Field Properties: General

[1] Button attributes include only Hidden and Don't Print.

7.7 Form Design

Creating an effective, easily understandable form requires careful planning during the design stages of content development. Unlike HTML fields, a PDF form field name is not visible to the user, although it is visible within Exchange 3.0 and later when the form tool is selected. Use the selected creator application to assign labels for each form field. These labels should be expressive—cueing the user to choose or enter specific information in the field. After converting the document to a PDF file, the form tool then can be used to actually add the form and form values. See Section 7.6.8, "Form Field Appearance," for additional design considerations specific to the border, color, and style of form field backgrounds and boundaries.

Note: FDF files can be used (via the Import or Submit actions) to alter the appearance of all or selected form fields. See Appendix C, "The Forms Data Format," for more information on FDF files.

7.7.1 Designing Forms to be Processed by a Server Script or Application

Construct a form for automatic calculation, checking, and other computations just as a form for any other use would be constructed. In order to compile and submit the form field data, a user interface feature (the submit button) must be added. As a standard interface feature, add a reset button to clear any changes made to the form field values. Information on processing and replying to the form is completed by the script or application script on the server.

Note: Because of the liberal use of forms on the World Wide Web, users are accustomed to clicking the Submit button when finished.

7.7.2 Designing Forms for Print Use

PDF files are an excellent file format for resolution-independent printing needs. A field's contents and appearance print like other PDF page objects. When designing any form, take into account the possibility that the form may be printed or used off-line. For these reasons, page dimensions and the use of color play a factor. PDF pages used as forms, which are regularly printed, are better served as standard paper sizes. Many users will not print forms in color. Use colors that print legibly on standard resolution printers. Pay careful attention to the background color of a form, as colored text may be much less visible when printed in grayscale than when viewed onscreen.

PDF form fields can be set with a Don't Print attribute to prevent selected fields (including their values) from printing. See Table 7.6—17, "Field Properties: General," for information on field attributes. The Don't Print attribute does not affect the submission of the form to a server's script or application, and it enables users to view and interact with form fields normally.

7.8 Thumbnails

Thumbnails are miniature representations of the pages in a PDF file. When Page and Thumbnail view is selected in any Acrobat viewer, thumbnails appear in the left-most margin (the overview window) of the Acrobat document window (where bookmarks are displayed when in Bookmark and Page view).

Thumbnails open directly to the page they represent. This is not an action and cannot be configured, nor can it be deactivated.

A user may open to a magnification of the page by clicking and sizing a boundary within the thumbnail of the destination page. The destination page then opens to the relative magnification of the boundary drawn by the user in the thumbnail.

7.8.1 Thumbnail Appearance

Thumbnails are colored, anti-aliased images proportionate to the dimensions of the page the thumbnail represents. Thumbnails cannot be scaled, although the margin where thumbnails are viewed can be enlarged or reduced.

If thumbnails have not been created for a document, a gray box proportionate to the page the thumbnail represents is displayed. These unrendered thumbnails have the same functionality of a fully-rendered thumbnail.

7.8.2 Thumbnail Sizes

For Internet publishing, the defacto rule for thumbnails is "do not publish with PDF." Thumbnails require too many kilobytes —around 3.5 kilobytes per page, per thumbnail—and they can be created later by the user if needed, or desired.

Note: When a monitor is set at 8-bit (256 colors), grayscale, or monochrome, thumbnails take less space in the PDF file.

7.9 Article Threads

Articles tie blocks of text together into threads. Use article threads in documents with more than a screen, column, or page-length of text (depending on layout). Articles are essential for PDF files served on the Internet. They magnify the story area to increase legibility and allow users to navigate through text by spanning several pages or columns. They also follow text that jumps to other pages of the document.

In Acrobat Exchange, select the article tool from the Tool menu and draw rectangular boundaries around each of the text areas in the article thread. The order in which the article threads are drawn defines the reading sequence. For large documents or those that make extensive use of columns and story jumps, use a PDF-savvy creator application (such as Adobe PageMaker or Adobe FrameMaker®) to automatically generate article threads.

Note: Adding author name, subject, keywords, etc., will add to the size of the PDF file unnecessarily. Avoid adding this information unless it is essential for document management.

Unlike other interactive objects that link to a single location (e.g., another page, magnification, etc.), an article opens an area of text that is defined by where in the article thread the user clicks; an article displays proportionately to the user's screen size and at the defined magnification preference for reading articles, if any. Subsequent clicks in the article may open to another area of the page, or an entirely different page. The end of the article links back to the where the user entered the article thread.

Click	Zoom	Action/Description
First click within article.	Between 100% to 800% (depending on monitor size[1]).	Zooms to display as much of the article as possible at the defined or default zoom. First line appears near the top of the document window.
Subsequent click(s)	Same as previous.	Scrolls down the page just under a full-window length (at the set magnification) to display the last line read at the top of the magnified area.[2] A flashing pointer appears in the upper-left corner of the document window to display from where the user should continue reading. (Could open to another area of the page, or an entirely different page.)
Final click	Previous magnification setting before clicking on article.	Resets magnification and links back to the page area in which the article thread was first clicked.

Table 7.9—1 Article Progression Description

1 With an Acrobat 3.0 or later viewer, the size of the Web browser's document window defines the magnification.

2 Users also can click and drag through the story.

Note: Once downloaded, clicking on an article does not request more information from the server. However, if an article jumps to another page (not cached), the server is contacted to download the target page before continuing.

7.9.1 Article Appearance

Article borders are invisible to the user. The boundary for an article thread is only visible in Acrobat Exchange when the article tool is selected.

Users are cued to the existence of an article when the cursor moves over an article. A small arrow (pointing down with a line at the top end of the arrow) is added to the hand cursor.

A line below the arrow in the hand cursor indicates that the end of the article thread and the story have been reached. An audible beep cues the reader that the end of the article has been reached, and the reader is returned to the view displayed before the article thread was entered.

7.9.2 Article Sizes

As with almost every enrichment, article threads add to PDF file size. One article thread box (of any size), adds 307 bytes to a PDF file. Subsequent article threads connected to the first article are smaller, approximately 180 bytes each. Out of all the enrichments, articles can add the most incremental volume to a PDF file because of their widespread use in text-heavy documents (newsletters, brochures, reports, etc.).

7.9.3 Article "Themes"

Article threads also can be used to dictate the sequence in which a user will experience other items in a PDF document.

Theme	Description
Order images or graphics	Opening order alternates between images and graphics, similar to a slide show.[1]
Order tables or charts	Follows the numbered order of the tables or charts.
Order by importance	Order text or graphic elements by importance, rather than by page or reading order.
Order by reference	Order opens from text to other text blocks or graphics as a link to an example, rather than a text reference.

Table 7.9—2 Article "Theme" Descriptions

[1] The article will enlarge the graphic or image at the same level of magnification that it does for text. Check the display quality of the graphic or image at 150% to 250%.

7.10 Notes

Use notes to append information, post changes, or call attention to an area of the document. Notes may be used to update an email address, indicate when a file will be posted to a site, or list a URL change.

Notes can be hidden or shown by other interactive objects by using the Show/Hide Annotation action. Creative use of the Show/Hide Annotation action can be combined with notes to display messages without taking up valuable screen real estate. See Section 7.10.5, "Other Note Uses," for more suggestions on how to use notes.

Notes may be added to PDF files with Acrobat Exchange, with PDF-savvy creator applications such as Adobe PageMaker or Adobe FrameMaker , or with pdfmark. Notes also can be imported from another PDF file.

Presently, few of the creator applications give control over the selection of a note's color, open or closed status, font, or point size. Adding notes by hand is tedious for large documents that require a great number of notes. However, manually inserting notes allows greater control over the characteristics of each note.

Add notes that appear with defined or default characteristics by selecting the note tool (Tools > Note). With the note tool selected, click anywhere in the PDF document to add a note. An individual note's characteristics can be changed by double-clicking the note's title bar (when opened), or by selecting the note and choosing Edit > Properties. Click once in the document window of an open note to display the text cursor, and then type or paste text in the note.

7.10.1 Note Appearance

A closed note appears as a miniature iconized version of a sticky note in one-of-eight predefined colors (or a custom color selected from a color picker). The magnification of a page has no affect on the text or the window dimensions of a note. Double-clicking a note icon opens the note.

The text in an open note appears in a miniature, resizable, scrollable document window. The title of the note—if any—appears in a colored title bar, which matches the color of the note icon. An open note window can be as large as four inches high by six inches wide. Text in a note can have a maximum of 65,535 characters.

Notes can be placed anywhere in the document, or off the page entirely. When saving a document in Acrobat Exchange, the open or closed status of a note is preserved—regardless of the Acrobat viewer used to open the document.

7.10.2 Note Size

Text in the body of a note and the title of the note are not compressed. This results in a nominal increase in file size.

Title	Color	Body Text	Size (in bytes)
"Untitled"	Custom[1]	(None)	292
"Untitled"	Custom	"How razorback-jumping frogs can level six piqued gymnasts!"	354

Table 7.10—1 Note Sizes

[1] Looks like the yellow note color of the popular sticky notes.

7.10.3 Note Preferences

Change note preferences to assign a particular style to a note. These preferences include a default note label, body text font, point size, and note color.

Item	Default	Options
Label	(Blank) or user name	Any text (maximum 31 characters).
Note color	Custom[1]	Eight built-in[2], custom colors with color picker.
Body text font	Helvetica	Fourteen-base Acrobat fonts, and fonts embedded[3] in the document.
Body text point size[4]	10	Any point size between 8 and 24 points.

Table 7.10—2 Note Preference Item Options

[1] Matches yellow note color of the popular sticky notes.

[2] Colors are black, white, red, green, blue, cyan, magenta, and yellow.

[3] Choosing a font that is not embedded in the PDF document means Helvetica will be substituted on computers that don't have the font installed.

[4] Only one body text font and point size can be chosen for a document.

7.10.4 Note Security

A PDF document can be configured to prevent users from adding or changing notes in a document. (This does not include the capability to open and close a note window.) Another security option is available that can prevent others from making changes in a document; however, it does not prevent the adding or altering of notes. See Section 7.11.2, "Conditional Security Options," for more details on note security options.

7.10.5 Other Note Uses

The note window has creative implications beyond its use as message containers.

Use	Description
Set form field buttons over areas with the mouse. Enter/Leave form action to show or hide a note.	When a user's mouse enters a text area using the form mouse enter action, the Show/Hide action displays a note providing just-in-time help and other context-specific information. When the user's mouse leaves the field area (by using the mouse Leave form action), the note is hidden.
Progressive disclosure.	Use notes to cover sections of a document with a text message to close the note ("Close Me") to progressively disclose points.
Layered notes.	Layer notes for similar progressive disclosure of information.
Hides links that require special configurations (plug-ins, networks, etc.).	Use an open note to cover media file action, instructing the user to download the movie file before playing the file and listing required hardware and software for playback (Movie Plug-in, sound card, video card, etc.).
Hides non-functional links.	Notes float over links, articles, form fields, and other interactive objects. Use note windows to cover objects if the object's action or destination is no longer available, or if the target file is password protected.

Table 7.10—3 Other Note Uses

7.11 PDF Security Options

Acrobat Exchange enables files to be secured with a password and with any of four conditional security options. A secured file is encrypted and requires the entry of the correct password before an Acrobat viewer will allow the user to open the PDF file.

Use the PDF client-level security options with traditional server security options (e.g., protected directories and IP address blockouts), to provide an even greater level of security.

Secure files by selecting the desired security options in the Security dialog box (both password, change option password, and conditional security options). Secure files immediately before saving or optimizing a PDF file for use on the Web.

Note: Importing a page into a secured file applies the security features to the imported page as well.

7.11.1 Owner Password

A second owner password can be used—different from the password used to open the file—to limit changing conditional security options. (The option to enter a password to change the preventive security features and to change the open password is hereafter called the "owner password.") Use the owner password on any PDF file with conditional security options.

7.11.2 Conditional Security Options

Conditional security options prevent users from taking certain actions with a PDF file (such as printing or copying text). However, they don't require the user to enter a password when opening the file. A file can be secured with either some or all of the conditional security options and an open password, or both the conditional options (in any combination) and an open password.

7.11.3 RSA Data Security Algorithms

Acrobat protects documents with passwords by using RSA Data Security's RC4 Symmetric Stream Cipher encryption algorithm. Visit the RSA Web site at http://www.rsa.com/.

Prevents	Password?	Description
Opening	Yes	Requires the user to enter a password to open the file.
Printing1	No, only to change	Prevents the document from being printed. Print menu and shortcut keys disabled.
Selecting text and graphics[1]	No, only to change	Prevents text and graphics from being copied.[2]
Adding and changing notes	No, only to change	Prevents the adding or changing of notes. Still allows the opening and closing of notes.
Document modification	No, only to change	Prevents the modification of a document (e.g., adding links, deleting article threads, extracting pages, etc.).

Table 7.11—1 Security Options

[1] Be sure to note somewhere in the document (perhaps a note on the first page) that this feature has been disabled, otherwise the file may appear to be "broken."

[2] Does not include text.

RC4 is a proprietary algorithm of RSA Data Security. RC4 is a variable-key-size symmetric stream cipher and is 10 or more times as fast as DES (Data Encryption Standard). (DES is the cipher that was defined and endorsed by the U.S. government in 1977, as an official standard.) Compared to other data protection schemes, RC4 is one of the more secure algorithms used to protect documents.

7.11.4 Security Option Size

Adding a security password to PDF adds only a couple hundred bytes to the file size.

7.11.5 Changing Security Options

If the PDF file is secured with an owner password, it must be entered before any security options can be changed. Set the security options (including passwords) and save the file, thereby replacing the old file. (See also, Section 6.1.6, "Checking Security.")

7.12 Open Preferences

Open preferences, applied to a PDF file in Acrobat Exchange, defines the PDF file's initial view, window options, and interface options. A PDF file can be configured with none, some, or all three of the open preferences described below.

7.12.1 Initial View Options

The Initial view defines the page number, magnification, page mode, and the display mode, and the page view at which the document will open.

Page view options

PDF documents can be configured to open with any one of the following four page view options.

Page number

Set the page number at which the PDF file should open. The default page is the first page of the document. Depending on the publishing strategy, the first page of a PDF file may contain more images and take longer to render than other pages (e.g., the cover

View	Description/Suggestions for use
Page Only View	Displays the page (no bookmarks or thumbnails). Makes the most efficient use of document window (and monitor) real estate.
Page and Bookmarks View	Displays the page and all bookmarks in the bookmark column (left of the document window). Bookmarks are useful navigational tools. They can be emphasized by opening to this view.
Page and Thumbnails View	Displays the page and all thumbnails that fit within the overview window (left of the document window). Thumbnails increase a file's overall size and require the Web browser to make additional calls to the server for the thumbnail data. If used at all, emphasize them by opening to this view.

Table 7.12—1 Open Preferences Page View Descriptions

of a magazine published concurrently on the Web and in print). Rather, set the page to open to the table of contents, or a page that renders quickly and provides navigational objects to open other parts of the PDF file.

Note: Changing the opening page number does not affect which page is displayed when a multi-page PDF file is embedded in an HTML document. By default, embedded PDFs always display the true first page (page one).

Magnification

A PDF document can be configured to open at a predefined (relative) or fixed (defined by a percentage) magnification. Relative magnification scales the page based on the variable size of the document window (either in a Web browser or Acrobat viewer document window). Fixed magnification opens the document at the defined magnification percentage, regardless of the user's window or monitor size.

Use the Magnification Open preference to zoom in on images and graphics. Enlarging graphics and images between 50% to 100% makes efficient use of bandwidth and rendering time by reducing the actual amount of data required to display the image or graphic without significantly reducing quality.

Alternatively, magnifying text areas (which progressive rendering displays first) provides seemingly immediate access to the content and allows image and font blitting (the update of a substitute font to the actual, fully-downloaded font) to occur off-screen while the download continues.

Magnification	Description/Suggestions for use
Fit Page	Fit Page increases or decreases the page's magnification to fit the whole page within the Acrobat viewer or Web browser document window.
Fit Width	Fit Width fits the entire width of the top of the document within the Acrobat viewer or Web browser document window.
Fit Visible	Fit Visible enlarges or reduces the page to fit the left-most and right-most images, text, or graphics within the Acrobat viewer or Web browser document window by hiding white space in the margins.
Fixed	Sets the page's magnification to a percentage. Choose from preset percentages (25, 50, 75, 100, 125, 150, 200, 400, 800) or enter a custom percentage.

Table 7.12—2 Open Preferences Magnification Descriptions

Page mode

Page mode determines how pages are viewed and scrolled within the Acrobat viewer and Web browser document window. The single column allows continuous scrolling through the document pages to give the file a HTML-like feel.

Mode	Description
Default	Displays the document by using the page mode set in the user's Acrobat viewer. The factory-set default is single page mode.
Continuous	Displays one page-at-a-time in the Acrobat viewer or Web browser's window.
One column	Pages are displayed in a continuous, scrollable, vertical column. Users with large monitors can view more than one page at a time.
Continuous—facing pages	Pages are arranged so that they are displayed side-by-side, in two continuous, scrollable columns. This view is useful for viewing page spreads or multiple pages of a document.

Table 7.12—3 Open Preferences Page Modes

7.12.2 Window Options

Use Window Options to better control the way a document opens in an Acrobat viewer—regardless of the user's monitor size. These options are not presently supported by Web browsers. The three window options can be used individually or together.

Mode	Description
Center Window on Screen	Displays the application window in the middle of the user's screen.
Resize Window to Fit Document	Sizes the application window to fit the document page.
Open in Full Screen Mode	Displays the document without menubar, toolbar, or status bar.

Table 7.12—4 Open Preferences Window Options

7.12.3 Interface Options

The interface option enables the opening PDF document to show or hide the Acrobat viewer's toolbar, menubar, and window controls. Only the Hide Toolbar interface option is supported by Web browsers.

7.13 Using Plug-ins to Automatically Add Navigational and Interactive Objects

Adobe Systems and third-party developers provide plug-ins (see Appendix I, "Acrobat Plug-ins"), used by Acrobat Exchange to automate, speed, and extend the creation of interactive and navigational objects.

Some plug-ins, which don't require the user to have the plug-in installed, automate or aid in the creation or editing of bookmarks, links, notes, article threads, and other objects.

Other plug-ins extend the types of objects that can be added to a PDF file. Forms, links, transitions between pages, and other interactive or navigational objects require a user to have the plug-in that originally created the object (or a player version of the plug-in) installed, otherwise the action of the object often won't work.

For an updated catalog of plug-ins for Acrobat and other Acrobat-related plug-ins for other applications, contact the Adobe Plug-in Source at 1-800-685-3547.

7.13.1 Object Automation Plug-ins

The table below, "Object Automation Plug-ins Product Information," lists a number of plug-ins for Acrobat Exchange. The list comprises those plug-ins that are useful in automating the creation or modification of navigational and interactive objects. These plug-ins bridge the gap between the need for highly usable PDF documents and non-PDF-savvy creator applications, by creating PDF objects after the application file has been converted to a PDF file. They are also useful tools for streamlining the tasks of fine-tuning and editing existing PDF navigational and interactive objects.

Plug-in	Platform	User-required	Company	Description
Aerial	Windows 3.x, Windows 95	Yes	Software Partners, Inc.	Adds custom object, hot-listing options, and a feature to print page portions.
Banner Printer Corporate	Windows 3.x, Windows 95	One of three/ none	Computerised Document Control Ltd	Adds "watermark" to printed page and options to control revisions.

continued

Table 7.13—1 Object Automation Plug-ins Product Information

Plug-in	Platform	User-required	Company	Description
Compose	Windows 3.x, Windows 95, Windows NT	No	Software Partners, Inc.	Automates bookmark and link creation, compiles PDF documents, and generates headers and footers.
InfoLinker	Windows 3.x, Windows 95	No	Alliant Defense Electronics Systems, Inc.	Automatically generates hyperlinks between text references and the referred document item.
InternetLink	Macintosh	Yes	University of Minnesota	Embeds Universal Resource Locators (URL) within a PDF file.
Movie Tool	Macintosh, Windows 3.x, Windows NT, Windows 95	Yes	Adobe Systems, Inc.	Incorporates multimedia objects into PDF file.
Re:Mark	Windows 3.x, Windows NT, Windows 95	Yes	Software Partners, Inc.	Adds an extensive number of object options including media files, notes, text, etc.
SuperPrefs	Macintosh, Windows 3.x, Windows NT, Windows 95	No	Adobe Systems, Inc.	Adds a number of features for cropping, bookmark management, and page tiling.
TranZform	Windows 3.x, Windows 95	Yes	VerTec Solutions, Inc.	Adds form functionality to PDF files (both creation and fill-in).
VerZions	Windows 3.x, Windows NT, Windows 95	No	VerTec Solutions, Inc.	Workflow and automation, cataloging, and indexing.
Volume Builder	Windows 3.x, Windows 95	No	Computerised Document Control Ltd	Allows the compilation of many discrete documents into a single volume.
Weblink	Macintosh, Windows 3.x, Windows NT, Windows 95, UNIX	Yes	Adobe Systems, Inc.	Embeds Universal Resource Locators (URL) within a PDF file.
xTools 1.1	Macintosh, Windows 3.x, Windows 95	Some	xMan Software	Suite of tools that manage links and add custom objects.

Table 7.13—1 (continued) Object Automation Plug-ins Product Information

7.14 Optimizing PDF Files for the World Wide Web

A PDF file may contain redundant images. Optimizing a PDF removes unneeded, redundant images, text, and line art from the PDF file. The process creates a pointer from each occurrence of the item to its first occurrence in the PDF file.

Optimization also creates a table entry for each "element" in a PDF file. These elements are ordered sequentially and are chunked together in page-by-page blocks. Elements listed in a table from a downloaded page are cached and reused if the same element appears in the page (and table) of another page.

Note: Optimize all PDF files—regardless of the intent to publish the PDF files on a World Wide Web site. Optimization adds only a few bytes to an average PDF file. These optimized PDF files work well on other media (e.g., LANs, WANs, and CD-ROMs) to allow concurrent publication or mixed media publishing efforts. Optimization can reduce dramatically PDF file size by removing redundant data.

7.14.1 Batch Optimization of PDF Files

Batch optimize collections of PDF files created with Acrobat Distiller 1.0, 2.0, 2.1, or 3.0 with Acrobat Exchange 3.0. Choose File > Batch Optimize... and select a directory that contains the PDF files to be optimized. The Optimize subdirectories option, which by default is on, will search through the directory and optimize all encountered PDF files. Batch optimization can also create or delete the batch of PDF file's thumbnails.

8

Publishing PDF Files on the Internet

For purposes of this book, Internet publishing is defined as the act of serving PDF files on the World Wide Web, Gopher, and FTP sites. Additionally, content can be distributed by sending email to subscribers with PDF files attached.

This chapter concentrates on what issues the Internet publisher should be aware of once content has been created and optimized. Whenever possible, this chapter explains—in the simplest of terms—the more technical requirements for Internet publishing with Acrobat. The following issues—explained in greater detail in this chapter—should be considered and implemented:

- Ensure that the sever is configured with the PDF MIME type.
- Mark PDF files with either an icon or the .PDF file suffix.
- Indicate the file size and the potential download time that is required—based on common modem transfer rates—for the first page (and perhaps the entire file).

- Uuencode PDF files sent as attachments via email.
- Don't encode or serve compressed PDF files; PDF files are compressed already. Encoding or compressing them rarely compacts the file and prevents online viewing of the PDF files.
- Maintain or create links that open to locations where users can download Acrobat viewers.
- Don't serve a PDF file as a home page. (The first page a user logs onto if entering a general URL, for example http://www.adobe.com/ .)
- Test the PDF file links. Consider using a Web-site management application (such as Adobe SiteMill), to manage the links within the site and out to other sites.
- Search enable large PDF files.
- Secure the server and, if necessary, secure the individual PDF files. Client- and server-level security present more flexibility and security over files.

8.1 Watched Directories over the Internet

With the growing dependence on intranets and the Internet as a means of disseminating information, Distiller can be configured to convert PostScript files to PDF files that come from authorized users, or anyone with access to a watched directory. Acrobat Distiller can identify "watched" directories on an Internet server; Distiller also can monitor the directories for changes. Users can access Distiller's In directory through a publicly accessible FTP upload directory (e.g., an incoming directory), or via HTTP file upload (see the Netscape HTTP File Upload Tutorial at http: //home.netscape.com/). When a file is uploaded to the monitored folder, Distiller converts the file (if it can be converted), to a PDF file and deposits the converted file in the Out directory. To enable users to retrieve the converted files, ensure that the Out directory is accessible via the Internet, or write a script to mail the resulting PDF back to the submittor.

Additional directories, each with different Distiller job options, allow conversion with varying job options. Users can submit a PostScript file to the directory with the appropriate job options attributes, and then wait for the converted file to appear in the Out directory.

Note: Some PostScript files, for security and font copyright purposes (see Appendix F, "Font Copyrights"), may need to be examined before conversion. Codes in PostScript files can contain destructive commands with virus-like effects. Fonts embedded in PostScript files can be extracted easily, so the distribution of fonts within PostScript files may or may not have the same attendant issues as fonts embedded in PDF files. Refer to the font licensing and copyright agreements for clarification.

8.2 Configuring Web Servers for PDF Files

To publish PDF files from a Web site, configure the Web HTTP server software to support the PDF file type. Properly configured servers, with properly configured browsers, will read the PDF file data or download the file. The server then launches an Acrobat viewing program either as a help application, as with Acrobat 2.1 and earlier, or as an in-line helper application or "plug-in", supported by Acrobat 3.0 and later.

Configuration Issue	Description
PDF Multipurpose Internet Mail Extension (MIME) Type	For Web browsers and servers to distinguish a PDF file from an ASCII text file, the server must be configured to identify the PDF MIME type. The PDF MIME type is specific to the PDF file format and is shared by FDF files.
Byte Ranges	To support progressive rendering of PDF files (page-on-demand downloads), the server software must support byte ranges. Byte ranges enable individual access to pages and data within a PDF file. Byte-range requests are much newer than the PDF MIME type registration, and some server software may not come preconfigured to support byte-range requests.
	Older server software supports byte-range requests with the aid of a very basic CGI script. Byte-range requests, initiated by Netscape Communications, is not specific to the PDF file format. Many other new file types on the Internet use byte ranges to progressively download and cache data.
Forms Data Format	To process and respond to FDF-encoded forms, applications and server scripts must be written or modified to read and respond to FDF files. See Appendix C, "The Forms Data Format," for more information about FDF files.

Table 8.2—1 Web Server Configuration Issues

8.2.1 Configuring the Server with the PDF MIME Type

The PDF MIME type was registered with the Internet in September, 1994. Most of today's Web server software is preconfigured to recognize the PDF MIME type. In addition to the PDF MIME type, the server will need to identify PDF files by the ".PDF" extension. Some servers also may need to be configured to handle a PDF binary stream. See the Adobe Acrobat Web site at http://www.adobe.com/acrobat/ to learn how to configure the

MIME type of older versions of NCSA HTTPD, CERN HTTPD, and MacHTTP Web server software.

Servers that don't recognize the PDF MIME type may corrupt PDF data. Others may handle the PDF files as text files. This will result in the PDF file writing to the browser window, rather than progressively or wholly downloading.

Note: PDF files read into a Web browser's document window as text still can be salvaged as long as the PDF file is not secured with a password. After the entire PDF file has been read into the browser's window, choose File > Save As... from the browser's menu. If the browser being used has the option to save the file as a source file do so. Make sure that the filename is preserved. Save As... saves the text from the browser's window as a file locally on a hard drive or network node. Open the PDF file with an Acrobat viewer. The Acrobat viewer may display a message that it is repairing the PDF file. The file should then open and function normally. If the Acrobat viewer displays a message that that PDF file cannot be repaired, it has been corrupted during the download. Try another means of downloading the PDF file (FTP, saving the link, etc.). If the file is protected with a password, the PDF file will begin to open, but any entered password—even the correct password—will not open the file. When this happens, there is no way to open the PDF file. Again, employ another method of downloading the file.

8.2.2 Serving PDF Pages on Demand

Servers that are configured for byte-range requests are able to download requested pages of a file, rather than the entire file. The process begins on the client side when an Acrobat 3.0 viewer, in cooperation with a Web browser that supports the HTTP extension, requests a range of bytes (perhaps page three of a five-page PDF file). Next, the Web server, which is configured to serve requested byte ranges, sends only the bytes needed to display the page. This is called "page-on-demand," or "page-at-a-time" downloading. Presently, Acrobat 3.0 viewers make whole-page byte requests, although they could be used to request specific objects on a page.

As the page bytes are read by the Acrobat viewer, the viewer caches and renders each page. Because the PDF file has been optimized, the first bytes of the page downloaded—after essential file information such as page dimension, orientation, page view, and security options—are for text and graphics, followed by interactive and navigational objects, images, and finally font data. This action is called "progressive rendering," as each part of the page is displayed as it is downloaded.

Note: The PDF file being served must be optimized, otherwise the whole file will be downloaded before it can be viewed.

Byte-range service is either built into the Web server software or retrofitted to other server software with the addition of a byte-service CGI script. The script, written in Perl, is available for DOS and UNIX-based servers. The CGI script is included with Acrobat 3.0; it also may be downloaded from the Adobe Web site at http://www.adobe.com/.

Note: WebSTAR, a MacOS Web server, plans to support byte-range requests by integrating the functionality into the server software through a plug-in rather than supporting the byteserver CGI script.

The server sees the byte ranges requested in the HTTP_REQUEST_RANGE environment variable. The syntax for these requests appears as “Range: bytes=0-100”. The returned bytes from the server are a multi-part MIME response with the 206 status code. This status code indicates that partial content is being returned by the server.

Generally, the service of PDF files via scripts is less secure than requesting file transfers via FTP. The CGI byteserver script, as of this writing, doesn't support the server security restrictions (such as password or IP access limitations). If the script can open the PDF file, it will return the requested file bytes.

Note: For more information about byte-range requests, see the Internet draft that detail byte-range requests with HTTP URLs proposed by Ari Luotonen of Netscape Communications Corporation and John Franks, Department of Mathematics at Northwestern University. (The document can be found at ftp://ds.internic.net/internet-drafts/draft-ietf-http-range-retrieval-00.txt.)

8.2.3 Installing the Byteserver Script

Install the byteserver CGI script where other CGI scripts are installed on the server. Most UNIX and DOS-based servers store CGI scripts in the cgi-bin directory. When installed, the script expects to see which file and which bytes are being requested in the PATH_TRANSLATED environment variable.

Note: Check the Adobe Acrobat Web site at http://www.adobe.com/acrobat/ for the most recent version of the byteserver script and installation instructions for serving PDF files with byte-range requests.

Note: Other servers support byte-range requests through plug-ins or other application-programming interface scripts and applications. Check the server's information about configuring server software for serving byte-range requests.

8.3 Configuring FTP and Gopher Sites for PDF Files

FTP and Gopher sites can serve PDF files. These types of Internet servers typically cannot process CGI scripts and therefore cannot be used to serve byte ranges. As a result, a Web server that allows progressive rendering and page-on-demand downloads is the best choice for publishing PDF files on the Internet.

PDF files—even if encoded as ASCII—should be downloaded (and uploaded to the server) as binary files.

Note: The PDF files served via Gopher or FTP servers will need to be downloaded completely before they can be viewed with an Acrobat viewer. These servers typically don't support byte-range requests, which facilitate progressive rendering and page-on-demand downloads.

8.3.1 Configuring a Gopher Server to Support PDF Files

Most Gopher servers come preconfigured with support for the PDF MIME type. These Acrobat 3.0-compatible servers include a custom icon for PDF files, so users can quickly identify PDF files by the Acrobat icon and better manage files on the server.

For Gopher servers that are not configured for serving PDF files, edit the descriptor code on the Gopher server. Add a "P" to the descriptor list to add support for PDF files. See the Gopher server documentation for full details about adding descriptor codes.

8.3.2 Configuring a FTP Server to Support PDF Files

Most FTP servers come preconfigured to support PDF files as binary encoded files. To add support for PDF file transfers in binary format, change the file type to binary and change Creator to PDF (or PDF%20 for the extra space).

8.4 Emailing PDF Files

Send PDF files as email attachments by uuencoding the PDF file. Uuencoding converts the PDF file into a transport-independent form that can be converted back to a PDF file after the file is received and decoded. Some mail transmission systems may not preserve certain 7-bit characters in ASCII-encoded PDF files and may change line endings as well. This can cause damage to PDF files.

Note: Another possible method of distributing PDF files, in addition to serving PDF files on the Internet, is to use email to send PDF files (or URLs where the PDF can be viewed) to subscribers. Be certain that the subscribers can receive attached files. Also consider the size limits many email gateways impose on attached files. Rather than sending the whole document, send only the table of contents, which includes links to the full document.

8.5 Serving PDF Files as Home Pages

A PDF file can be served as a home page by modifying the server's directory index to include the default PDF filename and the PDF-filename suffix (.PDF). However, unlike HTML, not all Web browsers support Acrobat viewers as in-line helper applications. In-line helper applications enable PDF files to be viewed directly in the Web browser window though a plug-in (such as Netscape Navigator), or with application communication (such as Microsoft's ActiveX). As a result, fewer users will be able to access pages served exclusively as PDF files.

There are a number of alternatives to integrating HTML and PDF files to maximize the content experience. Table 8.5—1, "Options for Home Page PDF and HTML Integration," outlines some options for integrating PDF and HTML home pages. Integration of HTML and PDF files helps the Internet publisher avoid alienating those without the capability to view PDF files either with an Acrobat 3.0-compatible Web browser, or as a downloaded file viewed in an Acrobat helper application.

8.6 Supporting PDF Files with HTML Markup

HTML files can open a PDF file (and vice versa), or have a PDF file embedded within them. Opening to a PDF file (or any other format the Web browser cannot read directly) passes control to an in-line helper application, or begins the download of the target PDF file. An Acrobat viewer-helper application (commonly an Acrobat Reader) is launched to view the file. In-line helper applications, like Acrobat 3.0 viewers, open the PDF file in the Web browser's document window.

Configuration	Acrobat 3.0-Compatible	Non Acrobat 3.0-Compatible
Embed a PDF file in HTML[1]	Displays the HTML document with the embedded PDF file.	Displays the HTML document. Area defined for the PDF file is blank. Web browser may issue a warning that the embedded item cannot be viewed.
Two versions of the home page. Initial page has links to PDF files or to the HTML version of the site (similar to the enhanced or text-only constructions).[2]	Follows the HTML link to view the home page (and parts of the Web site) as a PDF file.	Follows the HTML link to view the home page (and parts of the Web site), as an HTML file.
Uses a CGI script or Java applet to determine the Web browser's capabilities based on the environment (server-side included) and opens an appropriate file (PDF or HTML).	The script or applet senses that the Web browser can view PDF files in-line. A PDF home page is opened.	The script or applet senses that the Web browser cannot view PDF files in-line. The HTML home page is opened.

Table 8.5—1 Options for Home Page PDF and HTML Integration

[1] See Section 8.6.2, "Embedding PDF Files into HTML."

[2] Rather than designing the home page as an HTML document, and then converting it to a PDF file, design the home page with Acrobat, export the text as Rich Text Format (RTF), and mark up the text with HTML tags. Copy any graphics from the PDF version by using the Select Graphics option. Or use a creator application capable of generating both PDF and HTML documents from the same source file.

Opening PDF files to HTML files via a URL is detailed in Section 7.1.11, "World Wide Web Link Action." Opening HTML to PDF files is described in Section 8.6.1, "Linking from HTML to PDF Files."

PDF files may be embedded within HTML documents, much like GIFs or JPEGs are embedded in HTML documents. The in-line Acrobat helper application is required to view the embedded

PDF file. A warning is issued if the Web browser cannot render the PDF file within the HTML document.

Note: The limit on the number of total open PDF files for Acrobat-viewer applications applies here. Each embedded PDF file (used as an image) counts as an open file. A few PDF-source images will work fine, but 20 or 30 images may result in unloaded images or memory errors.

8.6.1 Linking from HTML to PDF Files

The syntax for linking from an HTML file to a PDF file is the same as linking from HTML to HTML (e.g., <a href="file-name.pdf"></a>). No height or width dimensions need be defined. Links to PDF files should be identified. See Section 8.8, "Web Site Design Issues and Etiquette for Publishing Content," for information on ways to best identify links to PDF files.

8.6.2 Embedding PDF Files into HTML

Single pages of PDF files may be embedded in HTML files as in-line graphics, much like GIF and JPEG images are used in HTML files. However, an embedded PDF file opens only to the first page (even if an open preference has been set to open the file at another page of a multi-page file). Links, notes, bookmarks, page modes (e.g., display thumbnails and bookmarks, etc.), other views, and interactive or navigational objects are not supported. Also, the Acrobat viewer toolbar is not displayed when an embedded PDF file is opened, nor are the toolbar's navigational and interactive features (or keyboard shortcuts). For all intents and

Source	Width and Height	Alignment
URL of source file[1]	By percent or pixel size	Left, Right, or Center
<Img Src="Example.pdf">	Height=100%, Width=350	Align=center

Table 8.6—1 In-line PDF File Syntax

[1] The Web browser loads the appropriate in-line helper application, based on the MIME type of the source file.

purposes, the PDF file is used as an image alternative to GIF, JPEG, and other common image formats.

Unlike viewing a PDF file with an Acrobat viewer, when the Web browser window is resized, the embedded PDF is resized along with the window (to remain at a defined width and height). An embedded PDF file is viewed according to required width-and-height dimensions that are set within the image source tag.

Embedded PDF files do not function like HTML links. Clicking an embedded PDF page opens the page in the Acrobat viewer. In the Acrobat viewer, the PDF page functions normally and the Acrobat viewer toolbar appears.

Note: Web browsers that support both frames and in-line viewing of PDF files can display a PDF file in one frame, and an HTML file—or other readable file formats—in another frame. Using frames to display a PDF file is a much more efficient way of integrating HTML with PDF, while getting the benefit of the interactive and navigational features found in PDF files.

8.7 Uploading PDF Files

PDF files are highly transportable across all types of media. After a Web server has been configured properly to serve PDF files either on the Web or by other Internet protocol servers (e.g., FTP or Gopher), the files are uploaded. Ensure that when the files are uploaded, the name and case sensitivity of the PDF files remain consistent. See Section 5.2.5, "Naming the PDF File," for more information on PDF file names.

8.7.1 PDF File Encoding and Compression Cautions

Do not Binhex, uuencode, .z, tar, or compress PDF files. Compressing (e.g., .zip, .sit, .z, etc.), or encoding (e.g., binhex, uuencode) a PDF file requires that it be decoded or uncompressed before it can be read. PDF files are compressed and decompressed by the Acrobat viewer. Applying additional compression to the file when uploaded often results in slightly larger archives than uncompressed PDF files.

8.7.2 PDF File Upload Formats

Move files to a Web, FTP, or Gopher server on the Internet by uploading the files as binary encoded files via a file transfer protocol (FTP is most common). An ASCII transfer may result in the corruption of binary encoded security elements.

Note: Some Internet service providers may allow uploading of PDF files and other large file formats from removable storage drives.

8.8 Web Site Design Issues and Etiquette for Publishing Content

Viewing PDF files in a Web browser requires correctly installed and configured software. Misconfigured Web browsers or Acrobat software may result in warnings or error messages that confuse or anger users. Additionally, as the Portable Document Format evolves, users must upgrade their Acrobat viewers to remain current with what the files have to offer. The recommended design and etiquette solutions help make users more receptive to the presentation of the information and make better use of the published content on a Web site.

8.8.1 Acrobat Viewer Sources

Where appropriate, provide links to locations where users can download PDF viewers. Adobe allows free distribution of the Acrobat Reader on removable media and the Internet. Web sites that distribute Acrobat viewers, rather than linking to Adobe distribution sites, should distribute the most current viewers. The Adobe Web site has Get Acrobat Now buttons for use on Web pages. These buttons link back to Adobe's central Acrobat 3.0 Reader distribution site.

Either link directly to Adobe's FTP site at ftp://ftp.adobe.com/ and open the Acrobat directory; or link to the Acrobat product page on the World Wide Web at http://www.adobe.com/acrobat/.

Adobe makes available graphical buttons for use on Web sites that serve PDF files. Check the Acrobat product page for the most up-to-date graphics.

Additionally, provide links to download locations for Acrobat 3.0-compatible Web browsers wherever appropriate.

8.8.2 File Size

A general rule of Internet etiquette is to use as little bandwidth as possible when communicating. Limit the bandwidth required to download PDF files by making them as small as possible during design and creation.

As a courtesy to all users—especially those with unreliable or low-bandwidth connections—indicate the approximate per-page file size (for page-on-demand downloading), and the number of pages in the PDF file. FTP and Gopher servers should indicate the total number of pages in the PDF file. (Most server software displays the PDF file size in the Gopher or FTP index.)

Note: Listing the number of pages is crucial. Users may not be inclined to download a 550-kilobyte file, but may be inclined to download a 85-page, 500-kilobyte file.

8.8.3 Assigning Icons to PDF Files

For Web sites, use an Acrobat PDF-file icon to indicate that the object's action opens a PDF file. Adobe has a number of PDF file icons in various sizes that are freely available for use in HTML documents. The icons can be found on the Adobe Acrobat Web site at http://www.adobe.com/acrobat/. Whenever possible, use the PDF file icon in Gopher or FTP directory indices.

Note: Enter "PDF File" in the PDF file icon image source tag (e.g., alt="PDF File"), as some users may not choose to load graphics, or may use software that doesn't allow in-line graphics.

8.9 Processing PDF Forms Data

Acrobat 3.0 introduces the capability to submit form data to a Web server. This form data can be either in the Forms Document Format (FDF), or URL-encoded form data (the format used by most HTML forms).

The processing of incoming form-value data can be accomplished with any server Common Gateway Interface (CGI) script or Java applet. The form values submitted by a PDF form are identical to the form data submitted by HTML forms. As a result, a single CGI script or Java applet can be written to process form data from both HTML and PDF forms. However, in instances when a response is sent back to the PDF form, the script must be capable of responding with a FDF file.

8.9.1 Processing FDF files

FDF files have two basic functions: 1) to represent a form's data for processing via the submit or export actions (see Section 7.1.10, "Submit Form Action"); and 2) to update or modify the data in an existing form. Through the Submit Form Data action, these two actions can be combined. The completed form is sent to a script or application by the user. The server processes the FDF data. To enable the Acrobat viewer to recognize the responses from the script or application, the URL must end in "#FDF."

The response also must be FDF data. The PDF form is updated or modified based on the new form data response, if any. The response can include basic form data or information to alter the form field, such as the form's name, value, options, appearance, form action, and action.

8.9.2 Populating PDF Forms with FDF files

Populating PDF forms with a FDF file requires the transmission of the file to the user. Rather than sending the entire PDF file or page, send only the FDF file. (When sending HTML forms, both the HTML and the HTML form's values and properties must be sent.) When received, the FDF file populates the form by setting the form field values according to the FDF file.

FDF files can populate a PDF form by the import FDF file action (see Section 7.1.3, "Import Form Data Action"). Additionally, with the assistance of a server CGI script or application, forms can be populated as a response to query from a form query.

8.9.3 Creating Scripts and Applications That Generate FDF Data

Scripts that process and create FDF data can be written like the scripts that process URL-encoded HTML data. Popular scripting and application programming languages (e.g., Perl, Java, C, etc.), can be used with FDF files. Script and applications that presently process HTML data can be modified easily to process and to respond with FDF data. For detailed information on the FDF file structure, see the most recent release of the PDF language spec. Also, check Adobe's Web site's developer area for information and sample data.

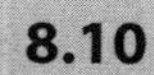

8.10 Search-Enabling PDF Files

Searching multiple PDF files or collections of PDF files on an Internet server is supported by third-party, search-engine solutions. A number of Internet servers and Internet search engines have announced or released products that index PDF files. The capabilities of these products vary. See Appendix B, "Internet Searching and Indexing Software," for more information.

All PDF search engines presently support full-text searches, which include Boolean, free text, and keyword queries. Others may support filtered categories, thesaurus matching, and word stems.

Feature	Description
PDF file thumbnail display.	Files found as a result of a query are displayed with title and thumbnail.
Automatic conversion of files to PDF.	Creator application files that are added to a directory to be indexed are converted to PDF files. Originals are maintained.)
Select text queries.	Text selected in a PDF file can be used as the text in a query.
Highlighted results.	Found terms are highlighted in the open PDF file.

Table 8.10—1 PDF-Specific Search Engine Features[1]

1 Searching Adobe Catalog-created .PDX files with the Search Plug-in (Exchange only) is best suited for LAN, WAN, and CD-ROM search solutions.

8.11 PDF File and Server Security

The built-in security features of PDF files reinforce the server's capability to protect documents (see Section 7.11, "PDF Security Options"). In addition to limiting access, a PDF file's limited actions security features prevent users from taking certain actions with a PDF file (see Section 7.11.2, "Conditional Security Options"). Server security commonly limits access by username and passphrase (or password), or by the user IP address, or both.

8.11.1 Server Security Options for Protecting PDF Files

Server security options can be engaged to prevent unauthorized users from accessing specified directories on a server. These security options are detailed in the server's documentation. The most common way to limit user access is by Internet Protocol (IP) addresses. Here access to a directory or site is denied, except to a few IP addresses (and the users connecting from those addresses). For most servers, this is accomplished by placing a configured .htaccess file in the secured directory. Another option is to require users who are connecting to the server to enter a predefined username and password (or passphrase). Only by entering the correct username and password combination is access allowed to the site or directory.

8.11.2 Securing Individual PDF Files on a Server

Upon gaining authorized access to a directory of PDF files, the PDF files in the directory can be configured to require a password or passphrase for access to the file. The files also can be configured to limit the actions a user can take with the file by setting the file's conditional security options.

The two-tiered security options provided by the server and individual PDF files allow a custom approach to security that is not possible with other file types. This approach provides protection for entire sites and directories, or the option to leave a site open—with little or no server security beyond the basics, and limited access to specified files.

8.12 Serving Multimedia Files

External data files, such as movie files and Forms Data Format files require no special configuration or optimization. In addition, these files can be linked to and from other non-byte served sites to lessen the load on other servers.

Note: Ensure that the action that opens the media file or FDF file from the PDF file is correct. Incorrectly opened movie files will display an error; an incorrectly opened FDF file may populate a form with the wrong data, no data at all, or display an error.

8.13 Dynamic PDF

PDF files can be generated on-the-fly, or initiated by interactive input from a user. Typically, forms allow the greatest flexibility when selecting options for dynamic output. However, other variables also can be used (e.g., a Web browser's environment, the time of day, a magic cookie, etc.).

8.13.1 Dynamically Merging a PDF Template with User Data

There is presently only one solution for generating dynamic PDF documents, which is to merge selected or inputted information with a template. The capability to generate a document based entirely on user input is some time off in the future. The ability to custom build a newsletter, a press release detailing specific issues in depth, or to generate a document that contains graphics selected from a catalog with an accompanying caption in a selected language may be more practical than a more free-form document. The level of customizable features seems to be reset with the number of input options available to the user.

The resources needed to create a dynamic PDF page—the PDF language specifications, Acrobat Exchange, and a C programming language compiler—are publicly available. Generating PDF files on-the-fly requires only some programming ability.

Note: See the dynamic PDF page example at http://www.best.com/~dglazer/adobe/ to see how PDF, HTML forms, and the C compiler can be used to generate dynamic PDF files based on user input.

8.13.2 Creating PDF "On-the-Fly"

Another solution for dynamic PDF generation—although not specifically Web-based—is to programmatically load .RTF or .MIF files into an appropriate application (e.g., Microsoft Word or Adobe FrameMaker), and convert to PDF using Acrobat Distiller.

9

Troubleshooting

This chapter has been arranged to follow the logical progression in using Acrobat software, from installing the software to viewing PDF on the Internet. This chapter contains listings of only the most common problems and their solutions. Many of the answers to these commonly asked problems/questions come from the Adobe technical support archives.

The tables outline the problem and offer the most common solution. Additional information, even step-by-step assistance for configuring the software, can be found in the full technical sheet. These technical sheets are available via fax or the Internet. For a list of technical support URLs or fax numbers, see Section 10.2.1, "Application and Technical Notes" and Section 10.3, "PDF-Related World Wide Web Sites."

Problems specific to Web server software, system software, and hardware, Post-Script printer drivers, creator application software, and hardware (scanners, CD-ROM writers, etc.) are not within the scope of this book. Check the software documentation, the software or hardware company, or contact Adobe Acrobat support for Acrobat-related assistance.

Note: As new software, hardware, and operating systems are introduced, it is likely that more problems and questions will arise. Adobe provides numerous channels for technical questions and troubleshooting. Also, use the many Acrobat-related newsgroups and listservs, which have a large number of very knowledgeable subscribers who may be willing to answer questions, troubleshoot a problem, or offer other assistance.

9.1 Troubleshooting Acrobat Software Installation and Launching

After installing or launching Acrobat software, some Acrobat features may not function or may fail. Table 9.1—1 lists some of the most common installation problems and feature failures. Also refer to the installation guide (residing with the Acrobat software installers) for detailed information and possible remedies.

Problem	Platform	Solution
Acrobat Reader doesn't load the Search Plug-in.	All	Acrobat Reader 2.1 and earlier versions do not support the Search Plug-in. Only a specially licensed version of Reader 2.1—Acrobat Search for CD-ROM—includes a Reader that can use the Search Plug-in.
Third-party plug-ins purchased to make changes in the PDF document do not load in Acrobat Reader.	All	Only Reader-enabled plug-ins (Weblink, Movie, and others) can be used with the Reader. Plug-ins that modify PDF files cannot be used with the Reader. The Reader cannot write to a PDF file, only read from it.
The installation of Adobe Acrobat appears to be successful, but no Acrobat program group or icons appear in Program Manager.	Windows	Disable any installed desktop managers (e.g., PC TOOLS, or Norton Desktop), reboot the computer, and reinstall Acrobat; or, create program icons manually; or use the File Manager to launch the Acrobat application's .EXE file. More information is available from the Adobe FaxYI #7416.
During startup, Acrobat Distiller for Windows 2.0 or earlier, displays the Starting Distiller status window, and then quits unexpectedly.	Windows	When Acrobat is installed on a 386 computer, ensure that the WEMU387.386 file (2/17/93; 28975 bytes), is installed in the WINDOWS directory and that the line "device=WEMU387.386" is present in the [386Enh] section of the SYSTEM.INI file. More information is available from the Adobe FaxYI#7443.
The error "Not enough free disk space to continue installation" appears while installing Acrobat Reader.	Windows	Do one or more of the following: 1) Make sure that there is a minimum of 4 to 8M free disk space available on the hard drive; 2) Ensure that the "Set temp=" line in the AUTOEXEC.BAT is valid; and 3) Ensure that there is write-access to the drive where the TEMP directory is located. More information is available from the Adobe FaxYI #7425.
The error "Cannot load the license agreement" appears while installing Acrobat Reader 2.1.	Windows	Do one or more of the following: 1) Make sure that there is a minimum of 4 to 8M free disk space available on the hard drive; 2) Ensure that the "Set temp=" line in the AUTOEXEC.BAT is valid; and 3) Ensure that there is write-access to the drive where the TEMP directory is located. More information is available from the Adobe FaxYI #7426.
The error "Cannot load the language library" appears while installing Reader 2.1.	Windows	Do one or more of the following: 1) Make sure that there is a minimum of 4 to 8M free disk space available on the hard drive; 2) Ensure that the "Set temp=" line in the AUTOEXEC.BAT is valid; and 3) Ensure that there is write-access to the drive where the TEMP directory is located. More information is available from the Adobe FaxYI #7427.
OS/2 version 3.0 (Warp) or Reader 2.1 displays the error "ATM cannot be found" when launching an Acrobat viewer.	OS/2	When using Acrobat on OS/2, ATM must be installed and running in enhanced mode. More information is available from the Adobe FaxYI #7481.

Table 9.1—1 Troubleshooting Acrobat Installation and Launching

9.2 Creator Application-Specific Troubleshooting

After converting a PostScript file to a PDF file, the resulting PDF file may not match the original document. It is also possible that some of the navigational and interactive objects may not appear. Additionally, when configuring a creator-application file to be converted to a PDF file, certain features that automate or aid the process may fail. Table 9.2–1 lists the most common creator application-related issues.

Problem	Platform	Solution
When opening a PDF file in Illustrator 5.5 (with the PDF Filter), text strings are disjointed or mispositioned.	All	Use a Level 2 PostScript-savvy printer driver and save the PostScript file as a Level 2 PostScript file. Level 2 PostScript drivers and PostScript-savvy applications that use Level 2 PostScript will reduce the disjunction of text to a minimal level.[1]
When saving a PDF file from Adobe PageMaker 6.0 to the root directory or main window (PC) or the hard drive folder (Macintosh) of another volume, the PDF file is located on the root directory of the volume where the PageMaker 6.0 publication is located, rather than the volume specified.	Macintosh and Windows	Save the PDF file in a folder (Macintosh) or directory (Windows) on the volume instead of the root directory; or, after saving the PDF file from PageMaker 6.0, copy the PDF file to the desired volume. More information is available from the Adobe FaxYI #116103.

continued

Table 9.2—1 Troubleshooting for Adobe Illustrator, Adobe PageMaker, and Microsoft Word

Problem	Platform	Solution
When creating a PDF file of publications in a book while Thumbnails is enabled and the "First page only" option is selected, Adobe PageMaker 6.0 creates a thumbnail for the first page of each publication in the book, instead of only the first page of the first publication.	Macintosh and Windows	Disable Thumbnails when creating a PDF file of a book publication. Alternatively, leave the First Page Only option selected in the Thumbnails pop-up menu in the Distiller PDF Job Options dialog box to enable the Create Adobe PDF Plug-in to create a thumbnail for the first page of each book publication. More information is available from the Adobe FaxYI #116104.
The page numbers listed in a table of contents of a PDF file created from PageMaker 6.0 are inaccurate. When clicking on a table of contents entry in a PDF file created from PageMaker 6.0, the Acrobat viewer jumps to an unexpected page.	Macintosh and Windows	The PageMaker 6.0 publication that created the PDF files contains blank pages. Select the Print Blank Pages option in the document Print dialog box for the printer style that is being used to create the PDF file, and then recreate the PDF by using the updated printer style. More information is available from the Adobe FaxYI #116310.
When a Microsoft Word 6.0 document that contains both portrait and landscape oriented pages is converted to a PDF file with Acrobat PDF Writer or Distiller, pages that were landscape oriented in the Word document become portrait oriented; or text is truncated on the right side of the page; or both occur in the resulting PDF.	Macintosh and Windows	Ensure that all pages in the Microsoft Word 6.0 file are the same orientation before creating a PDF file with either PDF Writer or when printing to disk as a PostScript file for use with Distiller. More information is available from the Adobe FaxYI #4491.

Table 9.2—1 (continued) Troubleshooting for Adobe Illustrator, Adobe PageMaker, and Microsoft Word

[1] Thanks to Gary Cosmini, Adobe Systems, Inc.

9.3 Troubleshooting the Conversion of PostScript Files with Acrobat Distiller

Converting PostScript files to PDF files is usually quick and simple. However, certain creator applications, printer drivers, fonts, and other operating system-related options may interfere with the conversion. Table 9.3–1 lists the most common error messages generated by Acrobat Distiller and some possible workarounds.

Problem	Platform	Solution
PostScript files don't distill correctly, resulting in discrepancies between the original document and the distilled document, or failure to distill at all.	All	Acrobat Distiller functions like a printer driver. Check to see if the document will print correctly. Documents that do not print correctly will not distill correctly. More information is available from the Adobe FaxYI #4403.
Distiller gives a LIMITCHECK or VMERRORS error.	All	LIMITCHECK or VMERRORS errors usually are caused by insufficient RAM. By default, Distiller is set up to use 6144K of RAM. Long documents or graphic-intensive documents may require more memory to process. Increase the amount of RAM allocated to Distiller. More information is available from the Adobe FaxYI #4403. LIMITCHECK errors from FrameMaker files with extensive cross-references are common. Acrobat Distiller 2.1 has a limit of 4000 named-destination links it can process. Convert the file in parts to reduce the total number of links processed at one time.
Distiller gives a LIMITCHECK error when using RUNFILE to combine multiple PostScript files into a single PDF file.	All	Multiple PostScript files can be distilled into one PDF file by using the RunFile procedure. One drawback to this is that all of the PostScript files included are loaded into Distiller's RAM partition and can cause a LIMITCHECK error. You can force Distiller to flush its RAM after processing each PostScript file by using the procedure in FaxYI #4403 rather than the RunFile procedure. More information is available from the Adobe FaxYI #4403.

continued

Table 9.3—1 Troubleshooting PostScript to PDF File Conversion

Problem	Platform	Solution
After inserting a page in Exchange or merging PostScript files together, by using the RUNFILE command, some of the document's characters display incorrectly.	Windows	The problem is that one document has one font character subset, while the merged document has another character subset. When merging PDF files that contain different character subsets of a font with duplicate names in Exchange, only one character subset can be used. Characters in the combined PDF file that are not included in the character subset display incorrectly. More information is available from the Adobe FaxYI #4410.
Distiller gives a %%[Error: configuration error; Offending Command: setpageparams]%% error when distilling a PostScript file.	All	Reduce the size of the page to be distilled. Distiller and Exchange support a maximum page size of 45 by 45 inches. More information is available from the Adobe FaxYI #4437.
Consistent, reproducible untraceable error when distilling a PostScript file.	All	Add debugging statements to the PostScript code to help isolate the cause of the error. When each page or EPS graphic in the PostScript file is preceded by a debugging statement, the Distiller's Message window indicates whether that element was processed successfully or resulted in a PostScript error. More information is available from the Adobe FaxYI #4439.
The following error appears in Distiller when you attempt to distill a PostScript file that contains text. "%%[Error: invalidfont; Offending Command: findfont]%% Stack: /Font /[fontname]"	All	Make sure that the folder or directory in which the base-14 Type-1 fonts are installed is listed in Distiller's Font Locations dialog box. More information is available from the Adobe FaxYI #4442.

Table 9.3—1 (continued) Troubleshooting PostScript to PDF File Conversion

9.4 Troubleshooting Web Server Errors

A number of non-Acrobat or PDF-file related errors may result when viewing or downloading PDF files. Most errors result from a malformed or incorrectly entered World Wide Web Link action URL embedded in a PDF or HTML file.

9.4.1 Server Errors

Server errors originate for a number of reasons. Hypertext Transfer Protocol, version 1.0, defines four server responses. These responses provide feedback to users as to why a requested action was not completed. HTTP 1.0 defines these responses numerically as a 5xx status code.

Status Code	Description
500 Internal Server Error	Something unexpected occurred on the server preventing it from fulfilling the request.
501 Not Implemented	The server could not fulfill the request. It doesn't support the requested function. In this case, the server doesn't recognize the request method and cannot support it.
502 Bad Gateway	The server has received an invalid response from the gateway.
503 Service Unavailable	Either the server is too busy to handle the request or maintenance has required that it be shut down for the moment. Generally, this is temporary. Note that other servers may refuse the connection and a 503 may not be used.

Table 9.4—1 5xx Status Code Server Errors

9.4.2 Client Errors

Client errors come from mistakes that seem to be made by the browser. Generally, these errors include malformed URLs and links to documents that don't exist. These errors are listed by HTTP 1.0 as 4xx status codes. These errors may be temporary.

Status Code	Description
400 Bad Request	The request could not be completed because the server cannot understand the syntax of the request.
401 Unauthorized	The request requires that the user have authorized access to the server.
403 Forbidden	The server understands the request, but won't perform the request.
404 Not Found	The server cannot find anything that matches the requested URL.

Table 9.4—2 4xx Status Code Client Errors

Possible causes of error "404 Not Found"

A 404 status message results when the target document the link points to doesn't exist. The target document has been moved, deleted, or renamed. Defuse the 404 error by checking the syntax of the link. With URL links in HTML, check the formation of the URL. Most links to other Web resources are formed with the transport protocol followed by the path.

Error 404 messages from URLs embedded in PDF files can be corrected the same way. Include the full URL, or suffix of the base URL. If the file was tested locally first, make sure that the paths from directory name to directory name remain consistent. Check the URL to ensure that it uses the correct form.

Note: Most Web servers are case sensitive, so check the capitalization of the directory name and file names. Also check spelling and the file names themselves. Some servers may truncate the file name to conform to the 8.3 file naming convention used by DOS and other operating systems.

9.5 Troubleshooting Browser Applications

Older versions of the listed Web browsers need to be configured to best handle PDF files. For optimal PDF viewing on the Internet, refer to Adobe's Acrobat site at http://www.adobe.com/ acrobat/ for the most recent recommended Web browser/Acrobat viewer version combination.

Problem	Platform	Solution
When selecting a PDF file link on an Internet server, NCSA Mosaic 2.0 displays a prompt to download the PDF file, rather than launching Reader or Exchange to display the PDF file.	Macintosh	Configure Mosaic to use Reader or Exchange as a helper application. More information is available from the Adobe FaxYI #4456.
When selecting a PDF file link on an Internet server, Netscape 1.1N displays a prompt to download the PDF file, rather than launching Reader 2.1 or earlier or Acrobat Exchange 2.1 or earlier to display the PDF file.	All	Configure Netscape to use Reader or Exchange as a helper application. More information is available from the Adobe FaxYI #7423.

Table 9.5—1 Troubleshooting NCSA Mosaic 2.0 and Netscape Navigator 1.1N

9.6 Troubleshooting the Display and Printing of PDF Documents with an Acrobat Viewer

Compatibility issues between Acrobat software and certain hardware or software combinations can cause certain PDF functions to fail or function abnormally. Refer to the Table 9.6–1, the Acrobat user guide, and the Adobe Acrobat Web site for detailed descriptions of noted compatibility issues and workarounds.

Problem	Platform	Solution
Documents with Helvetica or Times created on a Macintosh display and print differently on other machines, but look fine on the machine that created the file.	Macintosh	The machine that created the document uses Apple versions of Helvetica or Times, which contain different character-kerning information (information about the spacing between characters) than the Adobe versions of Helvetica or Times installed with the Acrobat viewers. More information is available from the Adobe FaxYI #4401.
The Adobe Acrobat software is installed and can open and view PDF documents, but cannot print.	All	A number of problems can cause your printer not to print: 1) The printer is not switched on; 2) The printer is not connected to your computer correctly; 3) The printer is broken; and 4) The printer is not selected with the Chooser (Macintosh). More information is available from the Adobe FaxYI #4400.
Acrobat documents will not print on a Personal LaserWriter NT printer.	Macintosh	Upgrade your printer to a Personal LaserWriter NT. The version of the PostScript language interpreter installed in the Personal LaserWriter NT cannot print the Multiple Master fonts used by Exchange and Reader to substitute for fonts not installed on a system. Contact an Apple dealer for Personal LaserWriter upgrade information. More information is available from the Adobe FaxYI #4400.
The printer stops printing before an entire document has printed. This problem happens when you try to print a page that requires more printer memory than is installed in your printer.	Macintosh	Either purchase more memory for your printer, or reduce the amount of printer memory required to print the document. The best solution is to purchase more printer memory. Have at least four megabytes of printer memory to print Acrobat documents. More information is available from the Adobe FaxYI #4400.

continued

Table 9.6—1 Hardware Compatibility Issues and Workarounds

Problem	Platform	Solution
Graphics (i.e., Quark-generated or imported graphics) in QuarkXPress documents converted to PDF, display and print as boxes with Xs through them when distilled by using Acrobat Distiller.	Macintosh	Make sure that Normal, not Rough, is selected as the Output option in Quark's Print dialog box when creating the *.PS file to be distilled through the Acrobat Distiller. More information is available from the Adobe FaxYI #4424.
Bitmap images in PDF files created with Distiller display and print with a distortion or a quilted pattern.	All	Reduce the amount of compression Distiller performs on the bitmap images. More information is available from the Adobe FaxYI #4415.
Patterns, fills, and lines become solid tints when converted to PDF format in Adobe Acrobat; PDF document using fills and lines when distilled results in very large file sizes; PDF documents using fills and lines renders slowly.	All	Use solid fills instead of pattern fills and dashed lines instead of pattern lines in documents to be converted to PDF format. Or, when creating a PDF file from a document created in an application that supports custom PostScript patterns (e.g., Macromedia FreeHand), use PostScript fills and lines. More information is available from the Adobe FaxYI #4417.
Bitmap images created with custom halftone functions (e.g., Adobe Photoshop images saved with customized dot shapes), display and print differently in Acrobat than from the application that created the file.	All	Resave the image with standard halftone functions. More information is available from the Adobe FaxYI #4432.
When attempting to display QuarkXPress 3.x PDF files created from PostScript files with bitmap smoothing, Acrobat viewers run out of memory.	Macintosh	Print the PostScript file again with bitmap smoothing off. More information is available from the Adobe FaxYI #4410.
After conversion, the PDF loses all color and only displays graphics and images in grayscale.	All	Select a color PostScript Printer Description (PPD) and print the file to disk with that driver. The selected driver is for a black-and-white printer that doesn't support color, thus resulting in a PostScript file absent of color.

continued

Table 9.6—1 (continued) Hardware Compatibility Issues and Workarounds

Problem	Platform	Solution
Text copied from PDF files created using Distiller from an Interleaf Publisher 5.0 or earlier PostScript file pastes into other applications as unrecognizable characters.	All	None. Interleaf Publisher is a DOS- or UNIX-based word processor that when printed to as a PostScript file, creates non-standard PostScript. Interleaf PostScript files do not contain the ASCII information required by Acrobat Reader or Exchange 2.0 or earlier to facilitate the Copy command. This results in PDF files with text that can be highlighted, but not pasted correctly into other applications. More information is available from the Adobe FaxYI #4433.
The width of a PDF file created from a QuarkXPress 3.31 PostScript file is truncated to 8.5 inches. For example, a page 11 by 22 inches in Quark is only 8.5 by 22 inches when printed to a PostScript file and then saved as a PDF.	Macintosh and Windows	In QuarkXPress, if Paper Width is grayed out in the Printer Setup dialog box (Windows) or Page Setup dialog box (Macintosh), create a custom printer file to remove the lines that cause the Paper Width option to be grayed out in QuarkXPress. More information is available from the Adobe FaxYI #4436.
When displayed in an Acrobat viewer, Distiller has cropped-page dimensions.	All	The file has insufficient page-size information (e.g., EPS files). Increase the default page size in the EXAMPLE.PS file so that the complete document is in the PDF's page area. More information available from the Adobe FaxYI #4441.
DOS users cannot print from Acrobat Reader 1.0.	DOS	Use only supported printers, or check the printer's documentation to see if it can emulate any of the printers listed in the Adobe FaxYI #7421.
Converted LaTeX or TEX documents have missing characters in the resulting PDF file.	Windows, UNIX	Configure TeX (or LaTeX) not to subset fonts when the PostScript file is generated. More information is available from the Acrobat Distiller 2.1 ReadMe.pdf.

Table 9.6—1 (continued) Hardware Compatibility Issues and Workarounds

10

Acrobat Resources

In addition to this book, there are a number of other resources for learning more about Internet publishing with Acrobat, or Acrobat in general. As of this writing, this chapter compiles and summarizes the known Acrobat resources available by phone, via fax, in print, and on the Internet. This chapter also includes information on a number of Acrobat-related technologies including the PostScript language, fonts, Adobe software and, more.

10.1 Acrobat Print Resources

There are a number of books that focus on Acrobat issues related to software and publishing PDF files. These publications provide a different perspective of Adobe's Acrobat technology, the PDF file format and its uses than this reference.

10.1.1 *Beyond Paper*

By Patrick Ames

Beyond Paper mixes the practical with the technical. The book is organized around a typical work day to illustrate the advantages of using the PDF file format. The book covers a number of common office document types and how these documents can be used as PDF documents. Technical information is presented relative to the tasks in each section.

Beyond Paper provides information about how humans work and how they interact with the software and hardware that create PDF documents. Technical information is sparse, but effective. Most technical details cover only version 1.0 of Adobe Acrobat software.

Adobe Press
1585 Charleston Road
Mountain View, CA 94039

Distributed by:
Macmillan Computer Publishing USA
201 West 103rd Street
Indianapolis, IN 46290
Telephone: (800) 428-5331

ISBN 0-56830-050-6

10.1.2 *Portable Document Format Reference Manual*

By Tim Bienz, Richard Cohn, and Jim Meehan

This manual is the published standard for the PDF file format. Targeted to application developers who want to produce PDF files directly, or create applications that read and modify PDF files.

This book provides information to Internet publishers who want to use pdfmark operators. Those publishers interested in creating dynamic PDF documents, perhaps through the use of a CGI script, will find the handbook indispensable.

This book is out of print.

Note: More information about the most recent PDF spec can be found at the Adobe Developer's Associaton at Adobe Web site at http://www.adobe.com/.

10.1.3 *Acrobat Quick Tour*

By Barrie Sosinsky and Elisabeth Parker

The Acrobat Quick Tour covers the basics of Acrobat PDF file creation and distribution. More detailed and technical information has been purposely left out, resulting in a book best suited for beginners. The book does not contain coverage of Acrobat Capture and Catalog.

The *Quick Tour* includes a section on Internet publishing, which covers file transfer and Reader MIME-type configuration issues. It also details some of the earlier sites serving PDF on the Internet.

Ventana Press
P.O. Box 13964
Research Triangle Park, NC 27713-3964
Telephone: (919) 544-9404

ISBN 1-56604-255-0

10.1.4 *Acrobat 2.1: Your Personal Consultant*

By Roy Christmann

This book presents technical information on the entire Acrobat 2.1 family of software. Much of the book is focused on the many new features added to version 2.1 of Adobe Acrobat. The book provides enough detail for the beginner to expert user.

An informative section describes how to use Web browsers and PDF files for Internet publishing. (Publishing PDF with 2.1 software is much different than publishing those same files today.)

Ziff-Davis Press
5903 Christie Avenue
Emeryville, CA 94608

Distributed by:
Macmillan Computer Publishing USA
201 West 103rd Street
Indianapolis, IN 46290
Telephone: (800) 688-0448

ISBN 1-56276-336-9

10.1.5 *Adobe Acrobat Handbook: Digital Publishing in the Post-Gutenberg Era*

By Kenneth Grant and W. David Schwaderer

This PDF handbook serves as one of the most comprehensive of the technical books on PDF. The focus is not on how to use the PDF file format, but how to make the various PDF applications work together. Specific to the Windows and Macintosh 1.0 versions of Acrobat software, Capture and Catalog are not covered.

Most of the information in the book can now be found in the Acrobat help files or in Adobe's various FAQ sheets. However, the book provides a lot of good information about using Acrobat software in general.

Sams Publishing
201 West 103rd Street
Indianapolis, IN 46290
Telephone: (800) 428-5331

ISBN 0-672-30393-0

10.1.6 *Web Publishing with Adobe Acrobat and PDF*

By Bruce Page and Diana Holm

Web Publishing with Adobe Acrobat and PDF explains the process of creating documents to be published simultaneously on CD-ROM, the Web, and in print by using Adobe Acrobat and common desktop publishing tools.

Other areas covered are configuring Web servers and browsers to support Acrobat PDF files, securing PDF files, and publishing PDF files on CD-ROM.

John Wiley & Sons, Inc.
305 Third Avenue
New York, New York 20258
Telephone: (800) 225-5945

ISBN: 0-471-14948-9

10.1.7 *Designing Interactive Documents with Adobe Acrobat Pro*

by John Deep and Peter Holfelder

This book/CD package includes background information and a graphical tutorial to illustrate how to use Adobe Acrobat Pro to create interactive documents by combining graphics and hypertext links. Examples demonstrate how to create everything from interactive advertising to dynamic electronic books that can be browsed on the World Wide Web. The accompanying CD-ROM contains an Acrobat viewer program for Windows, Macintosh, DOS, and UNIX; it also contains a hypertext copy of the book on Acrobat, sample Acrobat documents, and an interactive graphical tutorial for using Acrobat

John Wiley & Sons, Inc.
305 Third Avenue
New York, New York 20258
Telephone: (800) 225-5945

ISBN: 0-471-12789-2

10.2 Technical Support

Adobe provides technical support for all its products. Support is available via the Web, telephone, facsimile, or BBS. See the options listed below:

- The Adobe Web page: http://www.adobe.com/supportservice/.
- The Adobe Acrobat Web page for help: http://www.adobe.com/acrobat/gethelp.html.
- The CompuServe Forum. (GO ADOBE).
- America Online. Keyword: Adobe, Adobe Online Message Board, Adobe Acrobat Topic.
- Adobe FaxYI, (206) 628-5737. Request free technical notes by fax, 24 hours a day, 7 days a week. (For users outside of the U.S. and Canada, contact your local distributor.)
- Pay for support option (U.S. only), (900) 555-2276. Each minute is $2.00 plus toll, if applicable; charges appear on your monthly telephone bill.
- Adobe Automated Technical Support, (206) 628-2757. A full-time (24 hours a day, 7 days a week), computer-driven diagnostic system with answers to the most commonly asked questions.
- Adobe Electronic BBS, (206) 623-6984. Receive detailed instructions on how to use the BBS and FaxYI service by calling (206) 628-5737.

The most up-to-date phone numbers for support can be found at http://www.adobe.com/aboutadobe/phones.html.

Users of third-party products that either support the PDF file format directly, or are used to generate a PostScript file, which is then distilled into a PDF file, should consult the software manufacturer for technical support.

A number of Internet listservs and Usenet newsgroups focus on PDF specifically, as well as many of the related software programs used to create PDF documents. Other organizations have created sites on the Internet that provide information on plug-ins, PDF translators and viewers, and documents and databases that contain frequently asked questions (or FAQs) posted by users.

10.2.1 Application and Technical Notes

To supplement the information contained here, consult the application and technical notes from Adobe at the following URLs:

- http://www.adobe.com/studio/tipstechniques/
- http://www.adobe.com/supportservice/devrelations/devtechnotes.html
- http://www.adobe.com/acrobat/gethelp.html

10.2.2 Developer Support

Adobe's Support Group produces, distributes, and supports software development kits (SDKs) for Adobe products, including Acrobat. Members of the Adobe Developers Association (ADA) can purchase the Acrobat SDK, which includes support. Developer support also conducts a developer class for Acrobat developers. For further information see http://www.adobe.com/supportservice/devrelations/.

10.3 PDF-Related World Wide Web Sites

This information listed below can be used as general pointers to other PDF-related World Wide Web sites.

10.3.1 Adobe Systems

- General information: http://www.adobe.com/
- Software and information: ftp.adobe.com
- Adobe Acrobat: http://www.adobe.com/acrobat/
- Adobe PageMaker: http://www.adobe.com/prodindex/pagemaker/
- Adobe PageMill: http://www.adobe.com/prodindex/pagemill/
- Adobe FrameMaker: http://www.adobe.com/prodindex/framemaker/
- PPD Files for PostScript Printers: ftp://ftp.adobe.com/pub/adobe/PPDfiles/

10.4 Internet Discussion Lists

Internet discussion lists allow Acrobat publishers and users to exchange ideas, troubleshoot problems, and discuss new publishing solutions. Many of these list are frequented by Adobe staff, and Acrobat experts who often provide detailed information to the Acrobat publishing and user communities. There are a number of discussion groups specific to Acrobat and Acrobat-related topics. They can be found on commercial online services such as America Online or CompuServe, or on moderated Usenet or listserv lists.

10.4.1 ListServs

The following Acrobat listservs are for the public discussion of Acrobat and Acrobat-related topics. Listservs forward messages sent to the listserver to a subscriber's email account (much like receiving a personal email message). Some listservs have digests (all the postings sent to the listserver over a specified time are compiled into a single email message). Additionally, some of the listservs have searchable archives of frequently asked question (FAQs) files and databases for a quick orientation to the listserv's topic, or for researching previously discussed topics.

pdf-l

A list for discussing Acrobat hosted by EMERGE.

To subscribe to the list, send email to Majordomo@binc.net with the following command in the body of your email message, SUBSCRIBE PDF-L.

To subscribe to the digest, send email to Majordomo@binc.net with the following command in the body of your email message, SUBSCRIBE PDF-DIGEST.

More information on the pdf-l list is available at the EMERGE Web site at http://www.emrg.com/pdfl.html.

A hypermail archive of the pdf-l list can be found at http://wuecon.wustl.edu/~pdfl/.

acrobat-l

A list for discussing Acrobat hosted by Blue World Communications.

Find the Web-page subscription format at http://www.blueworld.com/lists/acrobat/.

To subscribe to the list, send a message to listproc@ucdavis.edu with SUBSCRIBE in the subject.

To subscribe to the digest, send a message to acrobat-request@blueworld.com with SUBSCRIBE DIGEST in the subject.

ucd-adobe

A list that discusses Adobe products and software, including Acrobat. Hosted by the University of California at Davis.

To subscribe to the list, send email to listproc@ucdavis.edu with the text SUBSCRIBE UCD ADOBE, your first name, and your last name.

To post messages to all subscribers on the list, send email to ucd-adobe@ucdavis.edu (not for subscribing to the list).

10.4.2 Usenet

comp.text.pdf: Discussion of the PDF file format and related applications and resources.

comp.text.frame: Desktop publishing with FrameMaker.

comp.text.desktop: Desktop publishing technology and techniques.

alt.aldus.pagemaker: Discussion of PageMaker use.

comp.graphics.apps.pagemaker: Discussion of PageMaker use.

comp.lang.postscript: Discussion of the PostScript page description language.

comp.sources.postscript: PostScript code and discussion of its use

alt.hypertext: Discussion of hypertext including uses, transport, etc.

comp.text.sgml: ISO 8879 SGML, structured documents, markup languages discussion.

comp.infosystems.www.authoring.html: Topics, tips and questions about HTML markup.

comp.fonts: Discussion of font usage.

comp.infosystems.www.authoring.cgi: Discussion on the programming of Common GateWay Interface scripts used by many WWW servers.

10.4.3 Acrobat Frequently Asked Questions (FAQ)

URL http://www.blueworld.com/acrobat.faq.fcgi compiled by Blue World Communications.

10.5 Acrobat Periodicals

The following publications (all available as PDF files) are published by expert Acrobat users and companies with several years experience using Acrobat and related software.

10.5.1 *Acrobatics*

Acrobatics: The Journal for Acrobat Users, published by Merlin Open Systems can be found at http://www.ep.cs.nott.ac.uk:80/~dre/merlin/acrobatics.html.

10.5.2 *Acropolis*

A magazine about Acrobat publishing is published by Magnetic Press and can be found at http://plaza.interport.net/acropolis/).

10.5.3 *Acrobat in Academia*

Published by the Douglas Stewart Company. This periodical can be found at http://www.dstewart.com/acrobat.html.

10.6 Acrobat-Compatible Viewer and Converter Applications

Other software developers have applications specifically for viewing, printing, interacting and navigating PDF files. Some of these applications are similar to Adobe Acrobat and its functions. The following section summarizes these products and their capabilities.

These applications often cater to special audiences. They may require different functionality such as support for Asian languages, or have specific needs (for example, PDF viewers that have been developed for computer platforms for which Adobe does not offer a PDF viewer).

Note: These products often operate on a much different product cycle from Adobe Acrobat products. Some may support features not yet available (or will never be available) in Adobe Acrobat. Carefully read each product's documentation and thoroughly test the compatibility of each file with the intended audience's systems and software in mind.

10.6.1 Zeon Corporation's DocuComp PDF Viewers and Producers

From Taiwan, Zeon Corporation's DocuCom products are similar to the Adobe family of Acrobat products. The DocuPlus bundle of PDF file creation and authoring tools includes a shareable Reader-clone called DocuReader, an Exchange-like tool called epPlus and epDriver, and a printer driver PDF converter similar to PDFWriter. Zeon Corporation's target market is the publishers who wish to publish PDF in Asian languages including Japanese, Korean, and Chinese. All DocuComp products are DBCS-enabled. This allows them to display, print, and embed Double Bytes Character Set fonts, a common Asian language font format. DocuComp products also make it possible to create multilingual documents from the same page. DocuComp products are available for Windows 95 and Windows 3.x.

Visit Zeon Corporation's Web site at http://www.zeon.com.tw/ for product information.

Classification	Application Name(s)	Description
Viewers	DocuReader	DocuReader's functionality is comparable to Adobe Acrobat Reader.
	epPlus	epPlus functionality is comparable to Adobe Acrobat Exchange. epPlus supports standard PDF interactive and navigational features and has a MediaClip feature, similar to the Movie Plug-in from Adobe. Additionally, epPlus adds a marker tool for free-form annotation and "painting" of PDF pages (often used for revision marking).
Producers	epDriver	Similar to PDFWriter, epDriver is a printer driver, used to convert documents to PDF from virtually any application.

Table 10.6—1 Zeon Corporation's DocuComp Family of Software by Class

Zeon Corporation

1/F, 34, Alley 4, Lane 69, Section 5, Ming-Shen E. Road
Taipei, Taiwan.
Telephone: 886-2-766-9840
FAX: 886-2-760-0355
http://www.zeon.com.tw/
3whome@zeon.com.tw

10.6.2 GhostScript

GhostScript, by Aladdin Enterprises, is a PostScript language interpreter that enables the viewing and printing of PDF files, as well as PostScript language files. GhostScript cannot be used to interact with or navigate PDF files.

GhostScript 3.33 includes support for PDF 1.1 files (with the exception of encrypted PDF files). GhostScript also can convert a PDF file to PostScript, which allows printing to PostScript and PostScript-compatible printers.

GhostScript 4.0 includes, ps2pdf, a PostScript to PDF conversion utility. See Aladdin's Web site for more information on the capabilities and platform availability of PostScript and the ps2pdf conversion utility.

Aladdin Enterprises

P.O. Box 60264
Palo Alto, CA 94306
Telephone: (415) 322-0103
Fax: (415) 322-1734
ghost@aladdin.com
http://www.cs.wisc.edu/~ghost/index.html

Platform	Operating System
UNIX	X Windows v.11 (release 4, 5, and 6, including Sun-3, Sun-4, Sun-386i, and Sun SPARCStation)
	Generic 80386/486/Pentium machines running Linux, 386/ix, FreeBSD, ISC UNIX, SCO UNIX, and Solaris; H-P 9000/300 and 9000/800; DECStation 2100 and 3100.
	VAX running Ultrix and OSF/1.
	Sequent Symmetry
	Convex C1 and C2
	Tektronix 4300
	SGI Iris Indigo
	4.4bsd UNIX systems (FreeBSD, NetBSD, Sparc, m68k (Apple, Amiga, Sun and Hewlett-Packard), VAX, and 386BSD
Sun workstations (Sun-3, SPARC, Sun-386i)	SunView
VAX	VMS with X11R4/5 and DEC C or GCC
AXP	
PC	MS-DOS 3.1, 3.3, 5.0, or 6.22[1]
	Microsoft Windows 3.0 or 3.1[1]
	DR DOS 6.0
	OS/2 2.0, 2.1 and Warp 3.0
Macintosh (both 680x0 and PowerPC) [2]	System 7.x

Table 10.6—2 Aladdin GhostScript Availability by Platform and Operating System

[1] With EGA, VGA, SuperVGA, or compatible graphics.

[2] For specific information on Macintosh implementation, see http://www.glyphic.com/glyphic/projects/macgs.html.

10.6.3 xpdf

xpdf, by Derek B. Noonburg, is a PDF viewer for UNIX and the X Window Systems.

Platform	Operating System
UNIX or X	x86, Linux 1.2.13, XFree86 3.1.1, gcc 2.6.3
PowerPC, AIX 4.1, gcc 2.7.0	
SPARC, SunOS 4.1.3, gcc 2.5.8	
MIPS, Ultrix 4.4, gcc 2.6.3	
Alpha, OSF/1 1.3, gcc 2.6.3	

Table 10.6—3 xpdf Availability by Operating System

xpdf is available from ftp://ftp.andrew.cmu.edu in the /pub-/xpdf/. Source code is available from ftp://ftp.x.org/contrib-/applications/xpdf-0.3.tar.gz and mirrors. The source code and Linux binary are also available from ftp://sunsite.unc.edu-/pub/Linux/X11/xapps/graphics/viewers/xpdf-0.3.tar.gz and mirrors.

derekn@ece.cmu.edu

http://www.ece.cmu.edu/afs/ece/usr/derekn/.home-page.html

10.6.4 Other Sites of Interest

PDF Viewers for NEXTSTEP computers can be found at ftp://peanuts.leo.org/pub/comp/platforms/next/Text/apps/.

10.7 PDF File Applications, Utilities, and Application-Specific Plug-ins

Adobe and other developers have created a wide variety of applications, utilities and application-specific plug-ins to expand or enhance the process and interaction of PDF files with other software. Most of the items described are available free or as shareware (requiring a modest payment for the use of the software).

10.7.1 Adobe Fetch PDF Plug-in

This update enables Fetch to catalog PDF files. Available for free download from Adobe's Web site at http://www.adobe.com/.

10.7.2 Illustrator 5.5 PDF Plug-in

Enables Adobe Illustrator 5.5 (Macintosh only) to read and write to the Acrobat PDF file format. Adobe Illustrator, version 6.0 and above, includes the Plug-in. Available for free download from Adobe's Web site at http://www.adobe.com/.

10.7.3 PDF2PS

A Perl script that converts PDF to PostScript is available at ftp://peanuts.leo.org/pub/comp/platforms/next/Unix/text/.

10.7.4 EPS Links Files

EPS Links (for Macintosh and Windows), outlines the process of creating links with EPS files within Adobe Illustrator using pdfmark and Acrobat Distiller. Available for free download from the Adobe Acrobat Web site at http://www.adobe.com/acrobat/.

10.7.5 Gymnast

Developed by Robert Schifreen, Gymnast (Windows only), converts ASCII text files to PDF documents (freeware). Available for Windows.

10.7.6 'PDF' Type Utility

PDF Type (Macintosh only) is a applet that sets the file type of a Windows or UNIX-produced PDF file to "PDF", so the file is recognized by Acrobat Exchange and Reader.

10.7.7 Tumbler

Tumbler (Macintosh only), by Lawrence D'Oliveiro (ldo@waikato.ac.nz) converts Apple's QuickDrawGX Portable Digital Documents (PDDs) to PDF files. Available from many of the Info-Mac archives or try http://www.emrg.com/.

Glossary

Acrobat 3.0-compatible Web browser: A Web browser that supports the Adobe Acrobat 3.0 Application Programming Interface (API), by enabling Web browsers to view PDF files within the browser's document window.

Adobe Type Manager (ATM): ATM enables scaleable PostScript fonts to appear smooth at almost any size onscreen and when printed.

anti-aliasing: The technique of smoothing and softening the edges of polygons by adding pixels in a lighter, yet complementary color along the curve or edge of the font or image. This results in a slightly blurry, yet more readable font or smoother looking image. For Acrobat 3.0, ATM facilitates anti-aliasing of text in a PDF file.

AppleEvents: Enables applications and users (through scripts), to send commands to other programs and the MacOS on a Macintosh.

Application Programming Interface (API): Often divided into classes (e.g., communications, messages, etc.), APIs facilitate prescribe actions on particular software operating systems. Acrobat 3.0 supports Netscape Communications' Navigator APIs, which enable the Acrobat viewer application to exchange information with the Navigator application.

ASCII (American Standard Code for Information Interchange): Developed by the American National Standards Institute (ANSI), ASCII is set of 128 characters that include letters, numbers, punctuation, and control codes all represented by a unique number. ASCII-encoded PDF files use only the ASCII-character set to describe the PDF file. This typically results in slightly larger files than those encoded with binary data.

authoring languages: Languages that enable non-programmers to create a custom presentation and to control the actions of navigational and interactive objects within the application. Primarily used by scripters or multimedia developers.

bandwidth: A capacity of a connection (including wires, and radio frequency transmissions), and the amount of data that can travel through the connection.

base URL: The highest non-variable directory in which other subdirectories are located.

base-14 fonts: The fonts that are included with Acrobat viewers that cannot—and need not—be embedded in PDF files. These fonts include: Helvetica (regular, bold, oblique, and bold oblique), Times (regular, bold, italic, and bold italic), Courier family (regular, bold, italic, and bold italic), Symbol (a symbolic font with Greek letters and mathematical symbols), and Zapf Dingbats (a symbolic font with dingbat characters).

binary: Data transmitted or stored as a bit pattern, rather than ASCII characters. Binary data are more compact and load faster. Acrobat Distiller enables PDF files to be saved as binary-encoded files (by default), or as ASCII-encoded files.

bitmap font: A raster font (also called a "screen font"). Raster fonts generally do not scale well and appear blocky at large sizes.

bitmap image: An image represented as a set of pixels arranged in a rectangular pattern.

bookmarks: Opens to locations, pages, URL and other objects of a PDF document (or documents). Also used by some Web browsers to mark URL locations.

Boolean: Logical operations involving TRUE/FALSE, and the operators AND, OR and NOT. Booleans are commonly used when constructing search queries.

byte range: A defined number of bytes in a file, which includes the first and last byte of a series of bytes.

cache: An area in RAM or on a hard drive where data is stored for frequent, quick access by an application. Acrobat viewers cache images and some font data in a directory on the user's system and in RAM. Acrobat viewers used in conjunction with a Acrobat 3.0-compatible Web browser, may use two or more caches.

CCITT (Comite Consultatif Internationale de Telegraphie et Telephonie): A Geneva-based, international committee that recommends telecommunications standards and compression/decompression standards. The committee is now known as ITU-T (International Telecommunications Union-Telecommunication). Acrobat Distiller offers CCITT image compression.

CGI (Common Gateway Interface): A standard convention for passing commands and data from the client to the server (and sometime back again). Often used to transfer information from a client's Web browser (e.g., HTML-based form, or imagemap) for processing. The CGI script responds by sending a response document, commonly in HTML format, back to the user.

CIE: A device-independent color space used to describe the entire visual spectrum.

clipping path: A function of the PostScript language that allows one shape to mask another.

CMYK: The process image colors (frequently used to describe printed images) which are Cyan, Magenta, Yellow, and Black (versus Red, Green and Blue for RGB).

creator application: As defined by this reference, creator applications are used to design, author, edit, or otherwise manipulate files specifically for preparing for conversion to a PDF file.

downsample: The reduction of the number of dots per inch of an image, which results in lower resolution.

dpi (dots per inch): Resolution measured as the number of pixels that can fit within an inch of space on printers, scanners, and other input or output devices.

embedded fonts: Inclusion of the font's information (width, height, stroke, and other information).

EPS (Encapsulated PostScript file): An implementation of the PostScript language that enables a PostScript language object to be transported as a whole and inserted in other (non-PostScript) documents.

File Transfer Protocol (FTP): A client-server network structure that enables the transfer of files across the Internet. Users may access file directories for downloading or uploading files to a server.

font: Measured in point sizes, fonts are the discrete styles of various glyphs, which include common alphanumerical glyphs (e.g., letters and numbers), and symbol glyphs (e.g., equations and scientific symbols).

font subsets: Font data capable of displaying only particular alphanumeric glyphs, and not the entire glyph set of the typeface or font.

Forms Data Format (FDF): Portable form data that may be imported into Acrobat viewers to populate form fields, or exported for later use or processing by a Web server (much like the server processes HTML form data).

GIF (Graphic Interchange Format): The most common graphic format on the World Wide Web, GIFs are compact, 8-bit images (256 colors or less), which are easily portable across common hardware platforms without conversion.

Gopher: A text-based client-server information service system for publishing information or files and searching databases. Most Web browsers include support for Gopher clients.

grayscale: Black-and-white photographic images using any of the 256 gray tones.

Greeked text: Text displayed as gray lines, rather than font glyphs (numbers, letters, symbols).

GUI (Graphical User Interface): Allows human-computer interaction via pointing to and clicking icons, menus, and via drag-and-drop procedures.

HTML: A subset of SGML, HTML is the coding language used to create hypertext documents published on the World Wide Web (and other media).

HTTP: A transmission protocol used by Web servers and Web browser clients that allows the transmission of hypertext documents such as those found on the World Wide Web, between a HTTP client and an HTTP server.

hypertext: Text, which is also a link, that when selected, displays other files or information related to the original word or phrase.

incremental update saves: Changes and additions to the PDF file are appended to the end of the PDF, thereby minimizing save activity. Typically increases the files size and requires a full save to optimize the changes.

InkJet: Used to describe printers that spray ink from a nozzle (typically CMYK, or just black ink).

intranet: A client-server network that functions much like the Internet (using a Web server and Web-browser clients to access information). Usually access is limited to a specific audience (e.g., corporate employees).

IP address: A unique string of four numbers, often separated by periods, which identifies a computer (or server) on the Internet.

Java: Sun Microsystems' programming language, which enables animation and other custom action to be added to Web sites. The Web browser client must be able to support Java applets (the applications created by the Java programming language).

JPEG (Joint Photographic Experts Group): A highly-compressed, high fidelity, color-rich image file format. JPEG supports variable degrees of compression. JPEG uses lossy compression, resulting in a lower-quality image as compression increases. Acrobat Distiller offers JPEG compression for color and grayscale images.

Kanji character set: Characters used for the Japanese language, which require special software to be used on personal computers.

kbps (kilobits per second): A modem or other connection's speed, measured in the number of bits transferred per second.

LaTeX: A widely-used language, from Leslie Lamport, commonly used to author scientific and mathematical documents. Based on Donald Knuth's TeX system.

legacy document: Proprietary archived documents.

lossless compression: A compression technique that removes redundant bits of information without affecting the quality of the image.

lossy compression: A compression technique that reduces the image's quality to reduce file size. The greater degree of compression, the lower the quality of the image compared to the original.

Lotus Notes: Notes is a client/server environment that enables users (or clients) to communicate and collaborate securely over a network with a document residing on a shared computer (or server).

LZW (Lempel-Ziv Welch) compression: A lossless compression scheme that compresses data with repetition of strings in the data resulting in no image quality loss.

macro: A file (commonly a text file) that contains a sequence of commands that can be executed as one command.

magic cookie: A protocol that stores and exchanges a small string of data between client and server. Netscape Navigator includes the magic cookie protocol that functions like an identification marker. The cookie can hold information (such as items selected to be purchased in a "shopping cart" implementation). The information expires after a prescribed amount of time.

Microsoft Video for Windows: Microsoft Corporation's proprietary digital video file format.

MIME: (Multipurpose Internet Mail Extensions). MIME types specify a file type. Used for both email file attachments and as a way for Web servers to publish different file types, allowing Web browsers users to select an application to read the file, based on the MIME type.

Multiple Master font: A category of Type 1 font where type characteristics such as weight (thickness) and width of each character can be modified without altering the font's design.

n-up printing: Enables two or more document pages to be printed on a single "sheet" of media (commonly paper).

navigation: The act of finding one's way round an information structure.

NetWare: Novell, Inc.'s networking system, which works with Adobe Acrobat PDF files.

NNTP (Network News Transfer Protocol): The underlying technology of Usenet news that enables clients to communicate with Usenet servers.

node: A computer connected to and accessible by a network.

OEM (original equipment manufacturer): A company that produces hardware to be marketed under another company's brand.

Optical Character Recognition (OCR): The process of converting shapes into text. OCR software works with input devices (e.g., scanners and fax machines), to convert paper-based documents into electronic text.

optimization: A PDF-specific process that removes redundant image data from a PDF file, resulting in a smaller PDF file when compared with the unoptimized original.

outline font: Each character of an outline font is represented by sets of equations or vectors that define the outline of the character. Outline fonts can be scaled to any size, and rotated to any angle.

passphrase: Comparable to passwords, however passphrases can contain more than one word. Good passphrases (like passwords) contain numbers, letters, and sometimes symbols.

PCL (or PCL - 3, 4, 5): Hewlett-Packard's Printer Control Language, an Escape Code printer language. PCL 5 has more capabilities than the previous PCL versions.

pdfmark: Inserted in PostScript language files to represent PDF features. Pdfmark is converted to PDF navigational and interactive objects when the PostScript file is converted to a PDF file.

PDFViewer: The Plug-in (or applet) that exchanges information between a Acrobat 3.0-compatible Web browser and an Acrobat viewer.

.PDX files (Portable Document Index): Files of indexed PDF documents by Acrobat Catalog or third-party PDX-compliant indexing applications. PDX files may be opened and searched by the Acrobat Search Plug-in.

PICT: A graphic file format commonly used for line-art and photographic-quality images and graphics.

plug-ins: Add-on software that expand, extend, or alter the feature set built into an application.

Portable Document Format (PDF): Adobe's open specification.

PostScript: The page description language from Adobe. PostScript language instructions are created by a software application in conjunction with a PostScript printer driver.

producer application: Specific to converting files to PDF files, applications include Acrobat Distiller,

PDF Writer, and other third-party software.

progressive rendering: Specific to PDF files, progressive rendering displays the first text portions of a PDF page (after downloading essential page and security information), then interactive and navigational objects, followed by images, then fonts and thumbnails as needed.

prospero: A protocol used for communication between clients and servers in the Archie system. It enables users to organize the contents of remote file servers into a customized, virtual file system.

QuickTime: A proprietary file format for storing and playing back sound, graphics, and video. Developed by Apple Computer, Inc., QuickTime viewers are available for both PC and Macintosh systems.

RGB images: Images that are described using the combination of the colors Red, Green, and Blue. Common for onscreen image displays.

RTF (Rich Text Format): Developed by Microsoft Corporation, RTF saves a text file with its basic formatting and some page layout, font information, and colored text. The file format is useful for exchanging word processing files among platforms and different applications.

server-side include: A set of tags embedded in HTML documents that are processed by the HTTP server as the documents are sent to a client's Web browser.

SGML (Standard Generalized Markup Language): A ISO standard (8879) for creating marked-up, structured documents.

SQL (Structured Query Language): An ISO, ANSI construction language capable of interactive queries and report generation for querying relational databases.

substitute fonts: A Type 1 font created by ATM to substitute for the original and unavailable font. ATM substitutes fonts from data contained in the ATM font database.

TCP/IP: (Transmission Control Protocol/Internet Protocol) A suite of protocols that defines and facilitates communication over the Internet.

Telnet: A program that accesses other machines, thereby enabling users to "log-on" to a host machine (often UNIX).

TeX: A typesetting language by Donald Knuth, widely used for writing mathematics. TeX files (.tex) may be processed to device-independent .dvi files, which can be viewed, printed or converted to a PostScript file.

TIFF (Tag Image File Format): A common interchange format for bit-mapped graphics of any resolution and color depth.

TrueType font: A scaleable outline font format.

Type 1 font: An outline font definition developed by Adobe for use with PostScript. Type 1 fonts include hint tables that help the fonts reproduce well—even at small point sizes or low resolutions.

Type 3 font: An outline font definition developed by Adobe for use with PostScript. Type 3 fonts do not include hint tables.

Usenet: Composed of newsgroups, the Usenet is a world-wide collection of discussion groups on a wide range of subject matter.

URL: (Uniform Resource Locator) The address of resources on the World Wide Web.

Uuencode: Uuencoding converts a file from binary to plain ASCII text, enabling it to be sent as an attached file via email.

WAIS (Wide Area Information Servers): Commercial software that indexes and allows users to search and access large amounts of information. Accessible both on small networks and the Internet.

XTension: Add-on feature enhancements specifically for QuarkXPress. Other software developers use a similar means of enhancing their software, often calling these add-on enhancements plug-ins, filters, macros, etc.

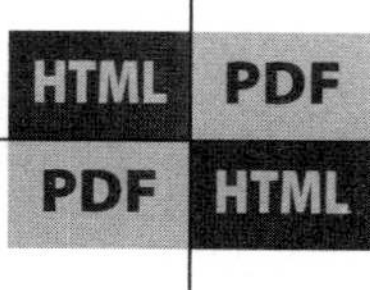

Appendices

The appendices include a wealth of information from relevant Adobe technical notes to lists of companies that provide Web server software designed to work with PDF files. The full text of the technical notes can be found at the Adobe Web site at http://www.adobe.com/. For the most complete list of third-party developers who have products that function with PDF files or Adobe Acrobat software, see Adobe's Acrobat Products and Services Guide on the Adobe Web site.

A

Appendix A: Web Server Software

This appendix lists and annotates the basic features of the Web servers that support PDF files as of this book's press date. A number of Web server manufacturers have integrated or announced their plans to support byte-range requests, which enable faster page-on-demand downloading of PDF files served on the Web. In addition to the companies listed below, other Web servers—most of which support CGI scripts—can also byte-serve PDF (and other file types) by simply adding the Perl byte-server script. (The Perl script is included with the retail version of Acrobat 3.0; also check the Adobe Acrobat Web page at http://www.adobe.com/ for availability and updates to the script.)

For information on other servers that support page-on-demand downloading of Acrobat 3.0 PDF files through byte-range requests, see the Adobe Web site at http://www.adobe.com/. Contact the companies below directly for the most recent, detailed information about their capabilities, features, and platform availability.

Web Server	PDF Support	Platforms/ Operating Systems	Contact
Microsoft Internet Information Server	byteserver CGI script	Intel (Microsoft Windows NT) Digital Alpha AXP MIPS PowerPC	Microsoft Corporation One Microsoft Way Redmond, WA 98052 Tel: (800) 426-9400 http://www.microsoft.com/
Netscape Internet Server	Built-in	Digital OSF HP-UX IBM RS/6000 AIX SGI MIPS IRIX Sun SPARC	Netscape Communications Corp. 501 E. Middlefield Rd. Mountain View, CA 94043 Tel: (415) 937-2555 Fax: (415) 528-4124 http://home.netscape.com/
Open Market WebServer	Built-in	Sun SPARC HP-UX Digital Alpha UNIX IBM RS/6000 AIX SGI MIPS IRIX	Open Market, Inc. 245 First Street Cambridge, MA 02142 Tel: (617) 621-9500 Fax: (617) 621-1703 info@openmarket.com http://www.openmarket.com/
O'Reilly & Associates WebSite	Built-in	Intel (Windows NT & 95)	O'Reilly & Associates 101 Morris St. Sebastopol, CA 95472 Tel: (800) 998-9938 or (800) 889-8969 Fax: (707) 829-0104 http://www.ora.com/
Quarterdeck WebSTAR	Plug-in	PowerPC (MacOS)	Quarterdeck Corporation 2550 Ninth Street, Suite 112 Berkeley, CA 94710 Tel: (800) 525-2580 Fax: (510) 548-0390 info@starnine.com http://www.starnine.com/

Table A.1—1 Web Server Software

B Appendix B: Internet Searching and Indexing Software

The following companies offer software that enable users on the Internet to search PDF files, as well as other standard text-based document formats. Other companies certainly will add support for searching PDF files (check the list of Internet resources listed in this book for information on companies that add support for PDF files). For the most recent list of searching and indexing software with PDF file support, visit the Adobe Web page at http://www.adobe.com.

Note: This appendix lists and annotates the basic features of the Web-based indexing software products that support PDF files as of this book's press date. Contact the companies directly for the most recent, detailed information about software capabilities, features, and platform availability.

B.1 Cascade Systems, Inc.

MediaSphere & MediaSphere /W3

MediaSphere/W3 allows Web browser clients to conduct queries using English-language phrases through natural language, keywords, and Boolean searches. Search results ranks relevancy by color, displays part of the caption, the query terms that were found, and an icon that indicates the file type (e.g., PDF, JPEG, etc.). A checkbox is also displayed that uses MediaSphere's Recycle action, which helps a user refine a search by presenting a list of the most relevant terms extracted from the selected entries in the search results list. The Lightbox view displays a thumbnail of the search results list, along with the caption (or the beginning of text—if it is a text or PDF file).

MediaSphere /W3 is an extension of MediaSphere, a multimedia library/archive system that fully integrates Adobe Acrobat. It can be configured to operate with a Macintosh co-processor to assist in the automatic creation of PDF files from popular Macintosh applications such as QuarkXPress. These pages are automatically indexed and stored along with the native layout files.

Cascade Systems Incorporated

300 Brickstone Square
Andover, MA 01810-1435
Telephone: (508) 749-7000
Fax: (508) 749-7099
info@cascadeinc.com
http://www.cascadeinc.com/

B.2 Excalibur Technologies Corporation

RetrievalWare EFS

RetrievalWare EFS is an information management system capable of conducting full-text retrieval of PDF files, HTML files, and number of other word processing and structured document formats. In addition to retrieving information, the software can manage, perform OCR, and create hierarchical-modular "file-rooms" for files. RetrievalWare EFS is available for Sun SPARC, HP 9000, IBM RS/6000, DEC Alpha, and Microsoft NT platforms.

Excalibur Technologies Corporation

1921 Gallows Road, Suite 200
Vienna, VA 22182
Telephone: (800) 788-7758
Fax: (703) 761-1990
info@excalib.com
http://www.xrs.com/

B.3 Excite, Inc.

Excite for Web Servers

Excite for Web Servers (EWS) allows users to both search and browse collections of HTML and PDF files (as well as several other file formats). Search results are ranked by confidence and can be sorted by subject. The query-by-example feature locates other documents that match a preferred found document. EWS is available for SunOS, Solaris, SGI Irix, HP-UX, IBM AIX, BSDI, and Windows NT platforms.

Excite, Inc.

1091 N. Shoreline Blvd.
Mountain View, CA 94043
Telephone: (415) 943-1200
Fax: (415) 943-1299
http://corp.excite.com/

B.4 Fulcrum Technologies, Inc.

SurfBoard

Fulcrum's SurfBoard supports the full-text searching of PDF documents with Boolean search operators, phrase searching, date ranges, wild cards, root-word stemming, and includes enhanced thesaurus support. Additionally, Fulcrum's Search-Objects enables users to save queries as bookmarks for later use.

SurfBoard is compatible with popular Web browsers and supports any CGI-compatible Web server running Windows NT.

Fulcrum Technologies Inc.

785 Carling Ave.
Ottawa, Canada K1S 5H4
Telephone: (613) 238-1761
Fax: (613) 238-7695
http://www.fulcrum.com/

B.5 Open Text Corporation

Livelink Search

Open Text's Livelink Search is based on the same software used by the Open Text index on the World Wide Web (use Open text at http://www.opentext.com/). Livelink Search can index PDF files and other common integrated file formats (including HTML, SGML, and around 40 other popular office file formats). This server-based indexing software works with a standard HTTP daemon. The search engine supports full Boolean, proximity and similarity searching, as well as full phrases (with no stop words). The search query can be configured by the user for specific elements of the document, and assign relative weights to search terms.

Livelink Search is available for Windows NT, Sun Solaris and Sun OS, HP-UX, AIX, SGI, and DEC OSF1.

Open Text Corporation

180 Columbia Street W., Suite 2110
Waterloo ON N2L 3L3
Canada
Telephone: (519) 888 9910
Fax: (519) 888 0677
info@opentext.com
http://www.opentext.com/

B.6 Personal Library Software

PL Web

PL Web supports the searching of PDF files and other common Internet file types with natural language and Boolean queries, relevance ranking of search results, and dynamic discovery. PL Web is available for Sun Solaris, HP PA-RISC, HP-UX, IBM RS/6000, IBM AIX, SGI IRIX, and Digital Alpha OSF/1. PDF files are supported on HP and Sun platforms only.

Personal Library Software

2400 Research Blvd., Suite 350
Rockville, MD 20850
Telephone: (301) 990-1155
info@pls.com
http://www.pls.com/

B.7 Verity, Inc.

Topic Internet Server

The Topic Internet server uses Verity's Topic architecture, which allows users to create queries using concept-based topics, Boolean, proximity, and field operators, fuzzy logic, weighted terms, and more. Topic also supports "find similar" requests.

In addition to the Internet, the Topic Internet server can be used to create indices and to retrieve documents on file systems, CD-ROMs, databases, and local networks. Catalogs created by the Topic Internet Server are in a standard Topic collection, which are compatible with other collections—including catalogs created by Acrobat Catalog. This standard catalog format allows Acrobat Catalog-generated indices to be used by the Topic Internet Server. Filters also turn more than 50 common office file types into searchable text, viewable in any Web browser.

Topic Internet Server is available for Sun Solaris, UNIX Sparc SunOS, HP-UX, RS/6000, Windows NT, SGI IRIX, MIPS, and DEC Alpha UNIX.

Verity SearchPDF for Web Servers

SearchPDF for Web Servers enables full-text search and retrieval of PDF files with search-term highlighting, and page-on-demand viewing from a Netscape plug-in and Acrobat 3.0-compatible Web browser. Found PDF documents are displayed in any Web browser that supports Acrobat 3.0 with search-term highlights. Based on the user's query, all the matching search terms are highlighted in the PDF file. This feature has been available for locally-indexed searching since Acrobat Catalog was introduced.

SearchPDF for Web Servers brings this functionality to the Web with External Markup Language (XML), which extends existing mark-up languages (e.g., HTML, and SGML) to enable term highlighting. The XML standard has been developed by Verity in conjunction with Adobe, Netscape, and other industry partners.

Note: The Highlight Server Plug-in (HLS), which enables search term highlighting in a PDF file, ships with Acrobat 3.0. Also see Appendix I, "Acrobat Plug-ins."

Web publishers who have created full-text indices with Acrobat Catalog can serve the indices on a Web server. The software supports up to four document collections created with Acrobat Catalog. SearchPDF for Web Servers comes with Simple, Standard, and Power query forms, templates for customized results lists, password security options. It is compatible and upgradeable to Verity's Topic Internet Server.

SearchPDF for Web Servers works with any CGI compliant Web Server. Available for servers running Sun Solaris, HP-UX, IBM AIX, and Windows NT.

Note: Verity offers the XML specification at no charge. See Verity's Web site at http://www.verity.com for more information.

Verity, Inc.

894 Ross Drive
Sunnyvale, CA 94089
Telephone: (408) 541-1500
info@verity.com
http://www.verity.com/

Appendix C: The Forms Data Format

The Forms Data Format (FDF) is the file format used for PDF Forms. With Acrobat Exchange 3.0 and later, FDF files can be created by exporting data from a form (choose File > Export > Export Form). FDF files also can be created by scripts and applications (or—albeit a lengthy process—by hand). Only Acrobat Exchange 3.0 and later with the AcroForms Plug-in can export and import FDF files.

The Forms Data Format (FDF) is based on the Portable Document Format, using many of the same syntax and objects as PDF. FDF files use the PDF MIME type (application/PDF), and it is registered as the same type on many platforms. Despite this compatibility with PDF files, an Acrobat viewer cannot display a FDF file, only import the data into its corresponding form fields. FDF files are much simpler than PDF files, as they contain only information about the data and any objects within the file. PDF search engines, given the simplicity of the file, cannot index FDF files.

FDF files are comprised of a one-line header (FDF 1.2 for Acrobat 3.0-created FDF files), a body that contains the form field data and other objects, and a trailer that contains additional information about the FDF file itself, and the final line of the FDF file. More information about the FDF file structure can be found in the most recent PDF language spec.

Experiment with FDF by focusing on the FDF file parts. To alter the form's appearance when importing a FDF file, create a form and export the form as a FDF file. Create another form with the same names as the fields in the first PDF file. Give these fields different appearances, values, options, etc. Export a FDF file for use as the second PDF file. Open both FDF files in a text editor. Copy the form data from the second FDF file over the first. Import the modified FDF file into the first PDF file to view the changes.

D Appendix D: Interapplication Communication and Web Browsers

Adobe Acrobat's capability to display PDF files within Acrobat 3.0-savvy PDF Web browsers is accomplished through interapplication communication (IAC). IAC allows the Acrobat viewer to render and manage live PDF files in the document window of other applications (e.g. Web browsers). All normal viewer navigational and interactive objects are available via the user interface and an optional Acrobat toolbar. In addition, IAC enables the other application to supply the Acrobat viewer with an interface for reading PDF files from data sources (e.g. Web servers).

In the case of Netscape Navigator (and other Web browsers that use the PDFViewer Plug-in), both the Web browser and an Acrobat viewer (either Acrobat Reader 3.0 or Acrobat Exchange 3.0) must be running simultaneously. Netscape Navigator uses the PDFViewer Plug-in, and the Acrobat viewer uses the External Window Handler Plug-in to facilitate communication between the two applications.

Note: Microsoft Internet Explorer uses ActiveX technology to communication with an Acrobat viewer, (See the Adobe Web site at http://www.adobe.com/ and Microsoft Corporation's Web site at http://www.microsoft.com/ for more information on ActiveX IAC specifics.)

For most interapplication communication, when a user clicks on a PDF file published on a Web server, the Web browser sends an IAC message to the Acrobat viewer (via the PDFViewer and External Windows Handler plug-ins). The message contains a handle to the Web browser's document window, where the PDF document will be rendered, and a handle to a stream from which the Acrobat viewer can read the PDF file's data. Via the external Window Handler, the Acrobat viewer sends back an IAC message to the Web browser that contains a request to read specific bytes from the data stream. The Web browser then sends the requested bytes to the Acrobat viewer, which in turn renders the PDF document in the Web browser's document window.

Note: IAC's communication and event handling is platform-dependent.

Applications that support Acrobat 3.0's IAC interface are called through a link with the PDFX library, which handles the details of the platform-dependent interface. PDFX is a cross-platform, C language interface (for Macintosh, Windows, and UNIX). It contains approximately 25 calls that applications like Web browsers use to invoke an Acrobat viewer to read data from a PDF file, to print, copy text and images to the clipboard, and handle events. On the Acrobat client, these calls are supported via the External Window Handler Plug-in.

Note: The Acrobat viewer, not the calling application, takes responsibility for the Print dialog box. This may affect the calling application's print actions.

Appendix E: Configuring QuarkXPress to Produce PDF Files

QuarkXPress users may find that using certain options available in QuarkXPress will result in PDF files of less than acceptable quality. These technical issues are related to the way QuarkXPress generates a PostScript file.

Adobe has addressed a number of these technical issues with solutions that, when followed, result in error-free conversion and high-quality PDF files. There are also a number of ways to customize QuarkXPress so creating PDF files with QuarkXPress is more efficient.

E.1 Creating a Custom Printer File for Distiller in Windows

1. Exit to DOS and change to the WINDOWS\SYSTEM directory.
2. Type "edit acrodist.ppd" to open the Distiller PPD file in MS-DOS Edit.
3. Locate the "*ModelName: 'Acrobat Distiller'" line and insert the word "Modified" before "Acrobat." For example: *ModelName: "Modified Acrobat Distiller".
4. Locate the "*NickName: 'Acrobat Distiller'" and insert the word "Modified" before "Acrobat." For example: *NickName: "Modified Acrobat Distiller".
5. Locate the section that begins "*%Custom Page Sizes" and delete the following lines from that section: *CustomPageSize True: " 4 dict begin pop % pop /Orientation value off the stack to fix bug in PageMaker 5.0

2 array astore /Margins exch def 2 array astore /PageSize exch def /ImagingBBox null def currentdict end setpagedevice" *End.

6. Press the Alt key to highlight the File menu and use the down arrow key to select "Save As...". Press the Enter key.
7. Name the file MODIFIED.PPD and save it.
8. When creating a PostScript file in Quark, select the "Modified Acrobat Distiller" PPD and enter the appropriate value in the Page Width: box at the bottom of the Printer Setup dialog box.

E.2 Creating a Custom Distiller Printer Description File for Macintosh

1. Open the Acrobat Distiller PPD in a text editor that saves in text-only format (e.g., TeachText, or Simple Text). The Acrobat Distiller PPD file is located in the Printer Descriptions folder in the Extensions folder found in the System Folder.
2. Locate the "*ModelName: 'Acrobat Distiller'" line and insert the word "Modified" before "Acrobat." For example: *ModelName: "Modified Acrobat Distiller".
3. Locate the "*NickName: 'Acrobat Distiller'" and insert the word "Modified" before "Acrobat." For example: *NickName: "Modified Acrobat Distiller".
4. Locate the section that begins "*%Custom Page Sizes" and delete the following lines from that section: *CustomPageSize True: " 4 dict begin pop % pop /Orientation value off the stack to fix bug in PageMaker 5.0

2 array astore /Margins exch def 2 array astore /PageSize exch def /ImagingBBox null def currentdict end setpagedevice" *End.

5. Use the Save As... command to save the file and name it MODIFIED.PPD.
6. When creating a PostScript file in Quark, select the "Modified Acrobat Distiller" PPD and enter the appropriate value in the Page Width box at the bottom of the Page Setup dialog box.

When creating a PostScript file from a QuarkXPress document using the Acrobat Distiller PPD file, the Page Width option in the Printer Setup dialog box (Windows) or Page Setup dialog box (Macintosh) is grayed out. As a result, page widths greater than 8.5 inches are truncated. The grayed-out Page Width option is caused by lines that were added to the Distiller PPD to make it compatible with Adobe PageMaker. Using a custom printer file without those lines makes the Page Width option available and allows the entry of the correct page width when printing a page larger than 8.5 inches from QuarkXPress (as noted in Adobe TechNote 4436.pdf).

F

Appendix F: Font Copyrights

Embedding fonts in PDF files without permission from the font's creator is a copyright violation. When distilled, if a font is set to be embedded in a document, the font's metrics are copied into the file and later used when the document is opened in an Acrobat viewer. Because the font data is copied directly into the file, the font information can be extracted from the file (with the exception of

Type 1C fonts). The result is widespread font copyright violation over the Internet. Even using font subsets includes the font's data within the file—again allowing others to remove the font data for use on their systems. This is an illegal act. It violates the copyright agreement between the publisher and the font vendor.

Note: It may be easy to claim ignorance to the use of a font in your documents. However, until a technological solution is created it is best to take a proactive position with all publishing efforts and work on alternatives to embedding the actual font data. At present, this is an ethical issue—later it may become a legal issue.

F.1 Companies That Permit Font Embedding

The following companies make their fonts available for legal embedding within a PDF document:

- Adobe Systems
- Any of the Adobe Originals fonts
- Any of the fonts in the Adobe Type Library
- Any fonts owned by Linotype-Hell AG
- Any fonts owned by Agfa-Gevaert
- Any fonts owned by Fundicion Tipografica Neufville
- Any fonts owned by Monotype Typography, Ltd.
- Any PrePRESS font or font from the Varityper Library, acquired by PrePRESS. Anyone who has purchased these fonts is permitted to embed that font in a PDF for purposes of viewing or reading that document.

- Typefaces from the Bitstream Typeface Library (BTL) may be used in the creation of portable electronic documents (embedded in PDFs and PostScript files), so recipients of those documents may read and print them. Bitstream Typefaces may not be included with (or embedded into) electronic document formats that allow the recipient to extract or freely gain access to those typefaces for future use. This requires Bitstream font users to subset (a font embedding job option in Acrobat Distiller 3.0) all Bitstream fonts or disable printing of the PDF document so the font may not be stripped from the PDF file.

Fonts in the public domain, custom fonts created internally, or fonts that have been authorized to be embedded electronically may be embedded in PDF files that will be published on the Web.

For fonts designed in house or a specially commissioned font, check the legal limits of the commission. While most privately designed fonts allow distribution via other media, specific contracts may dictate otherwise.

F.2 Getting Permission to Use a Font

For permission to use a particular font, contact the font company or designer that holds the copyright. When contacting the font company or designer, have specific document details. Often they will want to know:

- How many copies of the document will be distributed?
- Can the font be extracted? (All embedded fonts can be extracted from PDF files, with the exception of subset fonts.)

- Who is the audience (internal or external)?

A general license may require the payment of royalties.

If they refuse...

If the font company or designer denies a request to embed a font, the font must be removed from the document. Check your document after removing the font to see how well Adobe Type Manager substitutes the font. Perhaps there's really no need to embed the font, especially if ATM does a good job of substitution.

G Appendix G: Font Embedding Information

This appendix describes how embedded and substitute-font types such as TrueType, Type 1, and Type 3 fonts are handled on a wide variety of platforms.

G.1 How The Postscript Drivers Handle Fonts

The Distiller program processes PostScript language descriptions of documents. This means that before Distiller can process a document, the PostScript printer driver must convert all the non-PostScript language fonts in a document to either PostScript language fonts or graphics. Both the Windows and Macintosh versions of the PostScript printer driver can use TrueType fonts to create a synthetic Type 1 font with characters that look like the TrueType characters. Depending on how it is configured, the PostScript printer driver for Windows also can create a synthetic bitmapped Type 3 font for a TrueType font, or substitute an available Type 1 font for a TrueType font.

When a PostScript printer driver creates a PostScript language description of a document, it checks to see if the Type 1 fonts used in the document are present in the printer (either in printer ROM or in an attached device, such as a disk drive or CD-ROM drive). When the font is not present in the printer, the driver places a copy of the Type 1 font in the PostScript language file. When the font is present in the printer, however, the driver references it by name only.

Note: The latest version of the Apple LaserWriter printer driver and the Macintosh printer driver from Adobe for PostScript printers (PS Printer) have the option to include all the Type 1 fonts used in a document in the PostScript language file created for that document.

G.2 How Distiller Handles Fonts

The Distiller program deals with every type of font that can be used in a document. Documents created with Windows applications may contain PostScript language Type 1 and Type 3 fonts, Windows bitmapped and vector fonts, TrueType fonts, and PCL fonts. Documents created with Macintosh applications may contain PostScript language Type 1 and Type 3 fonts, Macintosh bitmapped fonts, and TrueType fonts.

In addition to font type, fonts are further classified by the set of characters included in the font. Character sets for Type 1 fonts, for example, include the ISO Latin 1, Expert, Small Capitals and Old Style Figures (SC & OSF), Symbolic, Cyrillic, and Kanji character sets. The ISO Latin 1 character set and the standard Type 1 character set include the standard English, French, Italian, and German alphabets; the Expert character set includes fraction and f-ligature characters for the English alphabet; and the Cyrillic character set contains the Cyrillic alphabet used by Slavic languages such as Russian and Ukrainian.

G.3 How Distiller Handles Type 1 Fonts

How the Distiller handles the Type 1 fonts in a PostScript language file depends on four scenarios:

- Whether a font that is referenced—but not embedded—in a PostScript language file is available to the Distiller;
- Whether the font is an Adobe font;
- Whether the font uses the ISO Latin 1 character set; or
- Whether the Distiller has been set up always to embed or never embed the font.

Depending on previously cited scenarios, the Distiller will handle a Type 1 font in one of three ways:

- Embed the font in the PDF file;
- Place a font descriptor for the font in the PDF file; or
- Report a findfont error and use Courier for the font.

When the Distiller embeds a Type 1 font in a PDF file, the font is available to Acrobat viewers for display and print purposes. The advantage to embedding a font in a PDF file is that the font is always available to Acrobat viewers. The disadvantage is that the file is larger. A typical Type 1 font is about 40 kilobytes in size.

A font descriptor includes the font name and information such as whether the font is serif or sans serif or italic, and the width of the vertical stems in characters. When Distiller places a font descriptor in a PDF file, Acrobat viewers can use the font if it is available on the viewing system. When the font is not available on the viewing system, the Adobe Type Manager (ATM) program uses the information in the font descriptor to create a substitute font with characters that look like the original font characters.

G.4 How Distiller Handles Type 3 Fonts

Type 3 fonts are typically custom or corporate fonts that include glyphs that Acrobat viewers cannot substitute. As a result, in order to display these font glyphs, all versions of the Acrobat Distiller embed Type 3 fonts in PDF files.

G.5 The Distiller Font Processing Table

The following table lists the various kinds of fonts used in Windows and Macintosh documents. The table also describes how Distiller handles each font type. Because Type 1 fonts referenced in a PostScript file may not be present on the system where Distiller is running, the table also shows how Distiller will handle fonts that are not present on the system that is running Distiller. For a full description of how Acrobat viewers display and print embedded and substitute fonts by platform and printer type (including PostScript and PCL printers) see Adobe Technical Note #4408 available from http://www.adobe.com/.

The table below (from Adobe Technical Note #4406) shows the default behavior of Distiller. Distiller can be set up, however, to embed a Type 1 font that is normally not embedded, and not to embed a font that is normally embedded.

Font Type	Result when font is present	Result when font is not present
Adobe Type 1, Base-14 fonts[1]	Font name placed in PDF file; only name is required because base-14 fonts are guaranteed to be present on viewing system.	Always present; installed with Distiller.
Adobe Type 1, ISO Latin 1	Font descriptor placed in PDF file.	Font descriptor placed in PDF file.[2]
Adobe Type 1, Expert	Font embedded in PDF file.	findfont error is generated; Courier used.
Adobe Type 1, SC & OSF	Same as either ISO Latin 1 or Expert.[3]	Same as either ISO Latin 1 or Expert.[3]
Adobe Type 1, Symbolic	Font embedded in PDF file.	Always present.[4]
Adobe Type 1, Cyrillic (with Macintosh version)	Font embedded in PDF file.	findfont error is generated; Courier used.
Adobe Type 1, Cyrillic (with Windows version)	Cyrillic character set not supported; Courier used.	Cyrillic character set not supported; Courier used.
Adobe Type 1, Kanji	Not supported.	Not supported.
Adobe multiple masters, ISO Latin 1	Font descriptor placed in PDF file.	Font descriptor placed in PDF file.
Adobe multiple masters, Expert	Font descriptor placed in PDF file.	PostScript error generated; file fails to distill.
Non-Adobe Type 1, ISO Latin 1	Font descriptor placed in PDF file.	findfont error; Courier used.
Non-Adobe Type 1, non-ISO Latin1	Font embedded in PDF file.[5]	findfont error; Courier used.
Type 3 outline font	Font embedded in PDF file.	Always present.[4]
Type 3 bitmapped font	Font embedded in PDF file.	Always present.[4]

continued

Table G.7—1 Font Processing by Acrobat Distiller (All Versions)

Font Type	Result when font is present	Result when font is not present
TrueType for Windows	Depending on driver setup and font size,[6] the PostScript driver: ■ Substitutes a Type 1 font, (which is handled as shown above). ■ Uses TrueType outlines to create a synthetic Type 1 font (which is handled as shown above). Do not use this option.[7] ■ Uses TrueType outlines to create a bitmapped Type 3 font, (which is embedded).	Synthetic Type 1 and bitmapped Type 3 font are always present (embedded in Post-Script language file). When the Type 1 font substituted for a TrueType font is not present, it is handled as shown above.
Macintosh TrueType	PostScript driver either creates a synthetic Type 1 font or downloads a TrueType rasterizer[8] in PostScript language file; in either case, the font descriptor for the synthetic font is placed in the PDF file.	Always present.[9]
Macintosh TrueType, Symbolic	Driver uses TrueType character outlines to create a synthetic Type 1 font; the synthetic Type 1 font is embedded in the PDF file.	Synthetic Type 1 font created for TrueType font is always present.[9] (Embedded in Post-Script language file.)
Macintosh bitmapped	PostScript driver uses character bitmaps to create a bitmapped Type 3 font; Type 3 font is embedded in the PDF file	Bitmapped Type 3 font created for bitmapped font is always present. (Embedded in Post-Script language file.)
PCL bitmap	When a PostScript printer is the active printer, Windows substitutes TrueType fonts for PCL fonts; see Windows TrueType.	Not applicable
PCL outline	When a PostScript printer is the active printer, Windows substitutes TrueType fonts for PCL fonts; see Windows TrueType.	Not applicable

continued

Table G.7—1 (continued) Font Processing by Acrobat Distiller (All Versions)

Font Type	Result when font is present	Result when font is not present
Windows bitmap	Windows converts to Courier when Post-Script language file is created; font descriptor for Courier placed in PDF file.	Not applicable
Windows vector	Characters converted to graphics when Post-Script language file is created; graphics are placed in PDF file.	Not applicable

Table G.7—1 (continued) Font Processing by Acrobat Distiller (All Versions)

[1] The base-14 Type 1 fonts are fonts that are built into PostScript printers.

[2] Distiller gets the font descriptor from the ATM font database. The ATM font database may not include font descriptors for newer fonts. Distiller can, however, obtain font descriptors from the fonts themselves—if they are available. See the Acrobat Distiller Online Guide for instructions on how to make fonts available to Distiller.

[3] SC & OSF fonts use the Expert character set. However, some SC & OSF fonts are programmed incorrectly and the Distiller processes them as ISO Latin 1 fonts. You can work around this problem by setting up Distiller to always embed problem SC & OSF fonts.

[4] The font is always present because PostScript drivers download fonts of this type to printers. Adobe drivers can, however, be set up to never download fonts. When a PostScript language file is created with this setting, a findfont error occurs and Courier is used.

[5] Some non-Adobe, non-ISO Latin 1 fonts are programmed incorrectly and the Distiller processes them as ISO Latin 1 fonts. You can work around this problem by setting up the Distiller to always embed problematic non-Adobe, non-ISO Latin 1 fonts.

[6] When the driver is set up to create synthetic Type 1 fonts for TrueType fonts, it creates bitmapped Type 3 fonts for the TrueType font sizes that have an em dash narrower than 16 points.

[7] Distiller 1.0 does not handle correctly synthetic Type 1 fonts created by the PostScript driver for Windows. Characters appearing in the original document may be lost in the resulting PDF file. Always set up the PostScript driver for Windows either to substitute an available Type 1 font for TrueType fonts, or to create bitmapped Type 3 fonts for TrueType fonts.

[8] The PostScript driver downloads a TrueType rasterizer, if the printer has 3M or more of memory. Otherwise, the driver uses the outlines of the TrueType characters to create a synthetic Type 1 font.

[9] Even when the PostScript driver is set up to never download fonts, it downloads synthetic Type 1 fonts created for TrueType fonts.

G.6 Where the Font Is Embedded

In a non-optimized PDF file created with Distiller or PDFWriter (versions 2.1 or earlier), the font data is dispersed throughout in the PDF file. Distiller writes the embedded font data into the PDF as it is encountered.

Acrobat 3.0's optimized files—required for page-on-demand downloading from the Web—place basic font table information in the first few lines of the PDF file's data. These font tables provide Adobe Type Manager with enough information to mimic the weight and height of the font used. After the rest of the text, graphics, navigation and interactive objects, and images are downloaded and cached by the Web browser, the embedded font data is downloaded. Once all the embedded font data is downloaded, the Acrobat viewer's in-line helper application updates the substituted fonts with the actual fonts—referred to as "font blitting."

Once downloaded, the font data (often the largest part of a PDF file) is cached and accessable by other pages of the same PDF file that uses the same font. Cached font data is not usable by other PDF files, even if they use the same font.

Note: Open PDF in a text editor to see how Acrobat orders the font, text, graphic and image information in either optimized or non-optimized PDF files.

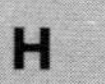

Appendix H: Setting Options in Distiller's Startup Directory

Apply custom modifications to a specific PostScript or EPS file before conversion by editing the startup script. These modifications can alter the job options set in Distiller, or override default conversions. To make these modifications, edit the Example.ps script found within Distiller's Startup directory.

Job options set in the Example.ps script will override those settings made in Distiller's job options. Modifying Distiller's job options will override preferences set in the Example.ps script.

The Example.ps script contains job option preferences and other commands that Distiller can read as it is launching. Editing this file while Distiller is running has no affect. All the options set in job options can be set in the Example.ps file. However, Acrobat Distiller 3.0 adds a number of interface features. In Distiller 2.1 and earlier versions, these features are accessible only by editing the startup script:

- Both the default page size and the page's measurement units (e.g., inches, picas, etc.), can be set from within Acrobat Distiller 3.0.
- Page orientation (portrait or landscape) can be configured by setting the width greater than the height for landscape, or the height greater than the width for portrait.
- Add a message that will be displayed in Distiller's window as Distiller launches.
- Convert CMYK graphics to RGB graphics (an Advanced conversion option in Distiller 3.0).

- Load specific fonts into memory; and
- Apply pdfmark operators to specific pages or the whole document.

Note: More detail about configuring the Startup script can be found in the Acrobat Distiller Online Guide.

H.1 Using Distiller to Set Page Sizes and Orientations

Distiller's default page size is 8 1/2 by 11 inches with portrait orientation (referred to as the bounding box). The bounding box in Reader or Exchange is seen as the size of the actual PDF page over the pasteboard or background.

Note: Selecting the Acrobat PPD file when setting up the printer driver will often yield the correct orientation and page size to match that of the original document. Other PPDs often don't pass Distiller the information it needs to set the document's bounding box (size and orientation). This is a common problem with many documents. Because the PPD can pass the information with the PostScript language file, configure Distiller to match the document's bounding box and orientation.

Setting custom page sizes: editing the Example.ps script

Before editing the Example.ps script, make a backup. Open the Example.ps file in a text editor.

Find the line:

```
% << /PageSize [612 792] >> setpagedevice
```

There are two steps involved in editing the script:

1. Make the line active as Distiller loads, which applies the changes in the active lines to Distiller's job options. To make the line active, simply remove the "%" from the line. This is true of all other lines in the script. The Example.ps file has no active lines by default.
2. Setting the page dimensions can be accomplished by entering the page size of the file in pixels. The default page size 612 by 792 pixels (8 1/2 x 11 inches). Change these numbers to reflect the desired size of the file.

Setting portrait and landscape orientations: editing the Example.ps script

1. Make the line active as Distiller loads, which applies the changes in the active lines to Distiller's job options. To make the line active, simply remove the "%" from the line. This is true of all other lines in the script. The Example.ps file has no active lines by default.
2. Set the page orientation by entering the page size of the file in pixels, width by height. Portrait orientation is 612 by 792 pixels (8.5 x 11 inches). Reverse the number's order to change to landscape orientation. Hence, 792 by 612 pixels gives is the same size sheet of the standard page size oriented as landscape, or 11 x 8 1/2.

I Appendix I: Acrobat Plug-ins

Acrobat plug-ins extend the PDF file format, automate the addition of navigational and interactive objects and modifications made to PDF files, or allow access to files—other than PDF files—for use within an Acrobat viewer. Most plug-ins are for Exchange, though some, like the Weblink or Movie Plug-ins, work with Acrobat Reader.

Other "enhancements," which could include QuarkXPress XTensions, filters, macros, plug-ins, etc., can extend the capabilities of a creator application. Those enhancements which have some relationship with the PDF file format or Acrobat software are listed here.

Plug-ins are developed either internally by Adobe Systems or by third party developers. Adobe-developed plug-ins are either integrated into the complete Acrobat family of software, bundled with Reader, Exchange, or both. Other plug-ins developed by Adobe have been distributed freely on Adobe's Web site. Third Party developers produce plug-ins for general or specific uses. Plug-ins which expand the capability of Acrobat and the PDF file format are available from a number of developers. Developers either sell their plug-ins as over-the-counter products or are developed to meet a specific customer's needs.

I.1 Alliant Defense Electronics Systems, Inc.

InfoLinker (Windows 3.x and later)

The InfoLinker plug-in automatically builds hyperlinks and bookmarks for PDF documents. InfoLinker can create links and bookmarks based on a pre-defined rule list, which may be applied to other documents with a similar structure. Links can be generated based on intelligent mapping between document references and the referred document item. References to tables, pages, and other document items are linked to the item to which they refer.

13133 34th Street North
Clearwater, FL 34622
Tel: (813) 572-1900
Fax: (813) 572-2395

I.2 Computerised Document Control Ltd

Banner Printer Corporate (Windows 3.x and later)

Banner Printer Corporate is a tool designed to assist with organizational control of documents that are published electronically, but where paper copies may be required. Banner Printer allows the addition of a "watermark" to the printed paper copy of the PDF file. The banner is not permanent and not visible when viewing the PDF document onscreen. This provides flexibility by allowing the printing of "controlled" or "uncontrolled" copies.

Volume Builder (Windows 3.x and later)

Volume Builder is a software tool that allows compilation of many discrete documents into a single volume. The volume's contents may be comprised of any document, single or multi-page, which is available electronically. In fact, any document that can be printed from the DOS, Windows, UNIX, or Macintosh environments—or can be imported into these environments as a Postscript File may be used in the Volume creation.

Custom headers and footers (which can include images, logos, etc.), may be applied to each volume. There are facilities to generate automatically a table of contents and to apply sequential page numbering to the entire volume.

Different volumes may be created from the same source documents. Volume definitions may be saved to provide easy update.

PO Box 5
Chepstow
Gwent
NP6 6YU
UK Tel: 01291 641554
Fax: 01291 641817

I.3 Adobe Systems Plug-ins

Weblink (Macintosh, Windows, UNIX)

Weblink enables publishers to embed a Universal Resource Locator (URL) within a PDF file, thereby allowing users to connect to any other supported file type on the World Wide Web from an Acrobat document. Weblink works with a user's Web browser to communicate across the Internet. The Weblink Plug-in and Exchange are an essential tools for Web publishers. The Weblink plug-in is required for users to view PDF files within a Web browser (via a plug-in, ActiveX, or other interapplication communications), or as a helper application (as with earlier version of the Acrobat Reader).

Weblink is included in the retail versions of Acrobat 3.0 software, with the free Acrobat Reader (version 2.1 and later) and may be downloaded for free from Adobe's Web site at http://www.adobe.com/. All versions of the free Acrobat Reader 2.1 support the capability to follow connections created by Weblink.

EWH (Macintosh, Windows, UNIX)

The retail version of Adobe Acrobat 3.0 and the free Adobe Acrobat Reader 3.0 includes the External Window Handler (EWH) plug-in. EWH implements the Acrobat viewer's IAC interface and is not compatible with earlier versions of Adobe Acrobat (e.g. 2.1, 2.0 or 1.0). EWH makes it possible for the Acrobat viewer to render PDF files in multiple windows from one or more calling applications (like Web browsers).

Import (Macintosh, Windows, UNIX)

This Plug-in allows Exchange users to import a variety of image types in black and white, grayscale and color. These images can be placed anywhere in on a PDF page. Useful for importing icons and other images for Internet-based publications.

Scan (Macintosh, Windows, UNIX)

The Scan Plug-in makes it possible to convert paper-based documents to PDF files using popular desktop scanners. For large volume jobs which use Acrobat Capture, a full-featured application for converting legacy documents to PDF files.

Touch-Up (Macintosh, Windows, UNIX)

The Touch-up plug-in allows the user to edit single lines of text, change font attributes and highlight/edit all bitmap suspects (resulting from using the Capture products). A very useful tool for creating styled hypertext-like text (colored, underlined text) or for making minor edits and updates in Internet documents.

HLS (Macintosh, Windows, UNIX)

The Highlight Server plug-in works with Verity's XLS technology to display highlighted terms in a PDF file viewed within a Web browser's document window. The page with the first matching term is displayed first, with one or more matching terms highlighted. The Acrobat toolbar can be used to navigate through the other pages or documents with matching terms. The plug-in has no function, it simply servers as a means for the Web server's search software to communicate the highlighted terms to the Acrobat viewer via the Web browser.

Optimizer (Macintosh, Windows, UNIX)

The Optimizer Plug-in facilitates progressive rendering of PDF pages downloaded (or downloading) from Web servers and reduces the file sizes of most PDF files by removing redundant text, images, and line art. For more information on optimization see Section 7.14, "Optimizing PDF Files for the World Wide Web." Optimization of PDF files is central to the technology which makes PDF files viewable in Acrobat 3.0-savvy Web browsers, and is therefore essential for Web publishing with Acrobat.

AcroForm (Macintosh, Windows)

The Acrobat Forms plug-in allows publishers to create, edit, fill-in, and print common form field types. The free Acrobat Reader can be used with the plug-in to fill-in, print and submit forms. Dynamic actions can be assigned based on when a user's cursor enters or exits a field, or when the mouse button is up or down.

Form data can be received from a Web server to update a form and its appearance dynamically, without resending the entire form.

Access (Windows)

The Access plug-in allows the blind and vision impaired customers to view PDF files in a separate Access View window, compatible with most Windows screen-reading programs. Additionally, Access exports PDF files to HTML 2.0 and formatted ASCII files.

Movie (Macintosh, Windows)

With Movie, Internet publishers can incorporate multimedia objects (including QuickTime and AVI video and audio files) into PDF files. Movie enables publishers to specify the placement, layout, and display of a digital video file.

Internet publishers who communicate with multimedia or with the aid of movie and sound files will find Acrobat's integration of digital media to be a simple, effective solution to presenting digital media across platforms and the Internet. Available for free download from Adobe's Acrobat Web site at http://www.adobe.com/acrobat/. Included with the retail version of Acrobat 3.0.

AutoClose (Macintosh, Windows)

The AutoClose Plug-in is an interface-less plug-in that automatically closes the least-recently used document before Acrobat's limit of 10 open documents is reached. AutoClose also enhances the Go Back stack—that is, it will automatically re-open a previously closed document if you "go back" to it.

Users browsing PDF documents on the Internet (and CD-ROM) will find the Plug-in essential to avoid the 10-file limit.

For Windows, there is an ini file (c:\windows\autoclos.ini) that by default appears as:

[AutoClose]

MaxDocs=9

The MaxDocs value equals the maximum number of PDF documents open at one time. AutoClose is an important plug-in for users browsing the Internet. Available for free download from Adobe's Acrobat Web site at http://www.adobe.com/acrobat/.

AutoIndex (Macintosh, Windows)

AutoIndex (AutoIndx) allows publishers to automatically add a search index to the user's search list when opened. The AutoIndex Plug-in must be installed.

To associate an index with a document, open the PDF document and choose:

File > Document Info > Index

Select the index to be associated with the document and click OK. Opening the file adds the selected index to the user's search list. Users can then search this index without explicitly adding it. The index is removed from the search list when the user quits the Acrobat viewer.

AutoIndex is useful for those publishers who wish to serve indices on hybrid CD-ROM/Websites (through the Search Plug-in). AutoIndex is part of the Acrobat 3.0 retail package and is available for free download from Adobe's Acrobat Web site at http://www.adobe.com/acrobat/.

OLE and MacOLE (Macintosh, Windows)

The OLE Plug-in enables Acrobat Exchange and Reader to act as an OLE server to view PDF documents embedded in other OLE-enabled container applications.

PDF documents can be incorporated into other documents created by OLE 1.0 or OLE 2.0 container application. Container applications allow data from other applications to be incorporated within their documents. For example, a brochure created in PageMaker on a Macintosh and converted to PDF can be embedded within a Lotus Notes database and viewed by someone on a PC running Microsoft Windows.

An excellent feature for intranet publishers using Lotus Notes.

Available for free download from Adobe's Acrobat Web site at http://www.adobe.com/acrobat/.

MonitorSetup (Macintosh)

The PDF language version 1.1 (associated with Acrobat 2.0 and 2.1 products) allows for device-independent color (DIC) specifications. This allows creators of PDF documents to specify the color of objects in a page description independent of the color characteristics of the destination device, for example a monitor or printer.

The result of using DIC is consistent color reproduction from device to device. This is important because of the significant color variations between different devices. Even two monitors can have widely different color characteristics. Note that not all colors in a given PDF document will be specified in this DIC manner. Currently, only PDF files created by Acrobat Distiller 2.1 or later contain DIC color specification on a global level and only images are affected (i.e., not line art). Acrobat Exchange 2.0 or later has an internal preference value associated with displaying colors in a calibrated manner. This preference value is not exposed by Acrobat Exchange's user interface. However, it can be exposed by plug-ins such as Monitor Setup.

Monitor Setup is essential for Acrobat 3.0 (or earlier) Internet or intranet publishers and designers who use the networks as a distribution channel to send color artwork to other sites. The DIC color specifications provide the color control needed for professional publishing.

Available for free download from Adobe's Acrobat Web site at http://www.adobe.com/acrobat/.

SuperPrefs (Macintosh, Windows)

SuperPrefs adds a new Super Preferences dialog box for Acrobat Exchange which replaces the standard Preferences dialog box items with the following items:

- File Open Behavior. Specifies the maximum number of documents to be open at any one time and the least recently used document to be automatically closed. Use the feature as a workaround to Acrobat 2.1's limit of no more than 10 open documents at one time.
- Acrobat Always On Top (Windows Only). Makes the

Acrobat Exchange window the topmost window at all times (similar to the Windows Help feature Always On Top).

- AutoSave Currently Open Docs (Windows only). Automatically saves whatever document is open when the application quits. The next time Acrobat Exchange is started, the documents will be opened automatically to the same page and position onscreen.
- Replace Rotate Dialog Box Replaces the standard Rotate dialog box with one that includes 180 degrees rotation, in addition to the 90 degree rotations that has always been offered.
- Cleanup Bookmarks. Checks for bookmarks that point to pages that have been deleted and removes them from the PDF file.
- Hot List. Creates a new menu item for instant access with a hot list of a user's favorite PDF files, listed by document path or title.
- Auto Tiling. Automatically tiles newly opened documents vertically, horizontally, or cascaded.

Internet Publishers will appreciate the Cleanup Bookmarks feature and the long overdue bookmarks menu. The rotate 180 degrees option saves publishers time when changing orientation from landscape to portrait (and vice versa).

Available for free download from Adobe's Acrobat Web site at http://www.adobe.com/acrobat/.

I.4 Crosswise Corporation

Trapeze (Macintosh, Windows)

The Trapeze family of plug-ins provides document distribution and real-time document conferencing. Trapeze File Exchange enables Acrobat 2.1 users to transfer PDF documents (or any standard file on a Macintosh or Windows system), to remote Acrobat 2.1 users over TCP/IP (the Internet), NetWare (Windows only), AppleTalk (Macintosh only), standard modems, and ISDN networks.

Files are compressed prior to transmission, and transfers are accomplished with the push of a button. Users are identified easily by means of a built-in address book.

Trapeze Live! extends the power of Acrobat across a network of Macintosh and Windows systems to provide "live" interactive review of PDF documents. Trapeze Live! users can simultaneously view, page, scroll, zoom, and search PDF documents while on the telephone. Trapeze Live! lets users review documents instantly with colleagues, managers, or suppliers. Call Crosswise for pricing of Trapeze Live! and other enhancements for Acrobat software that enable audio- and video-conference capabilities.

An important and useful plug-in for document conferencing over the Internet (and intranet). All parties in the conference must have the plug-in (Trapeze Live! for viewing, and Trapeze File Exchange for exchanging files).

105 Locust Street
Santa Cruz, CA 95060
Tel: (800) 747-9060, (408) 459-9060

Fax: (408) 426-3859
sales@crosswise.com (for sales information)
http://www.crosswise.com/
CompuServe: GO CROSSWISE
AppleLink: "Crosswise" or see Crosswise in the
Third Parties Folder

I.5 DigiDox, Inc.

DigiDox

The DigiDox toolkit includes database applications and a suite of Adobe Acrobat plug-ins that provide users with turnkey solutions for creating, distributing, and maintaining a library of collateral documents. DigiDox plug-ins for Acrobat enable incremental updating of remote PDF files, custom link actions, and more.

DigiDox tools and services can be scaled to provide affordable solutions for small departmental applications, such as fax databases for customer service, as well as company-wide literature collections.

Call DigiDox for pricing information and platform availability.

6870 60th Street, SE
Grand Rapids, MI 49512
Tel: (616) 554-2149
Fax: (616) 554-9676
digidox@aol.com

I.6 Software Partners, Inc.

Aerial (Macintosh, Windows)

Aerial, a plug-in for Acrobat Exchange that facilitates document navigation, allows users to search documents using the document's index, tag document's frequently referenced pages, jump to a page using its printed page number, mark pages with "paper clips" for quick reference, and print selected portions of a page.

- The Go To Document Page allows quick navigation to a document's page number. This feature navigates through documents using nearly all page numbering formats (including Roman numerals).
- The Index Manager allows users to enter text—even just a few characters—and the Index Manager displays a corresponding alphabetized list of the document's index entries representing the entered text. Index entries link to an entry's page by double-clicking the index entries found.
- Quick Tags maintains a customizable list of frequently accessed PDF documents and pages. The list requires no specific document to be opened.
- The print view tool enables a user to select a portion of a single page and to send the selected portion to the printer.
- The paper clip tool marks pages and allows the user to quickly flip back through them.

Aerial requires Acrobat Exchange 2.0 or later. Available for Windows 3.1 or later, and Macintosh running System 7.0 or later (features may vary slightly by platform).

Compose (Windows)

Compose automates the time consuming task of creating bookmarks and hypertext links. This plug-in quickly builds and repaginates composite documents and builds a library of PDF documents for easy selection.

- The compose bookmarks by example tool creates bookmarks based on a document's heading styles. Identify an example of each heading style to create a bookmark. Compose scans the entire document converting matching headings into hierarchical bookmarks.
- Create linked index pages from an existing table of contents and index pages. Compose even creates separate links for each page reference in the index.
- The copy link tool automatically copies hypertext links in a PDF file to another PDF file, eliminating the need to manually create each link on every page.
- Batch process files to set file security options and file open defaults, create thumbnails, and index lists.
- Link all instances of key words together to create hypertext links from one occurrence to the next.
- Compose checks the validity of a document's hypertext links and bookmarks and helps fix broken links.
- Automatically builds tables of contents for multiple PDF files. Compose creates a set of "open file" bookmarks that launch other PDF files using the general information fields, such as title and subject.
- Compose automates the assembly of large, composite documents by repaginating composite documents and electroni-

cally "whiting out" page numbers from the original documents, while overwriting new page headings and footers with customizable text and page numbers.

- Navigate document files by title.
- Compose can build a library of actual document titles and authors, not just a PDF's file name, to aid user navigation.

An important and useful tool for creating bookmarks and hypertext links. Internet publishers will appreciate the time it saves in creating links and bookmarks. Available for Windows 3.1 or later; call for Macintosh availability.

Re:Mark (Macintosh, Windows)

Re:Mark is a powerful tool for annotating PDF documents. Re:Mark adds a rich set of markup features to Acrobat, such as text highlighting, text strike-out, pop-up comments, and drawing tools. Its unique one-click, pop-up comment box lets you enter descriptive text for any Re:mark object. Use the ink drawing feature to sketch diagrams and highlight text right on the document, using a mouse. Cross out unwanted text with an "X" or write on the document.

The file attachment feature sends original source documents to reviewers and lets them attach materials. Attach any picture, bitmap, sound file, movie, spreadsheet, text file, or other file type anywhere in the document. And, since attachments become part of the document, they never get lost when the document is circulated for review. Attached files can be extracted as a separate file, copied to the clipboard, or launched with its associated application program. Re:Mark software's sound annotation records verbal comments right in the document. Re:Mark consolidates comments from multiple reviewers. Look at each reviewer's comments separately or combine them for a consolidated view. Re:Mark filters comments by author and object type.

Useful for intranet applications where online document editing and markup is essential; not very useful for Internet publishers as many features built into Re:Mark require the plug-in to be installed on each user's machine.

All plug-ins may be ordered directly from Software Partners.

2013 Landings Drive
Mountain View, CA 94043
Tel: (415) 428-0160
Fax: (415) 428-0163
http://www.buckaroo.com/
sales@buckaroo.com

I.7 University of Minnesota's InternetLink

InternetLink (Macintosh)

InternetLink is an Adobe Acrobat 2.1 Plug-in developed at the University of Minnesota. InternetLink, like Weblink, embeds a URL within a link using the InterLink action. InternetLink extends the capabilities of the Acrobat link tool to enable publishers to enter links in PDF documents that refer to URLs for Internet resources such as FTP, Gopher, netnews, and WWW servers. When a user selects one of the links that refers to a URL, InternetLink calls the appropriate helper application for FTP, Gopher, nntp or HTTP servers.

Available on Macintosh (Windows to follow), InternetLink sends an OpenURL AppleEvent to signal the appropriate network application to fetch the URL. The network application either displays the item referenced by the URL or calls a helper application to display the item. For example, TurboGopher renders text, Gopher searches and directories itself, but calls Acrobat to display PDF files. This means that you can use InternetLink and URLs to seamlessly link PDF documents residing on servers anywhere on the Internet.

Since only Web servers support the Amber technology that allows page-on-demand downloading and progressive rendering of PDF documents, adding a link to a 40-page PDF file located on a Gopher server will result in the launching of a Gopher application to download the entire file, then open an Acrobat viewer to view the PDF document.

The Weblink Plug-in is a better solution for connecting to Internet-based servers for both publishers and users.

The InternetLink plug-in software is available free via Gopher or anonymous FTP from ftp:// boombox.micro.umn.edu/.

Use this URL to gopher to the appropriate directory: GOPHER:// boombox.micro.umn.edu/11/gopher/Macintosh-TurboGopher/ helper-applications/.

I.8 VerTec

TranZform

TranZform is available as a two-part package (Definer and Fill-In). TranZform allows instantaneous interactive manipulation of forms throughout the business environment—totally independent of platform or software. With TranZform, PDF documents become interactive allowing everyone throughout the entire business setting—regardless of computer system or software—to input data directly into TranZform-predefined field areas or retrieve information from other databases directly into the same field areas. This information can then be embedded into the document or stored separately for archiving or data transmission purposes, achieving total manipulation of the original document.

TranZform eliminates the need for paper-based forms and saves processing time; offers extensive forms tracking functionality and makes forms interactive by retrieving data from PDF and by placing that data back into a database.

Publishers use the Definer Plug-in to set up the fill-in or database fields. Users with the Fill-In Plug-in can view and input data within these defined fields.

An excellent way to add HTML forms capabilities to PDF documents, but limited to those users who have only the Fill-In Plug-in. Excellent for intranet applications where the plug-in could be purchased for workstations where the documents would be viewed and printed. Call for platform availability information.

VerZions

VerZions is a plug-in that provides advanced document workflow solutions to automate, manage, and expedite the conversion of the printed page to an electronic format. VerZions can create a completely flexible, automated workflow environment to control each phase of the conversion process.

As an enhancement tool, VerZions progresses from document breakdown and separation through page scanning, PDF conversions and quality assurance, all the way to product reassembly including page numbering, indexing, and hypertext linking and archiving. After conversion, documents become even more interactive. Not only are they all in the same format, they can be searched and retrieved based upon information supplied by VerZions such as key words, date of origin, and destination. They also are fully available to users on any computer system throughout the organization.

Most useful to publishers creating documents for Internet use through collaboration. Call for platform availability information.

5601 Roanne Way, Suite 606
Greensboro, NC 27409
Tel: (910) 855 9555
Fax: (910) 855 1766

I.9 XMAN

xToolsOne (Macintosh, Windows)

XMAN's xToolsOne contains 10 Adobe Acrobat 2.1 plug-ins.

- xMarker's electronic ink places marks on Acrobat documents, tailoring editing needs by controlling color and pen width and noting the creator of electronic marks.
- xPrint Selection enables the user to select a specific portion of a page and print only that area.
- xSelect is a powerful and flexible tool that enhances Acrobat software's built-in text selection tool. Use xSelect to choose

text on a page within a user-defined rectangle.

- xAnnotations Window allows the examination of all objects in an Acrobat document. When the xAnnotations Window is displayed, a detailed list is created that includes the type of object, the page location, and the creation or last modification date. More specific object information is also available: the title is shown for text notations; the link's page number that the link jumps to; and the document's name the link will launch.
- xShowLink Borders shows all invisible link borders on a page so that other tools may be used with the link borders still visible. xShow Link Borders ensures access to all of the links in any given document.
- xPageMarker puts a marker on any page in a document. A corner of the page is folded down for easy reference. The xPageMarker notation is also added to the xAnnotations Window list.
- xFootnote creates a standard footnote in a single step. Select some text in a document, choose xFootnote from the menu, and xFootnote appends footnote information for the document and cuts the text to the clipboard for use in other applications.
- xDate Annotations ensures that a creation date is assigned all objects and makes tracking your revisions of links, marks, and notes easy.
- xMake Links turns linking a range of text into one easy step. Designed for table of contents and index text, xMake Links also will process tables of numbers. Select the text to be linked and click the xMake Links button on the Acrobat

toolbar. Links are automatically generated according to the settings selected in the Options dialog box.

- xMake Bookmarks turns a range of text into bookmarks in one easy step. Select the text to be processed and click the xMake Bookmarks button on the Acrobat toolbar. Bookmarks are automatically generated according to the settings chosen in the Options dialog box.

A good suite of tools for publishers creating documents to be published on the Internet. Some tools require the xTools Plug-in to be installed on the user's system.

276 Roosevelt Way
San Francisco, CA
94114-1432
Tel: (415) 986-1773
Fax: (415) 626-3359
mguthrie@aol.com
AppleLink: XMAN.RD

Appendix J: Acrobat-Related Creator Application Plug-ins

J.1 Cascade Systems Inc.

Cascade Systems Quark XTensions

Cascade Systems offers a series of four QuarkXPress XTensions:

- Story Threads allows setup and automation of article threads from Quark pages to PDF.
- Picture Compression overrides Quark picture compression attributes and replaces them with Acrobat Distiller preferences.
- Setting Annotations within Quark allows users to set up objects within a Quark document and have them automatically carry through to PDF.
- Bookmarks enables users to set up bookmarks within a Quark document and automatically carry them through to PDF files.

A must for any Internet publishers creating documents using QuarkXPress. Call for platform availability.

1 Corporate Drive
Andover, MA 01810
Tel: (508) 794-8000
Fax: (508) 794-0005
http://www.cascadeinc.com/

J.2 XMAN

PDF NAVigator (Macintosh)

PDF NAVigator is a PageMaker 5.0 plug-in for Macintosh computers that automatically adds the navigational capabilities of Acrobat to PageMaker documents. Bookmarks and links are generated for PageMaker Table of Contents and/or Index Stories.

Once a PageMaker document has been processed by PDF NAVigator and converted to PDF by Acrobat Distiller, simply click on a topic of choice in the document's index or table of contents and immediately transfer to the associated text in the body of the PDF document. In addition, PDF NAVigator automatically generates thumbnails of each page, crops pages to a custom page size, compresses text and graphics using LZW compression, and embeds fonts in an Acrobat documents—all from within PageMaker.

276 Roosevelt Way
San Francisco, CA
94114-1432
Tel: (415) 986-1773
Fax: (415) 626-3359
mguthrie@aol.com

AppleLink: XMAN.RD

Appendix K: Converting Other File Types to PDF

PostScript files are most easily converted to PDF files. With Acrobat Capture, a paper-based document can be scanned and the resulting TIFF files recognized and converted to PDF files.

With the wealth of electronic documentation used in business, education and government—and the relatively short time the Acrobat PDF file has been available—many publishers or librarians may be interested in the possibility of converting their existing electronic document archives to Acrobat PDF files.

This section describes the technologies and companies which provide electronic document conversion from other file formats and paper-based documents.

K.1 GenText, Inc.

AFP2PDF

AFP2PDF runs on a mainframe, workstation or PC to translate IBM Advanced Function Presentation data stream (AFPDS) files into the PDF files. AFP2PDF accepts AFCCU (Common Control Unit) AFP and supports both external and embedded AFP objects such as page segments, overlays, and mixed-mode line data. Support for GOCA and IOCA is coming soon. Users who have implemented the IBM Core Interchange Fonts will find a direct correlation to Adobe Type 1 fonts that gives the same look and feel to their documents. AFP2PDF also handles color.

9400 N. Central Expressway Suite 1640 LB 147
Dallas, TX 75231-5045
Tel: (214) 691-0300; Fax: (214) 691-0789
gentext@metronet.com

K.2 Alliant Defense Electronics Systems, Inc.

AnyImage

The AnyImage product line from Alliant Defense Electronics Systems enables users to electronically capture, store, retrieve, and view volumes of technical documentation. Through user-developed rules, the AnyImage InfoLinker product automatically can build hyperlinks and bookmarks for PDF documents. AnyImage InfoLinker uses Adobe Acrobat technology to convert large amounts of information into PDF, automatically apply hyperlinks, and deliver PDF files with Acrobat software.

13133 34th Street North
Clearwater, FL 34622
Tel: (813) 572-1900
Fax: (813) 572-2395

K.3 nett Information Products

nett InfoWare

nett InfoWare enables electronic collection, management, and distribution of Adobe Acrobat PDF documents over the Lotus Notes network or through electronic mail. nett InfoWare functions over both local area networks and wide area networks, connected via modems, X25 or TCP/IP, without requiring an online connection. nett InfoWare includes three applications.

- nett InfoWare Author allows authors to tag and submit their documents. It also automates the authorization process for their release into the distribution network, providing multilevel security.

- nett InfoWare Publisher facilitates conversion of documents submitted by nett InfoWare Author into PDF files and their proper filing into nett InfoWare databases for replication to recipients' sites.
- nett InfoWare Viewer is a powerful group and personal information manager and browser.

nett Information Products licenses nett InfoWare to corporations that require tight standardization and control of complex, rich-text document distribution—both internally and to customers and vertical information integrators servicing a market sector, such as health care and insurance.

8522 National Blvd.
Culver City, CA 90232
Tel: (310) 836-5225
Fax: (310) 836-5226
mhs.compuserve.com

K.4 The Xenos Group Inc.

Corridor AFP to PDF

Corridor AFP to PDF transforms IBM Advanced Function Printing datastreams (AFPDS) to PDF files, converting the datastreams into a portable, universally recognized format for viewing and printing with Adobe Acrobat products. The resulting output meets "light test" compatibility.

AFPDS to PDF accepts "mixed mode" (AAFPDS and IBM line mode) and "pure" (CCU-based, non-AFIG) AFP print streams; both external and embedded AFP objects such as page segments, Graphical Object Content Architecture (GOCA) files and overlays, and AFPDS at 240, 300 and 1,440 dpi. AFPDS to PDF accesses existing AFP resource libraries to select overlays, images and graphics. Normal library maintenance procedures remain in effect.

AFPDS to PDF does not create redundant resources, files or processes. The use of AFPDS to PDF provides for document portability over time, as all resources necessary for creating a document are stored with the text at the time of creation.

95 Mural Street, Suite 201
Richmond Hill, Ontario L4B 3G2
Canada
Tel: (800) 387-9781
Fax: (905) 709-1023

K.5 Elixir Technologies Corporation

Elixir

Elixir printing software brings the advantages of electronic documentation to mainframe users by converting documents to PDF—a necessity for large businesses in need of cross-platform communication.

Elixir's printing software provides PC-based WYSIWYG resource editing and conversion tools for use with IBM Advanced Function Printing (AFP) and Xerox Corporation's Metacode. Elixir outputs PostScript language files that are seamlessly converted into PDF files using Adobe Acrobat Distiller software.

180 Canada Larga Road
Ventura, CA 93001
Tel: (805) 641-5900 ext.140

K.6 Gateway Conversion Technologies

Gateway Conversion Technologies

Gateway Conversion Technologies offers advanced conversion technology for fast, accurate processing of hard-copy documents into electronic formats, including PDF.

Gateway also distributes PDF files along with Adobe Acrobat Reader and Acrobat Exchange software on a variety of media, such as tapes, diskettes and CDs.

P.O. Box 14385
Research Triangle Park NC 27709-9882
Tel: (919) 319-6500

K.7 Handmade Software Incorporated

Image Alchemy

Image Alchemy converts vendor-specific, computer platform-specific or standardized image files into a form that can be viewed by an Adobe Acrobat Reader or Acrobat software user.

Image Alchemy, the image conversion software from Handmade Software, converts more than 70 image-file formats to PDF, including formats used by scanners and facsimiles, or those posted to the Internet. Due to the compression supported by PDF, the files created with Image Alchemy may be substantially smaller than the originals, saving valuable storage space.

Image Alchemy also has a wide range of image transfer features, such as colorspace conversion and palette generation. Available for personal computers and workstations.

488 Kato Road Suite 110
Fremont, CA 94538
Tel: (510) 252-0101

K.8 GenText, Inc.

Meta2PDF

Meta2PDF runs on a mainframe, workstation, or PC to convert Xerox Metacode into PDF files. Meta2PDF accepts Xerox Metacode and line data conditioned with DJDEs. It supports both external and embedded objects, such as IMGs and FRMS. Fonts are supported by using a correlation table that maps the Xerox fonts to PostScript language fonts. The correlation table can be tailored to handle customized fonts. Meta2PDF also handles color.

9400 N. Central Expressway Suite 1640 LB 147
Dallas, TX 75231-5045
Tel: (214) 691-0300
Fax: (214) 691-0789
gentext@metronet.com

K.9 Rosetta Technologies, Inc.

Prepare

Prepare is a data conversion tool that supports a wide range of standard graphics and data exchange formats. Standard data in TIFF, MIL-R, C4, Sun Raster, HP-GL, CGM, IGES, DXF, and Adobe PostScript language formats now can be converted to PDF files.

File processing supports multi-page documents, and there are no restrictions on raster image size or resolution. Prepare supports automatic file type detection, batch processing, drawing merge and assembly, and vector to raster conversion. Available in Windows and UNIX versions.

15220 N.W. Greenbrier Pkwy.
Beaverton, OR 97006
Tel: (503) 690-2500
Fax: (503) 531-0401

K.10 Sys-Print, Inc.

Sys-Print

Sys-Print software produces PDF files, complete with bookmarks and links, from report-generated output such as mainframe "sys-out" data. Sys-Print enables large amounts of data to be stored, retrieved, and searched quickly and easily onscreen.

The software allows for fine control of output format through job specs and FCB parameters. MIS departments can benefit from this simple, revolutionary method to route information throughout a company. Since this information is distributed in PDF, the original presentation of each page is retained, complete with graphics and text. In addition, Sys-Print software uses PDF to reduce file size.

4151 Memorial Drive Suite 111-D
Decatur, GA 30032
Tel: (404) 296-7812

Index

B

C

H

I

T

X

Z

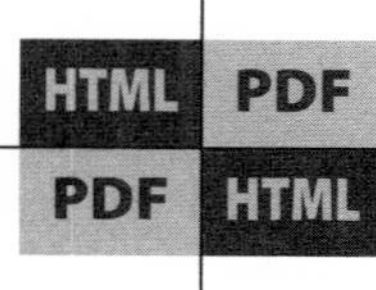

Acknowledgments

Harvey Alcabes, Ken Anderson, Rob Babcock, Rick Brown, Richard Cohn, John Dawes, Pam Deziel, Christopher Hunt, James C. King, Terry Kerth, Pete Koolish, Liz McQuarrie, Sally Phillips, Kevin Wandryk and Bob Wulff, all at Adobe Systems, worked with me during the research stages of this book, and later as Acrobat 3.0 was being developed. They answered questions and provided information about Acrobat 3.0 and PDF. Jena Yankovich provided the Acrobat 3.0 software crucial to completing this book.

Throughout the project Tim Bienz and Gary Cosmini provided technical review support, and Chris Warnock worked on many Web specific technical issues. These Adobe employees increased the technical accuracy of the book.

And Peggy Bogard, Judy Kirkpatrick, and Sarah Rosenbaum of Adobe spent hours reading various draft copies of this book. Their comments, suggestions, and time contributed were invaluable.

Thanks also to Joe Freda at PrePRESS SOLUTIONS, David Glazer, Stephanie Godek, Harold Grey at ITC, Denise Salis, Pat Soberanis, Tracey Thompson, and Joseph Treacy.

My gracious thanks to Karen Whitehouse, my editor, for working so hard on this project. She provided first-class editorial support throughout. This book is a testament to her diligent, careful work.

Finally, thanks to Patrick Ames, Publisher of Adobe Press. He began working with me on this project when Acrobat 3.0 was merely a two-page press release. He's reviewed countless drafts, and even entirely new incarnations of the book. His skills, support and belief in this project contributed directly to the quality of this book, and my ability to finish it.

About the Author & Adobe Press

Gordon Kent has a B.A. in Corporate Communications, a B.F.A. in Creative Writing from Roger Williams University in Bristol, Rhode Island, and a M.S. in Corporate Communications from Ithaca College, Ithaca, New York. Kent is manager of Information Technologies and Communications at the Northeast and Islands Regional Educational Laboratory at Brown University (LAB), a U.S. Department of Education-funded educational research facility. Kent designs, develops, and maintains the LAB's information dissemination activities using state-of-the-art collaboration and publishing technologies, which include the integration of both structured and dynamic documents. He teaches courses in corporate communications, technical writing, and electronic media at Roger Williams University's School of Arts & Sciences, Bristol, Rhode Island. He has worked as Communications Director for the National Association of College Broadcasters, performed radio research for Katz Communications, and has worked on projects for Apple Computer, Radius, and MTV.

Gordon Kent has established a Web site to support this book. Point your browser to http://www.novagraphix.com/Internet_Publishing_with_Acrobat.

Adobe Press books examine the art and technology of digital communications. Created within Adobe Systems Incorporated and published by Macmillan Computer Publishing USA, Adobe Press books are available wherever books about computers or the communication arts are sold. Visit the Adobe Systems web site at www.adobe.com for recent additions to the Adobe Press library.